D0456719

THE ROUGH GUIDE TO

Shanghai

This third edition updated by

Simon Lewis

ROUGH
GUIDES

roughguides.com

Contents

OPPOSITE YU YUAN GARDENS **PREVIOUS PAGE** ORIENTAL PEARL TOWER

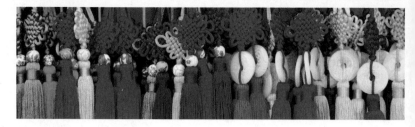

Introduction to
Shanghai

In the Roaring Twenties, Shanghai was a place of opportunity, famous for style, fashion, decadence and business panache. Now, after decades of postwar neglect, the city has shaken off its mothballs, and exactly the same is true today. The great metropolis is undergoing one of the fastest economic and urban expansions the world has ever seen. Suddenly Shanghai has China's largest stock exchange, the world's longest metro network and over a thousand skyscrapers, more than any other Asian city – with two thousand more on the way. The 2010 Expo served as a spur for a citywide convulsion of new infrastructure, including five new subway lines in as many years, and served notice to the world that the city had arrived. By 2020, it is expected to be the richest economic region in the world.

Faced with all those ads, neon signs, showcase buildings and vast shopping plazas, it's hard to imagine that you are in a communist country. Indeed, though dissent is quashed, as ever, outside the political arena anything goes these days, and consumer capitalism and instant gratification appear to be the prevailing ideologies; witness all the gleaming new restaurant and nightlife districts, the enthusiastic embrace of fashion, clubbing and fine cuisine, the gay bars and red-light zones.

Yet despite the rampant modernity, evidence of Shanghai's short and inglorious **history**, when it was carved up by foreign powers into autonomous concessions, is everywhere, and parts of the city appear distinctly European. Looking like a 1920s vision of the future, prewar Art Deco buildings – relics of hated foreign imperialism, now protected as city monuments – abound, standing in the shadows of brazen skyscrapers that share the same utopian aesthetic.

And Shanghai maintains its **international character**. The Shanghainese have always felt apart from the rest of the country and look abroad for inspiration as well as business; now, you'll find more English spoken here than in any other mainland city, see foreign

ABOVE COLOURFUL SOUVENIRS

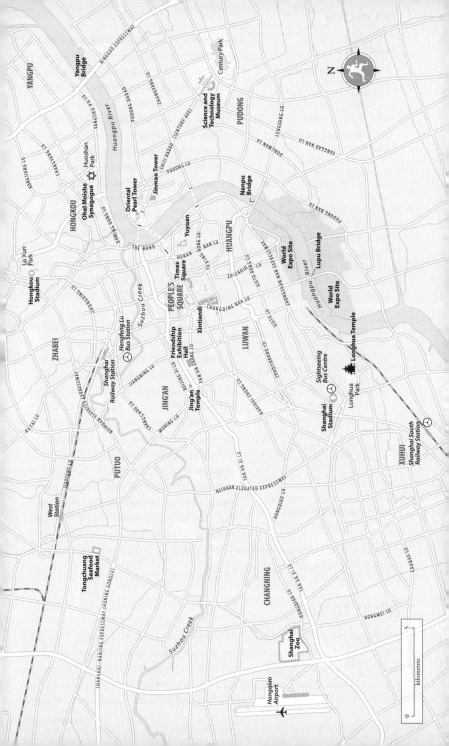

FACT FILE

- **Shanghai Municipality** encompasses 6300 square kilometres, which includes Shanghai city, eight surrounding districts and thirty islands.

- The city is **governed** by the Communist Party of China but enjoys a surprising degree of autonomy, to an extent which has begun to worry the central government in Beijing.

- The official **language** is Mandarin, but locals also speak a dialect called Shanghainese.

- The **population** of Greater Shanghai is 23 million, which includes 4 million migrant workers.

- Shanghai is the busiest **port** in the world, by cargo tonnage. The Shanghai region, including the adjoining provinces of Jiangsu and Zhejiang, accounts for almost a third of China's foreign **exports**, and a fifth of its **manufacturing output** is produced here. Each year, the city attracts a quarter of all China's foreign **investment**, more than any single developing country.

- The weight of its **skyscrapers** has caused Shanghai to sink 1.5 metres in twenty years, and the city continues sinking at the rate of 1.5cm a year.

- Shanghai's residents have the highest **life expectancy** of anywhere in China, at 82 years.

mannerisms such as handshaking and air-kissing, and observe the obsession with international luxury brands. But look closely and you'll also find a distinctly **Chinese identity** asserting itself, whether in the renewal of interest in traditional entertainments such as teahouses and acrobatics or in the revival of old architectural forms brought up-to-date for the city's young elite.

Like Hong Kong, its model for economic development, Shanghai does not brim with obvious attractions. Rather, its pleasures lie in some less-expected pursuits. Unlike most Chinese cities, Shanghai is actually a rewarding place to **wander** aimlessly: it's fascinating to stroll the elegant Bund, explore the pockets of colonial architecture in the former French Concession or get lost in the choking alleyways of the Old City, where traditional life continues much as it always has. The **art scene** is world class, and you can visit both flashy new art centres and ramshackle complexes of studios in abandoned factories. But perhaps the city's greatest draw is its emphasis on indulgence, and it's hard to resist its many temptations. The **restaurant** scene is superb, with every Chinese and most world cuisines represented; whether you treat yourself to the latest outrageous concoction at a celebrity restaurant or slurp noodles in a neighbourhood canteen, you may well find eating to be the highlight of your trip. There are so many great places to go for **nightlife**, from dive bars to slick clubs featuring international DJs, that some visitors rarely see daylight. And the **shopping** possibilities, at shiny malls, trendy boutiques and dusty markets, are endless; make sure you leave plenty of space in your suitcase.

What to see

First stop on every visitor's itinerary is the famous **Bund**, an impressive strip of colonial edifices lining the west bank of the Huangpu River. As well as allowing you an insight into the city's past, a wander along the riverside affords a glimpse into its future – the awesome, skyscraper-spiked skyline on the other side. Taking a river tour from here will give you a sense of the city's scale. Heading west from the Bund down the old consumer cornucopia of **Nanjing Dong Lu** will bring you to **People's Square**, the modern heart of the city, and home to a cluster of world-class museums, all worth a few hours of your time, and the leafy and attractive Renmin Park. Continuing west onto Nanjing Xi Lu brings you to the modern commercial district of **Jing'an**, where a couple of worthwhile temples, and the Moganshan Art District, provide welcome respite from all the relentless materialism.

Heading south from People's Square brings you to delightful **Xintiandi**, an upscale dining district housed in renovated traditional buildings, and a good introduction to the civilized pleasures of the **former French Concession**, which stretches west of here. As well as the best (and most exclusive) shopping, hotels and dining, on these incongruously European-looking streets you'll find a host of former residences of Shanghai's original movers and shakers.

But Shanghai's history was not all about the foreigners, as you'll find if you explore the **Old City**, south of the Bund, where most of the Chinese lived during the concession era. The old alleys are being torn down at speed, but you'll still find plenty of evidence of a distinctly Chinese way of life in the elegant old Yu Gardens, the bustling shopping bazaar that's grown up around them, and a clutch of backstreet temples. By way of contrast, across the river in **Pudong** you'll see very little that's less than a decade old; come here for the views from the elegant Jinmao Tower or huge new World Financial Centre. A clutch of sights on the city's **outskirts** are also worthy of exploration, among them Duolun Culture Street in the far north, Century Park and the Long Museum in the east, and Longhua Temple in the southwest.

After a week you might have had enough of Shanghai's hectic pace, in which case head out to the hinterland, which offers countryside, historic buildings and a chance to slow down. The tranquil Buddhist island of **Putuo Shan** and the cities of **Suzhou**, famous for gardens and silk, and **Hangzhou**, with its gorgeous lake, are well worth an overnight stop, while for a day-trip, don't miss a jaunt around one of the sleepy **canal towns**, such as Zhouzhuang or Wuzhen.

ARCHITECTURAL WONDERS OF SHANGHAI

Old Millfun (1933) This astonishing concrete slaughterhouse at 10 Shajing Lu, Hongkou, is reminiscent of an Escher drawing. It's being converted into an artsy complex of shops.

Fairmont Peace Hotel (1926) Designed by Palmer and Turner as Sassoon House, this is the city's most glorious Art Deco masterpiece, with a magnificent interior. **See p.43**

Customs House (1928) Huge, Doric columns accentuate this massive Neoclassical building's height, and lead the eye towards the massive clocktower. **See p.44**

Waibaidu Bridge (1908) This was China's first steel bridge, and remains its only camelback truss bridge. **See p.41**

Jinmao Tower (1998) This beautiful tapering tower uses the formal language of Chinese pagodas; the enormous barrel-vaulted atrium, lined with staircases arrayed in a spiral, is the city's most spectacular interior. **See p.77**

Tomorrow Square (2002) One of the city's characteristic landmarks, thanks to the pincers on the roof. **See p.52**

Oriental Arts Centre (2004) French architect Paul Andreu designed this building to look like a butterfly orchid, with the petals being the exhibition halls. Lights on the roof change colour with the cadences of the music being played inside. **See p.79**

World Financial Centre (2007) This 492-metre-high tower is a broad-shouldered wedge with very clean lines and a hole in the top – like God's own tent peg. **See p.77**

China Art Palace (2010) This extraordinary red, boxy crown was the grand Chinese showpiece of the 2010 Expo. It's now an art museum. **See p.80**

When to go

The best times to visit Shanghai are in **spring** and early summer (late March till the end of May) and **autumn** (mid-Sept till end of Oct). During these times, you can expect warm temperatures, blue sky and infrequent rain.

Summer (June to mid-Sept) is very hot and humid, yet you might need to carry an extra layer of clothes for when you go inside as it's common to find air-conditioning left on its fiercest setting. During the "Plum Flower Rain" season from mid-June to early July expect frequent showers, and up till September heavy storms are common – you'll certainly need an umbrella.

Winters are chilly and windy, though the temperature rarely drops below freezing and snow is uncommon. January is the coldest month.

Try to avoid visiting during the two "Golden Week" **holidays** – the first week of May and the first week of October – when pretty much the whole country is on holiday and tourist attractions become fearsomely busy. The city is lively during the run-up to **Chinese New Year**, which falls between mid-January and mid-February, but travel during this time is tricky and expensive as most people are going home. New Year itself is best avoided as just about everyone stays at home with their family and most businesses are shut.

AVERAGE TEMPERATURES AND RAINFALL

	Jan	Feb	Mar	Apr	May	Jun	Jul	Aug	Sep	Oct	Nov	Dec
Max/min °C	8/1	8/1	13/4	19/10	25/15	28/19	32/23	32/23	28/19	23/14	17/7	12/2
Max/min °F	46/34	46/34	55/39	66/50	77/59	82/66	90/74	90/74	82/66	74/57	63/45	54/36
Rainfall (mm)	48	58	84	94	94	180	147	142	130	71	51	36

Author picks

Our author has been to all the trendy bars, backstreet eating holes and destination restaurants; and he's cycled the city's length and breadth from thoroughfares to *longtangs*. Here is a list of his personal highlights.

Sip with the fast set Shanghai does after-dark glamour very well, and boasts some of the world's louchest cocktail bars. Head to a speakeasy such as *Senator*, tell them your mood and ask their expert mixologists to fix you up something appropriate. **See p.116**.

Look up Shanghai is a treasure-trove of fantastic Art Deco architecture, much of which, delightfully, is being spruced up after decades of neglect. Check out the *Fairmont Hotel* – inside and out – to bask in this most refined design aesthetic. **See p.43**

Get lost Dense with incident and colour, central Shanghai's streets reward the urban flâneur – they're architecturally diverse, busy with stylish or at least noteworthy people, and there's plenty of shade thanks to all those plane trees. Start in the French Concession and see how far east you can get. Jump in a cab when you've had enough. **See p.59**

Hang with the art crowd Don a black polo neck and statement glasses and see if you can schmooze your way into the smart art set – chat up the interns at the Moganshan galleries and you might get yourself invited to some private views. **See p.72**

Dine in style It is a shocking oversight that Shanghai still hasn't been visited by Michelin. When that's rectified, the city is certain to get a big haul of stars – some of the world's greatest chefs are working here. Try to get one proper fine-dining experience in: it'll be a lot cheaper than in the West and just as good. We recommend 8½, *Otto E Mezzo* and *Bombana*. **See p.102**

Get high At some point in your stay, try rising into the clouds. Pick a fine day or evening, and head up a skyscraper to a viewing platform or pricey hotel bar. The absolute best views, for the moment, are from the Shanghai World Financial Centre observation deck. **See p.77**

Our author recommendations don't end here. We've flagged up our favourite places – a perfectly sited hotel, an atmospheric café, a special restaurant – throughout the Guide, highlighted with the ★ symbol.

18

things not to miss

It's not possible to see everything that Shanghai has to offer on a short trip – and we don't suggest you try. What follows is a selective taste of the city's highlights: fascinating museums, spectacular buildings and a few ways just to indulge yourself. All highlights have a page reference to take you straight into the guide, where you can find out more. Coloured numbers refer to chapters in The City section.

1 THE BUND
Page 39
This strip of grand colonial mansions is fast becoming China's Champs-Élysées.

2 YU GARDENS
Page 55
This classical garden of pavilions, ponds and rockeries is a calm oasis at the heart of an olde-worlde Chinatown-style shopping centre.

3 SHANGHAI MUSEUM
Page 49
One of the best collections of paintings, jade, bronzes and other antiquities in the country, housed in one of the city's most stylish buildings.

4 XIAOLONGBAO
Page 102
These delicious dumplings are available from both street vendors and fancy restaurants.

5 TAILORING
Page 127
Tailored clothes to any design you can think of, all for a tiny fraction of the price you'd pay at home – Shanghai's best bargain.

6 SHANGHAI WORLD FINANCIAL CENTRE
Page 77
One of Shanghai's most beautiful buildings, with magnificent views from the lofty observation deck at the top.

7 SPA TREATMENTS
Page 28
Indulge yourself at one of Shanghai's world-class spas, such as the Banyan Tree. Because you're worth it (and it's much cheaper than at home).

8 FAKE MARKETS
Page 126
You know it's wrong but you can't resist. Stock up on name-brand knock-offs at bargain prices. A steal in more ways than one.

9 YUFO TEMPLE
Page 72
This lively temple, wreathed in incense smoke, is home to two very holy, and very beautiful, jade Buddha statues.

10 COOL BARS
Page 114
Linger over a cocktail at some of the coolest bars in the world.

11 XINTIANDI
Page 59
Upscale dining in a beautiful rebuilt neighbourhood of traditional *shikumen* (stone-gate) houses.

12 XI HU
Page 144

Hangzhou's charming lake, dotted with islands, crossed by causeways, and lined with pavilions and pagodas, is one of China's most famous beauty spots.

13 MOGANSHAN ART DISTRICT
Page 72

This old factory is a hive of studios and galleries, making it a great place to sample the city's vibrant art scene.

14 ACROBATICS
Page 120

Good old-fashioned entertainment with performers in spangly costume and plenty of oohs and aahs.

15 TIANZIFANG
Page 64

This charming network of historic alleyways now hosts dozens of artsy shops, designer boutiques and cosy cafés.

16 RENMIN PARK
Page 52

A bucolic beauty spot at the heart of the city, with a lovely lotus pond and bamboo groves.

17 FINE DINING
Page 99

Indulge yourself in a sumptuous feast in refined surroundings: the city boasts some really standout restaurants.

18 PROPAGANDA POSTER CENTRE
Page 66

This evocative museum showcases the bad old days of collective farms, five-year plans and pigtails.

Itineraries

Shanghai has distinct districts, but the centre is pleasingly compact and easy to stroll around, if you don't mind crowds. Each of the below itineraries can be covered in a day, mostly by walking, with a few short hops by metro.

THE BUND TO RENMIN PARK

This is the classic Shanghai walk: heading from the Neoclassical elegance of the Bund, along brash shopping streets, to a park fringed with standout sights, it offers a sampler of all the city's flavours.

❶ Huangpu Park This compact park alongside the Huangpu River is the perfect vantage point to take in Shanghai's two iconic skylines: the trim parade of the Bund's neocolonial edifices on this side and the dizzying modernity of Pudong's skyscrapers across the water. **See p.41**

❷ Afternoon tea at the Peninsula Hotel A great way to sample the luxuries of an iconic hotel without breaking the bank. Take in the sumptuous, marble-columned lobby in the company of the local smart set, over tea, pastries and a glass of champagne. **See p.105**

❸ Peace Hotel This historic hotel is once more the city's premier luxury destination. Don't miss the magnificent Art Deco lobby. **See p.43**

❹ Nanjing Dong Lu This vivid pedestrianized high street is jammed with stores: you might not want to buy anything but it's great for people-watching – and at night it's a river of neon. **See p.46**

❺ Renmin Park This surprisingly quiet and civilized retreat is right in the middle of the city. Stop off for a coffee by the lotus pond at *Barbarossa* (see p.104) before checking out a show at the Museum of Contemporary Art (see p.52). **See p.52**

❻ Park Hotel Ladislav Hudec's slim, tapering Art Deco masterpiece might have long since lost its crown as highest building in the city, but it's still one of the most striking – and clearly an inspiration for modern structures such as the Jinmao Tower. **See p.164**

❼ Shanghai Museum This stylish modern museum has a couple of floors that are worth anyone's time – check the Qing furniture and Tibetan masks. **See p.49**

❽ Shanghai Urban Planning Exhibition Hall Their vision might be questionable, but you can't fault the ambition – raise an eyebrow at the scale and scope of the plans for Shanghai's future, dramatically presented with models. **See p.51**

A GRAND TOUR OF THE FRENCH CONCESSION

The following elegant streets and districts are great for strolling – you'll quickly see why Shanghai got that "Paris of the East" moniker. If you want to stop off for coffee or dinner, you'll be spoilt for choice.

❶ Xintiandi This complex of upmarket restaurants in a complex of pastiche traditional architecture is very attractive – and wildly popular. Check the Shikumen Museum before splashing out at *T8* or the more affordable *Crystal Jade*. **See p.59**

❷ Fuxing Park One of the city's rare green spaces is a great place to unwind, and you'll likely see groups of elderly locals playing instruments or singing. **See p.63**

❸ **Tianzifang** The narrow *longtang* alleys here are a warren of cute boutiques, cafés and knick-knack shops. Browse in Harvest Studio for homeware, Nuomi for elegant womenswear, then hit the *Bell Bar* for a stiffener. **See p.64**

❹ **Maoming Nan Lu** The French Concession is deservedly famous for its fashion stores. This street is dotted with proficient tailors who will knock up a *cheongsam* or a suit for a very reasonable price. **See p.65**

❺ **Fuxing Xi Lu** This sedate street has a winning mix of bars, boutiques and villas, many in prewar buildings. Browse at Urban Tribe (see p.129), dine at *Lost Heaven* (see p.108), then catch a gig at *Cotton's* (see p.115).

❻ **Yongkang Lu** This leafy residential strip hosts some of the city's best ex-pat oriented bars and cafes, such as *Café des Stagiaires* (see p.110) and *Volcan* (see p.110). It's all appealingly boho and low key; in the evening the clientele from all venues spill onto the street to mingle. **See p.114**

PUDONG

It's hard to credit now, but thirty years ago Pudong was mostly paddy fields. Today it's where the city grows fastest and wildest, a forest of skyscrapers and new build.

❶ **Jinmao Tower** It might have been literally overshadowed of late by taller neighbours, but this stylish modern take on Art Deco is still the most glamorous skyscraper on the Lujiazui block. Lovely interior too; check out the observation deck and the *Hyatt* lobby. **See p.77**

❷ **Shanghai History Museum** This little museum in the bowels of the Pearl Orient Tower has a diverse selection of artefacts and dioramas that do a great job of bringing to life the city's turbulent twentieth-century history. **See p.77**

❸ **Science and Technology Museum** This huge museum has an IMAX cinema and some good displays, including a great one on China's space programme. Lots of interactive and imaginative exhibits. **See p.79**

❹ **Fake market** You'll find plenty of choice at this busy market specializing in fake designer-label clothes, shoes and watches. Bargain assertively but politely and you'll grab some real steals. **See p.126**

❺ **Century Park** This well-maintained park is big enough to make for a proper escape from the teeming urban jungle. Hire a tandem and cycle sedately around the lake. **See p.79**

❻ **Long Museum** A long way out, but worth the trip: Shanghai's newest museum displays the choicest items from a billionaire's collection of historical objets d'art and modern Chinese paintings. **See p.80**

MANSIONS AND VILLAS

Shanghai is blessed with some fantastic foreign-built mansions and villas from the Concession era. Many languished for decades and have only recently been renovated and repurposed, often as restaurants, bars and hotels.

❶ **Mansion Hotel** It might look the height of respectability now, but this genteel five-storey mansion, now a hotel, was once the home of Shanghai's most notorious gangster, Du Yuesheng. There's a fifth-floor bar if you want to linger. **See p.95**

❷ **Arts and Crafts Museum** This gracious white mansion, reminiscent of the White House, is one of Ladislav Hudec's masterpieces (see p.162). it's now a charming museum, exhibiting some great ivory carvings and snuff bottles. **See p.66**

❸ **Normandie Apartments** This striking landmark block of flats, built in 1934, has an unusual wedge shape, like the prow of a ship. **See p.162**

❹ **Song Qingling Residence** The private home of Song Qingling – a central figure in early twentieth-century Chinese politics – is now a museum of her life. After looking over the exhibits inside, check out the limos in the garage and the fine gardens. **See p.67**

❺ **Coconut Paradise** Many of the smaller French Concession villas have been converted into restaurants. This Thai restaurant, in an old French house, is one of the most successful, with a fantastic ambience. **See p.111**

❻ **Sun Yat Sen Residence** This old mansion has been turned into a museum of the great man; you can safely whizz over the exhibits, but linger in the refined house and surprisingly Western-style garden. **See p.63**

❼ **Ruijin Hotel** These urbane houses were built by a newspaper magnate; they then became a government guesthouse. Today the complex operates as a high-end hotel – the well-groomed grounds are perfect for a restful stroll. **See p.64**

STREET SCENE IN THE OLD CITY

Basics

Getting there

Shanghai now has direct flights from many European capitals as well as from a number of American and Australian cities. The cost of flights varies with the season, with fares at their highest between Easter and October, around Christmas and New Year, and just before the Chinese New Year (which falls between mid-January and mid-February).

You can often cut costs by going through a **specialist flight agent** – either a consolidator, who buys up blocks of tickets from the airlines and sells them at a discount, or a **discount agent**, who may also offer special student and youth fares plus travel insurance, rail passes, car rentals, tours and the like. Prices quoted below assume midweek travel – flying at weekends tends to be slightly more expensive.

Flights from the UK and Ireland

The only nonstop flights to Shanghai **from the UK** are with Virgin (Ⓦvirgin-atlantic.com), British Airways (Ⓦba.com), Air China (Ⓦairchina.co.uk) and China Eastern (Ⓦflychinaeastern.co.uk), leaving from London Heathrow (11hr). Flying from other UK airports or **from the Republic of Ireland** you'll either have to catch a connecting flight to London or your airline's hub city.

Return **fares** for direct flights from the UK start at around £500 in low season, rising to around £800 in high season. If you're flying from the Republic of Ireland, reckon on €1200 in low season, €1700 at peak times. Indirect flights can work out cheaper; Air China and Lufthansa (Ⓦlufthansa.com), both of which stop in Frankfurt, are worth considering, as is Aeroflot (Ⓦaeroflot.co.uk), which stops over in Moscow, Emirates (Ⓦemirates.com), which stops over in Dubai, and China Southern (Ⓦcs-air.com), which stops in Paris. Less-fancied airlines such as Qatar Airlines (Ⓦqatarairways.com) offer the most competitive fares, though you may have a lengthy stopover.

Flights from the US and Canada

There's no shortage of flights to Shanghai **from the US and Canada**, with direct flights from San Francisco, Los Angeles, Chicago, Detroit, New York, Vancouver and Toronto, operated by Delta (Ⓦdelta .com), American Airlines (Ⓦamericanairlines.com), United Airlines (Ⓦunited.com), Air Canada (Ⓦair canada.com), Air China (Ⓦairchina.com) and China Eastern (Ⓦflychinaeastern.com) It takes around thirteen hours' flying time to reach Shanghai from the west coast; add seven hours or more to this if you start from the east coast. In low season, expect to pay around US$1000 from the west coast or US$1400 from the east; less for an indirect flight. In high season if you book your ticket early you probably won't need to pay more than US$300 above these low-season fares.

Flights from Australia, New Zealand and South Africa

From Australia, there are direct flights to Shanghai from Sydney and Melbourne (about 11hr) with China Eastern (Ⓦflychinaeastern.com), Emirates (Ⓦemirates.com) and Qantas (Ⓦqantas.com), but you can usually expect to pay over Aus$1100. The cheapest flights are with carriers such as Malaysia Airlines (Ⓦmalaysia-airlines.com) and Royal Brunei (Ⓦbruneiair.com), costing around Aus$900 in low season, with a stopover in Hong Kong or Singapore. Flying from Perth to Shanghai can cost as little as Aus$900 in high season. Travelling **from New Zealand**, Air New Zealand (Ⓦairnewzealand.com) flies direct from Auckland to Shanghai; flights cost around NZ$2200 in high season.

Flying **from South Africa** requires a change of planes. A flight from Johannesburg with a stopover in Hong Kong will cost around ZAR10,000 in high season.

AGENTS AND OPERATORS

China Highlights China ☎ +86 773 2831999, Ⓦchinahighlights .com. China-based company that offers three- to five-day tours of Shanghai and the surrounding area.

A BETTER KIND OF TRAVEL

At Rough Guides we are passionately committed to travel. We believe it helps us understand the world we live in and the people we share it with – and of course tourism is vital to many developing economies. But the scale of modern tourism has also damaged some places irreparably, and climate change is accelerated by most forms of transport, especially flying. All Rough Guides' flights are carbon-offset, and every year we donate money to a variety of environmental charities.

China Odyssey China ☎ +86 773 5854000, 🖰 chinaodysseytours
.com. Operates short city tours, plus longer trips taking in other
destinations in China.

North South Travel UK ☎ 01245 608291, 🖰 northsouthtravel
.co.uk. Friendly, competitive travel agency, offering discounted fares
worldwide. Profits are used to support projects in the developing world,
especially the promotion of sustainable tourism.

On the Go Tours UK ☎ 020 7371 1113, 🖰 onthegotours.com.
Runs group and tailor-made tours that include Shanghai as part of a jaunt
around China.

STA Travel UK ☎ 0871 2300 040, US & Canada ☎ 1800 781 4040,
Australia ☎ 134 STA, New Zealand ☎ 0800 474 400, South Africa
☎ 0861 781 781; 🖰 statravel.com. Worldwide specialists in
independent travel; also student IDs, travel insurance, car rental, rail
passes, and more. Good discounts for students and under-26s.

Trailfinders UK ☎ 0845 058 5858, Republic of Ireland ☎ 01 677
7888, Australia ☎ 1300 780 212; 🖰 trailfinders.com. One of the
best-informed and most efficient agents for independent travellers.

Travel China Guide US & Canada ☎ 1800 892 6988, all other
countries ☎ +800 6668 8666; 🖰 travelchinaguide.com. Chinese
company with a wide range of three- and four-day group tours of
Shanghai and around.

Arrival

**Whatever your arrival point in Shanghai,
you are almost guaranteed a further
long journey into the centre. Fortunately,
there are excellent bus and metro
connections to speed you to your final
destination, and few shady cabbies,**
though you should always catch a
licensed cab from a taxi rank.

By plane

Arriving by air from abroad, you'll touch down
at glossy **Pudong International Airport** (PVG;
☎ 6834 1000, 🖰 shairport.com), 40km east of the
city along the mouth of the Yangzi River. There
are two terminals at present, with a third due to
open in 2015. Banks and ATMs are on the upper
floors. There are left-luggage offices in both
arrivals and departures (6am–11.30pm, ¥30 per
hour, ¥45 per day).

You'll be pestered in the arrivals hall by
charlatan taxi drivers; ignore them and instead
make for the official taxi rank, on your right as
you go out, opposite exit 15. A cab into the centre
should cost around ¥160 and take just under
an hour.

The most convenient public transport into town
is the **airport bus**, which leaves from opposite the
exit gates. There are eight routes, with departures
every fifteen minutes from 6am to 7.30pm, and a
reduced service afterwards till 11pm; tickets cost
¥20–30. Bus #2 is generally the most useful as it
goes to the Jing'an Temple metro stop in the city
centre. Bus #1 goes to Hongqiao Airport (see p.21);
bus #3 runs to Xujiahui; bus #4 heads to Hongkou
Stadium, in the north; bus #5 makes for Shanghai
Railway Station; bus #6 goes to Zhongshan Park;
and bus #7 to Shanghai South Railway Station. The

SHANGHAI TRANSPORT TERMINALS

AIRPORTS

Pudong Airport	浦东机场	pǔdōng jīchǎng
Hongqiao Airport	虹桥机场	hóngqiáo jīchǎng

TRAIN STATIONS

Hongqiao Station	上海虹桥火车站	shànghǎi hóngqiáo huǒchē zhàn
Shanghai Station	上海火车站	shànghǎi huǒchēzhàn
Shanghai South Station	上海火车南站	shànghǎi huǒchēnánzhàn

BUS STATIONS

Hengfeng Lu Bus Station	恒丰路汽车站	héngfēnglù qìchēzhàn
Pudong Bus Station	浦东汽车站	pǔdōng qìchēzhàn
Qiujiang Lu Bus Station	虬江路汽车站	qiújiānglù qìchēzhàn
Shanghai Long Distance Bus Station	上海长途客运总站	shànghǎi chángtú kèyùn zǒngzhàn
Shanghai South Bus Station	上海南站	shànghǎi nánzhàn
Shanghai Stadium Sightseeing Bus Centre	上海体育馆旅游集散中心	shànghǎi tǐyùguǎn lǚyóu jísàn zhōngxīn

only one with a drop-off in Pudong is bus #5 (at Dongfang Hospital).

You can also take the **subway** straight into town, although this isn't as convenient as it should be, as the trip takes an hour and a half (so isn't any faster than the bus) and you'll have to wait for up to twenty minutes to change trains onto Line #2 at Guanglan Lu station.

The most exciting way to get into town is on the **Maglev** (see box, p.21), though it's not recommended if you have heavy luggage, as there are escalators and corridors to deal with both at the airport and at your arrival point at Longyang metro station.

If you're heading straight out of the city, make for exit 18, opposite which **long-distance coaches** depart hourly for Suzhou, Hangzhou and other destinations; tickets cost around ¥80 to each of these places.

Otherwise, take an airport bus (every 30min; daily 6am–7.30pm; ¥22; 45min) from the terminal at 1600 Nanjing Xi Lu, opposite Jing'an Temple metro or get the subway.

Hongqiao Airport

Most domestic flights land at the newly refurbished **Hongqiao Airport** (SHA; ☎6268 8899, ⓦshairport .com), 20km from the Bund. It's on the subway, on lines 2 and 10. There are two terminals, with most arrivals at the new terminal 2, which is attached to Hongqiao train station. Luggage storage is available at arrivals and departures (7am–11pm; ¥30 per hour, ¥45 per day).

A taxi to Nanjing Xi Lu costs about ¥45, taking about 45 minutes, and to the Bund about ¥60. Buses leave from the car park: bus #1 goes to Pudong airport; the airport shuttle goes to Jing'an Temple subway stop in the city centre; bus #925 makes for People's Square; and the #941 heads to the main train station.

Getting to the airports from town

Airport shuttle buses for Pudong and Hongqiao airports leave from the terminal at 1600 Nanjing Xi Lu, opposite Jing'an metro station (every 30min; daily 6am–7.30pm; ¥20–22; 45min). The fastest way to get to **Pudong International Airport** though is to take the metro to Longyang Lu on line #1 and then get the Maglev (see box, p.21). You could take the subway the whole way (see p.22), or a taxi will cost around ¥160. To get to **Hongqiao Airport**, which handles most domestic flights, take subway line #2 or catch a cab (¥60 or so from the centre; 45min).

THE MAGLEV

The most glamorous way to get into town from Pudong airport is on the **Maglev train** (daily 7am–9pm; every 20min), suspended above the track and propelled by the forces of magnetism. It whizzes from the international airport to Longyang Lu metro station, in eight minutes, accelerating to 300km per hour in the first four minutes (though it is capable of much higher speeds than this), then immediately starting to decelerate. Tickets cost ¥50 one way, or ¥40 if you show a plane ticket, and a return is ¥90. Note that the Maglev terminal is three minutes' walk from the airport, and that Longyang Lu is still a long way from the centre of town.

Plane tickets

International and domestic plane tickets can be bought from any hotel or travel agent for a small commission, or online at ⓦelong.net or ⓦenglish .ctrip.com (☎40 06199999). You'll need to provide a phone number to confirm the booking.

By train

The city's main train station – **Shanghai Railway Station** – is in the north of the city. Its vast concrete forecourt is always a mass of encamped migrants, and it's not a particularly safe place to hang around at night. The best way to get out of the station area is by metro (lines #1, #3 and #4 run through it) or taxi, the latter not likely to cost more than ¥15–20 into the city. There's an official rank outside the station.

If you've come on a slow train from Hangzhou, or many destinations in the south of the country, you'll arrive at the impressive **Shanghai South Station**, which is on metro lines #1 and #3. And if you've come on the fast train from Beijing, Suzhou or Hangzhou, you'll arrive at the new **Hongqiao Station**, which is on subway lines #2 and #10.

You can **buy tickets** for departure or trips out of town from the station itself, from one of the numerous booking offices or, for some destinations, on the web (see p.134). Most hotels will book tickets for you for a small fee.

By bus

Hardly any tourists arrive in Shanghai by bus. If you do you'll probably be dropped at either Shanghai

South Railway Station, at the main train station or at the long-distance bus station behind the main station. Some buses arrive at **Hengfeng Lu Bus Station** – again, a short walk from the main train station. If you're unlucky, you might be dropped at **Pudong Bus Station**, in the far east of the city; a cab from here to town will cost ¥100 or so – it's cheaper to catch a cab to the nearest subway station, Chuansha Lu, a couple of kilometres southwest. A few services use the **Qiujiang Lu Bus Station**, next to the Baoshan Lu metro station. Sightseeing buses that serve the canal towns and Putuoshan use the **Sightseeing Bus Station**; regular long-distance buses depart from the **South Bus Station** (see p.134).

City transport

The city's infrastructure was massively upgraded for the 2010 Expo, and is now the best in mainland China. The subway is fast, extensive, air-conditioned and easy to navigate. Taxis are cheap and plentiful and drivers are honest, which means that it's easy to avoid the overcrowded bus system.

Cycling is a good way to get around, though bikes are banned on most of the major roads in the daytime. **Walking** is more rewarding than in most Chinese cities – there are few of the tedious boulevards that tend to characterize Chinese city centres – but the sheer density of the crowds can be intimidating. Crossing the road is more stressful than it

should be as traffic is allowed to turn right even when the green man is flashing – you really have to stay on your toes. It's impossible to rent a car without a Chinese driving licence, and anyway you'd have to be nuts to voluntarily drive on these streets; you'd be much better off hiring a driver.

If you're short on time, there are plenty of **tours** of Shanghai on offer, which can be a great way to see the sights. A cruise on the Huangpu is one of the highlights of a visit to Shanghai and shouldn't be missed (see p.45 and p.76). The train is the best way to get to most of the sights beyond the city, although for some you may have to take the bus (see p.134).

By metro

The clean, modern **metro** operates from 5.30am to 11pm and includes both underground and light rail lines. The system is easy to find your way around: station entrances are marked by a red "M" logo, all stations and trains are well signed in English and stops are announced in both English and Chinese over an intercom when the train pulls in.

There are twelve lines at the moment, with a couple more being built, although only three or four are particularly useful for visitors. **Line #1** runs north–south, with useful stops at the main railway station, People's Square, Changshu Lu (for the Old French Concession), Xujiahui and Shanghai Stadium. **Line #2** runs east–west with stops at Jing'an Temple, Henan Lu and, in Pudong, Lujiazui and the Science and Technology Museum. The lines intersect at the enormous People's Square station (take careful note of the wall maps here for which

USEFUL SHANGHAI BUS ROUTES

NORTH–SOUTH

#18 (trolleybus) From Lu Xun Park, across Suzhou Creek and along Xizang Lu.
#41 Passes Tianmu Xi Lu, in front of the main train station, and goes down through the Old French Concession to Longhua Park.
#64 From the main train station, along Beijing Lu, then close to the Shiliupu wharf to the south of the Bund.
#65 From the top to the bottom of Zhongshan Lu (the Bund), terminating in the south at the Nanpu Bridge.

EAST–WEST

#3 From the Shanghai Museum across the Huangpu River to the Jinmao Tower.
#19 From near Gongping Lu wharf in the east, passing near the *Pujiang Hotel* and roughly following the course of Suzhou Creek to the Jade Buddha Temple (Yufo Si).
#20 From Jiujiang Lu (just off the Bund) along Nanjing Lu, past Jing'an Temple, then on to Zhongshan Park subway stop in the west of the city.
#42 From Guangxi Lu, near People's Square then along Huaihai Lu in the Old French Concession.
#135 From Yangpu Bridge in the east of the city to the eastern end of Huaihai Lu, via the Bund.
#911 From the Yu Gardens to Huaihai Lu.

exit to use). Lines #4 to #7 are much less used by visitors, and mainly serve commuters. **Line #8** runs north–south, with handy stops at Hongkou Stadium, Qufu Lu, and Laoximen (for the Old City).

Tickets cost from ¥3 to ¥10 according to the distance travelled. Stations have vendors and touchscreen machines (there's an option for English). The vendors sell a **stored-value card** for a refundable ¥20, which you can top up with as much as you like.

By bus

Shanghai has more than a thousand **bus** lines, all air-conditioned, and with services every few minutes, although they're often overcrowded, and you should be careful of pickpockets. Buses operate from 5am to 11pm, after which time night buses take over. Set **fares** are ¥2; you pay on board. There are onboard announcements in English, but be careful not to miss your stop as the next one will likely not be for another kilometre.

Services with numbers in the 300s are night buses; those in the 400s cross the Huangpu. Most large fold-out city maps show bus routes, usually as a red or blue line with a dot indicating a stop. **Sightseeing buses** for tourist sights in the outskirts leave from the Sight Seeing Bus Station near Shanghai Stadium (see p.134). For a sightseeing bus tour, check out the Big Bus Company (see p.23).

By taxi

Taxis are ubiquitous (until you need one when it's raining) and very cheap – the rate is ¥2.4 per kilometre, a little more after 10pm, with a minimum charge of ¥14, or ¥18 at night. Drivers rarely speak English so you'll need your destination written down in Chinese characters. Otherwise, if you're heading anywhere near an intersection, just say the name of the two roads.

The driver should flip the meter down as he accelerates away – if he doesn't, say **dabiao** (dā biǎo). Having a map open on your lap deters unnecessary detours but you shouldn't be paranoid as Shanghai cabbies are a decent bunch on the whole. If you get into a dispute with one, take his number, written on the sign on the dashboard – just the action of writing it down can produce a remarkable change of behaviour.

The best **taxi company** is Dazhong (☎6318 3880). Their well-trained drivers wear uniforms and white gloves and drive newish Santanas. They also hire out cabbies at a day rate (around ¥600).

By bicycle

Cycling is a great way to get around the city, but cyclists need to be wary as traffic is not well disciplined, and you'll no longer be one of a crowd of cyclists, as these days most locals seem to have abandoned bikes for scooters and cars. Pedestrians provide the biggest hazard, though, thanks to their tendency to step right out in front of you. Ringing your bell will elicit no response, so you need to yell – shouting in English gets a better response than trying to do it in Chinese (perhaps it sounds more alarming). Note that major thoroughfares are closed to cyclists between 7.30am and 5pm.

There are few places to **rent bikes**; the two *Le Tour* youth hostels (see pp.97–98) are the only easily accessible ones, while the *Captain Hostel* (see p.97) rents out bikes to its guests. Your best bet is China Cycle tours (☎62726507, ⓦchinacycletours.com), with prices starting at ¥100 per day for a city bike (¥350 for a week); ¥150 for a mountain bike (¥500 for a week). They'll deliver to, and pick up from, your hotel, and rent you a helmet for ¥20 a day or ¥50 a week. A couple of companies run **cycling tours** of the city or out to the canal towns (see p.24).

Tours

The government-run tourist office, CITS (see p.37), runs a wide range of tours and trips, as well as selling tickets for onward travel. Much better value, however, is the private company **Jinjiang Tours** (191 Changle Lu, by the *Jinjiang Hotel*; ☎5466 7936). Their convenient day-long coach tour of Shanghai whizzes round all the staples – Old French Concession, People's Square, Jade Buddha Temple, Yu Garden, the Bund and Pudong – for ¥400 (including lunch but excluding entrance fees). Their English-speaking staff can also arrange tours to other sights in the city centre or further afield.

A handy way to see the city if you're short on time is the **Big Bus** (ⓦbigbustours.com). These sightseeing tours aboard a double-decker bus trundle you round the major sights, including the Shanghai Museum, Xintiandi, the Jing'an Temple, the Cool Docks and the Yu Gardens; tickets cost ¥350 and are valid for 24 hours, so you are free to get off at any of the 22 stops, have a nose around, then get on the next bus. One handy place to get on is at the north side of People's Square, opposite Madame Tussauds (metro exit #7). A second (less interesting) route takes you round the inessential sights of Pudong.

Tickets can be bought through the website or a hotel, and include a free one-hour cruise down the

Huangpu (see p.45) and entry to the Jinmao Tower Observation Deck.

The **Sightseeing Bus Centre** next to the Shanghai Stadium (by entrance #5), in the far south of the city, is the place to head for tours of the outlying areas, such as to the local canal towns (see p.135). Tickets can be bought up to a week in advance. For guided English-language **walking tours**, contact Newman Tours (☎1381 7770229, ⊕newmantours.com; ¥260, depending on tour). As well as tours of the French Concession and the Bund, they offer an imaginative, if perhaps tenuous, evening Ghost Tour.

Also worth considering for those short on time are the half-day and one-day **cycling tours** offered by China Cycle tours (☎1376 1115050, ⊕china cycletours.com; ¥300–400 per person) which breeze around the major sites. For **overnight cycle tours** further afield, to canal towns or Moganshan, check out Bohdi Bikes (Building 15, floor 3, 271 Qianyang Lu; ☎52669013, ⊕bohdi.com.cn). Finally, Shanghai Insiders (172 Jinxian Lu; ☎1381 7616975) offer intriguing tours in the sidecar of a vintage BMW motorbike (¥900 for two hours).

The media

Sadly, China's opening up and speedy development has not resulted in any softening of the Communist Party's authoritarian instincts, and all media is heavily censored. Journalists and bloggers who stray off message are often slung in jail, usually on a charge of "revealing state secrets". The Chinese state has put a mind-boggling amount of effort into fencing off the internet: more than two million people are employed in policing public opinion.

Newspapers and magazines

Xinhua, the Chinese news agency, is a mouthpiece for the state, whose propaganda you can read in the English-language **newspapers**, *China Daily* and *Shanghai Star*, available from most newsagents, including the ones on subway platforms. Both have a handy section listing mainstream cultural events.

Imported publications (sometimes censored) such as *Time*, *Newsweek* and Hong Kong's *South China Morning Post* can be bought at the bookshops of four- and five-star hotels and are sometimes available at the Charterhouse bookstore (see p.131). If you are moving or doing business here, you'll find plenty of books offering help and advice at the Foreign Language Bookstore (see p.131). Gourmands will also find in-depth dining guides.

You can pick up glossy free **leaflets**, containing basic tourist information at the upmarket hotels and at the airport. Much more useful, though, are the free **magazines** aimed at the expat community, such as *City Weekend*, *Time Out Shanghai* and the once great, but now rather pedestrian *That's Shanghai*. All have listings sections including restaurants, club nights and art happenings, with addresses written in *pinyin* and Chinese, but no maps. The magazines are free, and you can pick them up at most expat hangouts such as the Old French Concession, Xintiandi or *Barbarossa* in People's Park.

The internet

If the Chinese regime was discomfited by news faxes sent from abroad during the Tian'anmen massacre in 1989, imagine the headache the internet is giving them. Tireless as ever in controlling what its citizens know, the government has built a sophisticated **firewall** – known as the "Golden Shield Project", but nicknamed the new Great Wall of China – that blocks access to undesirable websites. The way the firewall is administered shifts regularly according to the mood of the powers that be. In general, you can be pretty sure you won't be able to access stories deemed controversial from sites such as the BBC or CNN, or anything about Tibetan freedom or democracy.

Virtual private networks (VPNs)

The firewall isn't impenetrable, however; it's simply meant to make getting information deemed controversial enough of a hassle that most Chinese people won't bother. You can get around it simply by subscribing to a **Virtual**

Private **Network**, or **VPN**, such as WiTopia, Hotshot Shield or Ultrasurf, all of which cost a few pounds a month and offer a free limited period trial. Technically, of course, this is illegal, but the government pays no attention to foreigners who do this – and just about every foreign business in China runs a VPN. For Chinese nationals, it's a different matter, and you will never find a public computer, such as one in an internet café, hotel or business centre, running one.

Internet cafés and wi-fi

Shanghai has plenty of **internet cafés**, usually full of kids playing Starcraft. They're generally located in backstreets, not on the ground floor, and never signposted in English – look for the net character, **wǎng** 网. Prices are cheap (around ¥3 an hour), and all places are open 24-hours, but are also heavily regulated – you are required to show your passport before being allowed near a computer. There are a couple on Nanyang Lu, behind the Shanghai Centre, and another on Yunnan Nan Lu, just south of the intersection with Huaihai Zhong Lu. Shanghai Library at 1555 Huaihai Zhong Lu (Ⓜ Hengshan Lu; daily 7am–2am) has a ground-floor room full of computers at ¥4 per hour.

All large **hotels** have business centres where you can get online, but this is expensive, especially in the classier places (around ¥30/hr). Better value are the **backpacker hostels** (see p.96), where getting online costs around ¥5 per hour or is free. But the best deal is to tote a **laptop** – just about every café has free wi-fi, as does *McDonald's*.

USEFUL WEBSITES

China Business World Ⓦ cbw.com. A corporate directory site with a useful travel section, detailing tours and allowing you to book flights and hotels.

Chinasmack Ⓦ chinasmack.com. A mix of serious and weird culture and news stories, taken from Chinese blogs and translated. The best introduction to Chinese internet culture.

City Weekend Ⓦ cityweekend.com.cn/shanghai. Up-to-date listings and light-hearted, informative features aimed at expats.

Expat Shanghai Ⓦ expatsh.com. Bags of useful info for the baffled big nose – how to register your pet, what's on TV, and so on.

Shanghai-ed Ⓦ shanghai-ed.com. Clunkily designed but useful site aimed at expats, with a large classified and jobs section.

Shanghaiist Ⓦ shanghaiist.com. News and a forum, with lots of quirky local gossip; entertaining and informative.

Smartshanghai Ⓦ smartshanghai.com. The definitive nightlife site, with plenty of restaurant reviews too; up to date, with events listings, bitchy user reviews, maps to show where venues are (a rare plus) and a personals section.

Taobao Ⓦ taobao.com. Just about anything you could want is on this eBay-style marketplace – there are almost a billion listings, and it's one of the world's most visited websites. It's not easy to for a non-Chinese speaker to find their way around, so use a guide like Ⓦ taobaofieldguide.com.

That's Shanghai Ⓦ thatsmags.com/shanghai. Extensive website that's rather more useful than the accompanying print magazine, *That's Shanghai*, with a good "community" section as well as listings and features.

Time Out Ⓦ timeoutshanghai.com. Hip listings magazine for expats, with in-depth restaurant reviews.

Yesasia Ⓦ yesasia.com. Online shopping for Chinese movies, CDs, books, collectables and so on.

Zhongwen.com Ⓦ zhongwen.com. A dictionary site useful for students of Chinese and anyone struggling to communicate in Chinese.

Radio

On the **radio** you're likely to hear the latest ballads by pop-robots from the Hong Kong and Taiwan idol factories, or versions of Western pop songs sung in Chinese. The **BBC World Service** can be picked up at 12010, 15278, 17760 and 21660kHz. **Voice of America** can be tuned into on 5880, 6125, 9760, 15250, 15425, 17820 and 21840kHz.

Television

You'd have to be very bored to resort to Chinese **television** for entertainment. Domestic travel and wildlife programmes are frequently shown, as are song-and-dance extravaganzas, the most entertaining of which feature dancers in weird fetishistic costumes. Gung-ho Chinese war films, in which the Japanese are shown getting mightily beaten, at least have the advantage that you don't need to speak the language to understand what's going on. Pop idol-type shows are tremendously popular, though they are sometimes taken off the air by censors for vulgarity. You'll see lots of tacky dating shows too. These too are surprisingly controversial; a girl who rejected a paramour of modest means by saying "I'd rather be crying in the back of a BMW than happy with you on your bike" managed to provoke national uproar and split opinion in the city right down the middle.

The only English-language programmes are news; CCTV9 is an English-language **news** channel, while local broadcaster SBN has a news update at 10pm daily. CCTV5 is a sports channel and often shows European football games. **Satellite TV** in English is available in the more expensive hotels, and most mid- and top-range hotels will have ESPN, BBC and CNN.

Festivals and public holidays

The rhythm of festivals and religious observances that used to mark the Chinese calendar was interrupted by the Cultural Revolution, and only now, nearly fifty years on, are old traditions beginning to re-emerge. The majority of festivals celebrate the turning of the seasons or propitious dates, such as the ninth day of the ninth lunar month, and are times for gift-giving, family reunions and feasting.

Traditional **festivals** take place according to dates in the Chinese lunar calendar, in which the month starts when the moon is a new crescent, and the middle of the month is marked by the full moon; by the Gregorian calendar, these festivals fall on a different date every year.

Public holidays have little effect on business, with only government departments and certain banks closing. However, on New Year's Day, during the first three days of the Chinese New Year, and on National Day, most businesses, shops and sights will be shut, though some restaurants stay open.

JANUARY/FEBRUARY

New Year's Day Jan 1.

Spring Festival Starts between late Jan and mid-Feb. Chinese New Year celebrations extend over the first two weeks of the new lunar year (see box below).

MARCH & APRIL

Shanghai Literary Festival ⓦ m-restaurantgroup.com/mbund /literary-festival.html. Held over three weekends in March at the *Glamour Bar* (see p.115), the city's literary festival has attracted some of the world's most fêted writers, making it a high point in the cultural calendar.

Guanyin's Birthday March 19, 2014; April 7, 2015; March 27, 2016. Guanyin, the goddess of mercy and probably China's most popular Buddhist deity, is celebrated on the nineteenth day of the second lunar month; festivities are held at the Yufo and Baiyunguan temples.

Qingming Festival April 4 & 5. "Tomb Sweeping Day" is the time to visit the graves of ancestors, leave offerings of food, and burn ghost money – fake paper currency – in honour of the departed.

MAY

Labour Day May 1. Labour Day is a national holiday, during which all tourist sights are extremely busy.

Youth Day May 4. Commemorating the student demonstration in Tian'anmen Square in 1919, which gave rise to the nationalist, anti-imperialist May Fourth Movement. Go to the First National Congress of the CCP and you'll see hordes of youths being indoctrinated.

JUNE

Children's Day June 1. Most school pupils are taken on excursions on this day, so if you're visiting a popular tourist sight, be prepared for mobs of kids in yellow baseball caps.

SPRING FESTIVAL

The **Spring Festival**, usually falling in late January or the first half of February, is marked by two weeks of festivities celebrating the beginning of a new year in the lunar calendar (and is thus also called **Chinese New Year**). In Chinese astrology, each year is associated with a particular animal from a cycle of twelve and the passing into a new astrological phase is a momentous occasion. New Year falls on January 31 in 2014 (Year of the Horse), February 19, 2015 (Year of the Sheep) and February 8, 2016 (Year of the Monkey). There's a tangible sense of excitement in the run-up to the festival, when Shanghai is perhaps at its most colourful, with shops and houses decorated with good-luck messages and stalls and shops selling paper money, drums and costumes. However, it's not an ideal time to travel – everything shuts down, and most of the population is on the move, making travel impossible or extremely uncomfortable.

The first day of the festival is marked by a family feast at which *jiaozi* (dumplings) are eaten, sometimes with coins hidden inside. To bring luck, people dress in red clothes (red being regarded as a lucky colour) – a particularly important custom if the animal of their birth year is coming round again – and each family tries to eat a whole fish, since the word for fish is a homonym for surplus. Firecrackers are let off to scare ghosts away and again on the fifth day, to honour Cai Shen, god of wealth. Another ghost-scaring tradition you'll notice is the pasting up of images of door gods at the threshold.

The most public expression of the festivities – a must for visitors – is at the **Longhua Temple** (see p.88), held on the first few days of the festival. There are food and craft stalls and plenty of folk entertainments such as stilt walkers and jugglers. The highlight is on the evening of the first day, when the Longhua bell is struck.

Dragon Festival June 2, 2014; June 20, 2015; June 9, 2016. A one-day public holiday held on the fifth day of the fifth lunar month. Traditionally, a time to watch dragon boat racing and eat treats wrapped in leaves.

Shanghai International Film Festival Mid-June; ⓦ siff.com. With takings at the Chinese box office increasing by 30 percent every year, and Western film-makers desperate to get into bed with moneyed Chinese producers, this festival has become increasingly important. Much better programming in the cinemas than usual, and plenty of glamorous parties, if you can blag an invite.

SEPTEMBER

Moon Festival Sept 8, 2014; Sept 27, 2015; Sept 15, 2016. Celebrated on the fifteenth day of the eighth lunar month, this is also known as the Mid-Autumn Festival, and is a national holiday. It's a time of family reunion, celebrated with fireworks and lanterns; in Shanghai there is an evening parade along Huaihai Lu. Moon cakes, containing a rich filling of sweet paste, are eaten: all the fancier restaurants will have them on the menu.

Shanghai Biennale ⓦ shanghaibiennale.org. An increasingly big deal on the international arts scene, the Biennale is held every other year (2014; 2016) between September and November. The main venue is the Power Station of Art.

OCTOBER

National Day Oct 1. On which everyone has three days off to celebrate the founding of the People's Republic, and state TV is even more dire than usual, packed with programmes celebrating the achievements of the Communist Party. During the "golden week" expect massive crowds everywhere – it's not a convenient time to travel.

Double Ninth Festival Oct 2, 2014; Oct 21, 2015; Oct 9, 2016. Nine is a number associated with *yang*, or male energy, and on the ninth day of the ninth lunar month qualities such as assertiveness and strength are celebrated. It's believed to be a good time for the distillation (and consumption) of spirits.

NOVEMBER

Shanghai International Arts Fair ⓦ artsbird.com. This month-long fair sees a variety of cultural programming at the city's arts venues. At its best when the Shanghai Biennale is in town (see p.27).

Sport and activities

Head to any public space in the morning and you'll see citizens going through all sorts of martial arts routines, playing ping pong and street badminton, even ballroom dancing. Sadly though, facilities for organized sport are fairly limited.

Spectator sports

The Chinese say they're good at "small" ballgames, such as squash, badminton and of course table tennis, at which they are world champions, but admit room for improvement in the "big" ballgames, such as **football**. Nevertheless, Chinese men follow foreign soccer leagues avidly, with games from the European leagues shown on CCTV5 and BTV. The standard of the domestic football league is improving, and decent wages have attracted a fair few foreign players and coaches. In season (mid-March to November) Shenhua, Shanghai's best team, play every other Sunday at 3.30pm in the 35,000-seat Hongkou Stadium in the north of the city at 444 Dongjianwan Lu (see p.84). Tickets cost ¥80 and can be bought on the day, either from the kiosk or from a tout, or in advance from ⓦ mypiao.com.

Basketball has a massive following, thanks largely to some astute marketing by the NBA. You can see the Shanghai Sharks play at the Yuanshen Sports Centre, which is on subway line #6; the season runs from November to April. Tickets cost from ¥80 and are available on the night or in advance from ⓦ mypiao.com.

Shanghai has an impressive **Formula One** track at Jiading, west of the city (ⓦ icsh.sh.cn). Races are held there every September; tickets start at ¥50.

Activities

Golf

There are plenty of courses outside the city; the most prestigious is the Shanghai West Golf Club (☎ 0512 57203888, ⓦ shanghaiwest.com). The Lujiazui Golf Club in Pudong (☎ 68871200) has a driving range and organizes competitions at city courses.

Gyms and yoga

Most large hotels have **gyms**, with facilities at the *Westin* and *Pudong Shangri-La* being particularly impressive. Good private gyms include Megafit in the basement of the Hong Kong Plaza (☎ 53836633) at 300 Huaihai Zhong Lu and Total Fitness on the 5th floor at 819 Nanjing Xi Lu, near Taixing Lu (☎ 62553535).

Yoga has taken off in a big way with the smart set (though they wouldn't be seen dead practising the similar home-grown tradition of *tai ji*). The most fashionable yoga studio is Yplus at 299 Fuxing Xi Lu, near Huashan Lu (☎ 63406161, ⓦ yplus.cn).

MASSAGE AND SPAS

Shanghai has superb massage and spa facilities, with something for all budgets. They are the perfect places to go to unwind from the stresses of a noisy, overcrowded city, for a post-work gossip or even to cap a night out on the town. They are generally open from 10am till 10pm, but may open later.

Every neighbourhood has a **foot masseur** – you can spot one by the poster of big feet in the window. For around ¥25 you'll get your toes and legs bathed, then thoroughly rubbed and pummelled for around forty minutes. For a little extra they'll paint your nails or squeeze your blackheads. Above this, there are plenty of mid-range places, which offer a reasonably priced service in a fairly clinical environment. Shanghai even has a **massage neighbourhood**, Dagu Lu, in Jing'an off Maoming Bei Lu (see map, pp.70–71), which comprises a whole strip of upscale massage venues, offering every imaginable treatment. The branch of Dragonfly (see below) is perennially popular.

At the upper end of the scale, the city has some fantastic **spas**, with lavish decor and ambience and well-trained English-speaking staff. Look out for discounts and special offers advertised in the expat magazines.

MASSAGE

Dragonfly 206 Xinle Lu ☎54039982; 20 Donghu Lu ☎54050008; 458 Dagu Lu ☎62371193, ⓦdragonfly.net.cn; daily 10am–2am. This popular chain offers aroma oil massage to relieve muscular aches and restore energy, as well as shiatsu and Chinese massages (all starting at ¥188 per hour). There's even a hangover relief massage (¥358 for 2hr).

Green Massage 58 Taicang Lu, near Jinan Lu ☎53860222, ⓦgreenmassage.com.cn; daily 10.30am–2am. Offers shiatsu and cupping among a wide range of inexpensive treatment massages, which start at around ¥188. Handily located just around the corner from Xintiandi.

Huimou Massage No.1, Lane 117, Ruijin Er Lu ☎64664857; daily 11am–2am. Cheap and friendly; foot massage ¥60, body massage ¥80, and an aroma oil massage is ¥184 for an hour. They can also arrange house calls, for which the same rates apply plus the cost of return taxi fare.

Yiheyuan Massage 656 Jianguo Xi Lu ☎54651265; daily 10am–2am. Inexpensive foot, body, aroma oil and traditional Chinese massages, starting at ¥60.

SPAS

Anantara Spa 3rd Floor, Puli Hotel, 1 Changde Lu, near Yan'an Lu ☎32039999; daily 10am–midnight. One of the best high-end spas, with a mix of Chinese and Thai techniques. A two-hour full body massage will cost ¥1500, a green tea wrap a little less.

Banyan Tree Spa The Westin, 3rd Floor, 88 Henan Zhong Lu ☎63351888, ⓦbanyantreespa.com; daily 10am–midnight. Choose from a menu of Thai-style oil massages, themed around the elements; prices start at ¥880.

ESPA Ritz Carlton Hotel, 55th Floor, IFC Mall, 8 Century Avenue ☎20201888; daily 9.30am–10pm. This luxurious spa even has perfumed showers, and the relaxation rooms offer great views. English-speaking therapists specialize in treatments inspired by Chinese traditions, such as the Jade facial, which will set you back just over ¥1200.

Hilton Spa Hilton Hotel, 250 Huashan Lu ☎62480000; daily 10am–10pm. Reasonably priced, no-nonsense and a bit more clinical than the other top-end places, this place is popular with men. Treatments include Chinese and Swedish massages and facials, from ¥600.

Mandara Spa JW Marriott, 6th Floor, Tomorrow Square ☎53594969, ⓦmandaraspa.com; daily 10am–10pm. Specialities include a hot stone massage (¥1080 for 90min) and something called a "Mandara Magic" (¥1880 for three hours), which includes a floral bath and a facial.

Swimming

Try the **Olympic-size pool** in the International Gymnastic Centre at 777 Wuyi Lu (Mon–Fri 3.30–9.30pm, Sat & Sun 8.30am–9.30pm; ☎51083583) or the smaller Pudong Pool at 3669 Pudong Nan Lu (Mon–Fri 3.30–9pm, Sat & Sun 9am–9pm; ☎58890101). One of the best of the luxury hotels for swimming is the *JW Marriott* (see p.93), which offers indoor and outdoor pools with views over People's Square. Entry is ¥150.

For fun, you can't beat the **Dino Beach water park** at 78 Xinzhen Lu, near Gudai Lu, Qibao town (daily June 19–Sept 5 9am–9pm; ¥200 (pay half after 6pm); ☎64783333, ⓦdinobeach.com.cn; ⓜLianhua Lu), with its slides, wave machines and 50m-long artificial beach. Rather incongruously, there are sometimes indie music gigs and raves here.

Culture and etiquette

toilet	厕所	cèsuǒ
man	男	nán
woman	女	nǚ

Shanghai is cosmopolitan and sophisticated, and its inhabitants on the whole well-mannered – there's certainly much less spitting and queue-jumping than elsewhere in China. But because the streets are so crowded there is a widespread public brusqueness that can take some getting used to. Pushy vendors will shout at you, jump in front of you or even tug your arm, and it takes a while to train yourself to simply ignore them, as the locals do.

As for personal appearance, skimpy **clothing** is fine (indeed fashionable), but looking scruffy will only induce disrespect. All foreigners are – correctly – assumed to be comparatively rich, so why they would want to dress like peasants is quite beyond the Chinese.

Shaking hands is not a Chinese tradition, though it is now fairly common between men. Businessmen meeting for the first time exchange business cards, with the offered card held in two hands as a gesture of respect – you'll see polite shop assistants doing the same with your change.

If you **visit a Chinese house**, you'll be expected to give your hosts a small gift. Ornamental trinkets and the speciality foods of your country are suitable as presents, though avoid giving anything too practical as it might be construed as charity.

For **restaurant** etiquette, see p.100. Pricier restaurants will have no-smoking sections, but normal restaurants, cafés and bars usually don't. **Public toilets** are sanitary on the whole, but if you blanch at going local, visit any decent hotel – there are always Western-style toilets in the lobby. You'll soon become familiar with the characters you need to know (see box, p.29).

Sex and gender issues

Women travellers in Shanghai usually find the incidence of sexual harassment much less of a problem than in other Asian countries. Chinese men are, on the whole, deferential and respectful. Being ignored is a more likely complaint, as the Chinese will generally assume that any man accompanying a woman will be doing all the talking.

In terms of sexual mores pretty much anything goes in Shanghai these days – the gay scene, as tame as it is, is the best in the country (see p.117), though public displays of homosexual behaviour will raise an eyebrow. **Prostitution**, though illegal, is widespread, with plenty of hairdressers and massage parlours operating as ill-disguised brothels. Single foreign men are likely to be approached inside hotels; it's common practice for prostitutes to phone around hotel rooms at all hours of the night, so disconnect the phone. Bear in mind that China is hardly Thailand – the legal consequences may be unpleasant if you are caught with a prostitute. AIDS is common and the public remains largely ignorant of sexual health issues. Condoms are widely available, however.

Travelling with children

Children in China are, on the whole, indulged and pampered, and thanks to the one-child policy, each "little emperor" is accompanied by six doting adults – his or her parents, plus two sets of grandparents. It's common to see little brats doing whatever the hell they like, but they have a lot less fun when they're old enough to be thrown into China's education sweatshop, where it's also made clear that when they grow up they're expected to look after those six adults in their dotage.

Foreigners with kids can expect to receive lots of attention from curious locals – and the occasional admonition that the little one should be wrapped up warmer. Local kids don't use **nappies**, just pants with a slit at the back, and when baby starts to go, mummy points him at the gutter. Nappies are available from modern supermarkets such as Parkson (see p.101), though there are few public changing facilities. High-end hotels have **baby-minding services** for around ¥150 an hour.

Sights that children would enjoy include the Ocean Aquarium and Century Park in Pudong (see p.76), the zoo (see p.89), acrobat shows (see p.49), Dino Beach and the Shanghai and Science and Technology museums (see p.79). If you're tired of worrying about your kids in the traffic, try taking

> **Tipping** is never expected, and though you might sometimes feel it's warranted, resist the temptation – you'll set an unwelcome precedent.

them to pedestrianized Xintiandi, the malls, Tianzi-fang or Moganshan Art District.

Travel essentials

Costs

Though there's a minority in Shanghai who throw their money around – and plenty of places to spend it – it's quite possible to live cheaply, with most locals surviving on salaries of around ¥3500 a month.

Generally, your biggest expense will be accommodation. Food and transport, on the other hand, are cheap. The minimum **daily budget** you can comfortably maintain is around US$40/£25/¥250 a day, if you stay in a dormitory, get around by subway, and eat in local restaurants. On a budget of US$80/£50/¥500 a day, you'll likely have a better time, staying in a room in a hostel or cheap business hotel, taking taxis, and eating in decent restaurants. To stay in an upmarket hotel and eat in the trendiest places you'll need a budget of around US$220/£140/¥1400 a day.

It used to be government policy to **surcharge foreigners** on public transport fares and admission tickets for sights. This is no longer the case but the practice lives on, and you might find price discrimination being exercised by unscrupulous shopkeepers. **Discounts** on some admission prices are available to students in China on production of the red Chinese student identity card or ISIC card. An international youth hostel card gets a small discount at hostels.

High-end restaurants and hotels add a ten or fifteen percent **service charge** (annoyingly though, it rarely goes to the staff).

Crime and personal safety

The main problem likely to affect tourists visiting Shanghai is **getting scammed** (see box below). In terms of personal safety, Shanghai is safer than most Western cities but you do need to take care as tourists are an obvious target for petty **theft**. Passports and money should be kept in a concealed money belt, and it's a good idea to keep around US$300 separately from the rest of your cash, together with your travellers' cheque receipts, insurance policy details, and photocopies of your passport and visa. Be wary on buses, the favoured haunt of pickpockets.

Hotel rooms are on the whole secure, dormitories less so – in the latter case it's often fellow travellers who are the problem. Most hotels should have a safe, but it's not unusual for things to go missing from these.

On the street, flashy jewellery and watches will attract the wrong kind of attention, and try to be discreet when taking out your cash. Not looking obviously wealthy also helps if you want to avoid being ripped off by street traders and taxi drivers, as does telling them you are a student – the Chinese have a great respect for education, and more sympathy for foreign students than for tourists.

The police

The police, or **PSB** (Public Security Bureau) are recognizable by their dark blue uniforms and caps, though there are a lot more around than you might at first think, as plenty are undercover. They have wider powers than Western police forces, including establishing the guilt of criminals – trials are often used only for deciding the sentence of the accused,

---

WARNING: SCAM ARTISTS

Getting scammed is the biggest threat to foreign visitors, and there are so many professional con artists targeting tourists that you can expect to be approached many times a day at places such as **Yuyuan Bazaar**, around **People's Square** and on **Nanjing Dong Lu**.

Commonly, a sweet-looking young couple, a pair of girls, or perhaps a kindly old man, will ask to practise their English, offer to show you round or just ask you to take a photo with their camera. After befriending you – which may take hours – they will suggest some refreshment, and lead you to a teahouse. Following a traditional-looking tea ceremony you will be presented with a bill for thousands of yuan, your new "friends" will disappear or pretend to be shocked, and some large gentlemen will appear. In another variation, you will be coaxed into buying a painting (really a print) for a ridiculous sum. Remember never to drink with a stranger if you haven't seen a price list.

though China is beginning to have the makings of an independent judiciary. Laws are harsh, with execution the penalty for a wide range of serious crimes, from corruption to rape, though if the culprit is deemed to show proper remorse, the result can be a more lenient sentence.

The police also have the job of looking after foreigners, and you'll most likely have to seek them out for visa extensions (see p.32), to get a loss report, or complain (uselessly) when you've been scammed in a teahouse. They are often extremely helpful, but can be officious. A convenient police station is at 499 Nanjing Xi Lu, beside the Chengdu Bei Lu overpass.

Customs allowances

You're allowed to **import** into China up to 400 cigarettes, two litres of alcohol, twenty fluid ounces (59ml) of perfume and up to 50 grams of gold or silver. You can't take in more than ¥6000, and foreign currency in excess of US$5000 or the equivalent must be declared. It's illegal to import printed or filmed matter critical of the country, but don't worry too much about this, as confiscation is rare in practice.

Note that **export restrictions** apply on any items over 100 years old that you might buy in China – though as you'd be hard pressed to buy anything that old in Shanghai, you needn't be unduly concerned about the process – the "antiques" you commonly see for sale are all fakes (see p.126).

Electricity

The electricity supply runs on 220 volts, with the most common type of plug dual flat prong. Adaptors are widely available from neighbourhood hardware stores, or any of the tech malls (see p.130).

Entry requirements

Visa applications

To enter China, all foreign nationals require a **visa**, available worldwide from Chinese embassies and consulates and through specialist tour operators and visa agents, and online. Recently, the Chinese embassy has outsourced its visa services to a Chinese visa service application centre (W visaforchina.org). These will process your application much quicker than the embassies used to, and they accept postal applications, but they charge substantial administration fees – as much as the cost of the visa itself. They are usually not far from the embassy or consulate and are open Monday to Friday.

> ## EMERGENCY NUMBERS
> **Police** ☎110
> **Fire** ☎119
> **Ambulance** ☎120
> Note though that in an emergency you are generally better off **taking a taxi** (see p.23) to the nearest hospital than calling for an ambulance.

Single-entry tourist visas (L) must be used within three months of issue, and cost US$30–50 or the local equivalent. The standard L visa is valid for a month, but the authorities will sometimes grant a two- or three-month visa if asked (which costs the same), though they might refuse at times of heavy tourist traffic. To apply for an L visa you have to submit an application form, either one or two passport-size photographs, your passport (which must be valid for at least another six months from your planned date of entry into China, and have at least one blank page for visas) and the fee. Recently visa processes have become much more stringent, and offices now also demand proof of entry and exit – such as a flight booking – and proof of accommodation bookings for at least part of the trip (though these can be cancelled later). If you intend to stay with friends, you must provide photocopies of their passport information and visa page and a letter of invitation.

If you apply in person, processing should take between three and five working days. Postal applications are a little more expensive and take longer. You'll be asked your occupation – it's not wise to admit to being a journalist or writer as you may be forced to apply for the inconvenient journalist visa (J), which restricts your movements. And you'll also be asked where you intend to visit; this is not binding, and is not checked, so don't put down any sensitive areas such as Tibet or Xinjiang.

A **business visa (F)** is valid for six months and can be for either multiple or single entry; you'll need an official invitation from a government-recognized Chinese organization to apply for one (except in Hong Kong, where you can simply buy one). **Twelve-month work visas (Z)** again require an invitation, plus a health certificate from your doctor.

Students can get an F visa if they have an invitation or letter of acceptance from a college in Shanghai, though this is only valid for six months. If you're intending to study for longer than six months, you need to fill out an additional form, available from Chinese embassies and online, and will also need a health certificate; then you'll be issued with an **X** visa which allows you to stay and study for up to a year.

Visa extensions

Once in China, a **first extension** to a tourist visa, valid for a month, is easy to obtain; most Europeans pay ¥160 for this, Americans a lot more, nearly ¥1000. To apply for an extension, go to the gleaming "Aliens Entry Exit Department" of the PSB (Public Security Bureau) at 1500 Minsheng Lu, in Pudong, near Yinchun Lu (🚇 Science and Technology Museum; map p.76; Mon–Fri 9–11.30am & 1.30–4.30pm). The visa office is on the third floor. You'll need a passport photo (a shop offers a photo service on the ground floor), proof of your address in Shanghai – so take some hotel receipts – and proof that you have plans to leave the country, so show a plane ticket if you have one. The officious staff will keep your passport for at least a week – note that you can't change money, or even book into a new hotel, while they've got it. **Subsequent applications** for extensions will be refused unless you have a good reason to stay such as illness or travel delay. They'll reluctantly give you a couple of extra days if you have a flight out of the country booked.

Don't **overstay your visa** – the fine is ¥500 per day, and if you're caught at the airport with an out-of-date visa the hassle that will follow may mean you miss your flight.

CHINESE EMBASSIES AND CONSULATES

Australia 15 Coronation Drive, Yarralumla, Canberra, ACT 2600 ☎ 02 6273 4780, ⓦ au.china-embassy.org. Also consulates at Toorak, Surry Hills, Camperdown and East Perth.

Canada 515 St Patrick St, Ottawa, Ontario K1N 5 ☎ 613 234 2682, ⓦ chinaembassycanada.org. Also consulates in Calgary, Toronto and Vancouver.

New Zealand 2–6 Glenmore St, Wellington ☎ 04 474 9631, plus a consulate in Auckland ☎ 09 525 1589; ⓦ chinaconsulate.org.nz.

Republic of Ireland 40 Ailesbury Rd, Dublin 4 ☎ 01 269 1707.

South Africa 220 Hill St, Arcadia, Pretoria ☎ 1234 24194, ⓦ chinese-embassy.org.za.

UK 31 Portland Place, London W1B 1QD ☎ 020 7631 1430, consulate at Denison House, Denison Rd, Victoria Park, Manchester M14 5RX ☎ 0161 224 7480; ⓦ chinese-embassy.org.uk.

US 2300 Connecticut Ave NW, Washington DC 20008 ☎ 202 328 2517, ⓦ china-embassy.org. Also consulates in Chicago, Houston, Los Angeles, New York and San Francisco.

FOREIGN CONSULATES IN SHANGHAI

Your consulate can help if you have lost your passport, need some local reading material or are moving here and need some advice.

Australia 22nd Floor, 1168 Nanjing Xi Lu ☎ 52925500, ⓦ shanghai.china.embassy.gov.au.

Canada Room 604, West Tower, Shanghai Centre, 1376 Nanjing Xi Lu ☎ 62798400.

New Zealand 15th Floor, Qihua Building, 1375 Huaihai Zhong Lu ☎ 64711127, ⓦ nzembassy.com/china.

Republic of Ireland 700A Shanghai Centre, 1376 Nanjing Xi Lu ☎ 62798729, ⓦ embassyofireland.cn/ireland/consulate.htm.

South Africa Room 2706, 220 Yanan Zhong Lu ☎ 53594977, ⓦ dfa.gov.za/foreign/sa_abroad/sac.htm.

United Kingdom Room 301, West Tower, Shanghai Centre, 1376 Nanjing Xi Lu ☎ 62797650, ⓦ ukinchina.fco.gov.uk.

US 1469 Huaihai Zhong Lu ☎ 64336880, ⓦ shanghai.usconsulate .gov.

GOVERNMENT TRAVEL ADVICE

Australian Department of Foreign Affairs ⓦ dfat.gov.au, ⓦ smartraveller.gov.au.

British Foreign & Commonwealth Office ⓦ fco.gov.uk.

Canadian Department of Foreign Affairs ⓦ dfait-maeci.gc.ca.

Irish Department of Foreign Affairs ⓦ foreignaffairs.gov.ie.

New Zealand Ministry of Foreign Affairs ⓦ mft.govt.nz.

South African Department of Foreign Affairs ⓦ dfa.gov.za.

US State Department ⓦ travel.state.gov.

Health

The most common health hazard in Shanghai is the **cold and flu infections** that strike down a large proportion of the population in the winter months, but **diarrhoea** can also be a problem. It usually strikes in a mild form while your stomach gets used to unfamiliar food, but can also be a sudden onset accompanied by stomach cramps and vomiting, which indicates food poisoning. In both instances, get plenty of rest, drink lots of water, and in serious cases replace lost salts with oral rehydration solution (ORS); this is especially important with young children. Take a few sachets with you, or make your own by adding half a teaspoon of salt and three of sugar to a litre of cool, previously boiled water. While down with diarrhoea, avoid milk, greasy or spicy foods, coffee and most fruit, in favour of bland foodstuffs such as rice, plain noodles and soup. If symptoms persist, or if you notice blood or mucus in your stools, consult a doctor.

To avoid stomach complaints, eat at places that look busy and clean and stick to fresh, thoroughly cooked food. Beware of food that has been pre-cooked and kept warm for several hours. Shellfish is a potential hepatitis A risk, and best avoided. Fresh fruit you've peeled yourself is safe; other uncooked foods may have been washed in unclean water. Shanghai's **tap water** can be a little suspect – too many heavy metals – so try to avoid drinking it. Boiled or bottled water is widely available.

Finally, note that though Shanghai is a pretty permissive place, there is widespread ignorance of sexual health issues. Always practise **safe sex**.

Hospitals, clinics and pharmacies

Medical facilities in Shanghai are pretty good: there are some high-standard international clinics, big hotels have a resident doctor, and for minor complaints, there are plenty of pharmacies that can suggest remedies. Most doctors will treat you with Western techniques first, but will also know a little Traditional Chinese Medicine (TCM).

Chinese **hospitals** sometimes charge high prices for simple drugs and procedures that aren't necessary – they'll put you on a drip just to administer antibiotics – so be wary of price gouging. In an emergency you're better off taking a cab than waiting for an ambulance – it's quicker and will work out much cheaper. Some English is spoken at the Ruijin Hospital (197 Ruijin Er Lu; ☏64664483), while the Huashan Hospital (12 Wulumuqi Zhong Lu; ☏62489999, 🖥sh-hwmc.com.cn) has a specialist foreigners' clinic on the eighth floor (☏62483986; 8am–10pm daily).

The United Family Hospital on 1139 Xianxia Lu (24-hr hotline ☏22163999, 🖥shanghai.ufh.com.cn) is a complete hospital staffed by English-speaking doctors trained in the West. They also have a clinic in Pudong at 525 Hongfeng Lu. Expect to pay around ¥700 as a consultation fee at each of the above.

Expats with medical insurance use **private clinics** – reliable, English speaking, international standard, and expensive. The largest is Parkway (24-hr hotline ☏64455999, 🖥parkwayhealth.cn), with seven clinics. The most central are at Tomorrow Square, 389 Nanjing Xi Lu (Mon–Sat 9am–5pm) and 2258 Hongqiao Lu (Mon–Fri 9am–7pm, Sat & Sun 9am–5pm). A consultation here will cost around ¥1000. Parkway manages one hospital, the East International Medical Centre (150 Jimo Lu, near Pudong Dadao; 24-hr hotline ☏58799999, 🖥seimc.com.cn).

Dental treatment will often not be covered on your insurance – never mind, treatment is a little cheaper than in the West. Head to Parkway (see above) or you'll find it a little cheaper at the Shanghai United Family Hospital (also above) – expect more of a wait here. A couple of surprisingly affordable dentists where you can expect treatment from English-speaking staff include KOWA (11th Floor, HONI Plaza, 199 Chengdu Bei Lu, near Weihai Lu ☏80 09881120; 3N1–3N5, Jinmao Tower, 88 Century Avenue ☏51082222, 🖥kowa-dental.com/en; both daily 8.30am–8.30pm) and CAD (Block G,

Zhonglian Villa, 1720 Huaihai Zhong Lu, near Wuxing Lu; ☏64377100; daily 9am–6pm).

Pharmacies are marked by a green cross. Be wary of backstreet pharmacies as counterfeit drugs are common (check for spelling mistakes in the packaging or instructions). There is a 24-hour pharmacy at 201 Lianhua Lu, Changning (☏62941403), and another outside the Huashan Hospital (see above). Watson's (daily 9am–9pm) is a good place to head for over-the-counter medicines – there are large branches at 787 Huaihai Zhong Lu and 616 Nanjing Dong Lu, in the basements of the Times Square Mall on Huaihai Lu, Raffles Mall on Fuzhou Lu and Westgate Mall on Nanjing Xi Lu.

MEDICAL RESOURCES FOR TRAVELLERS

IN THE UK AND IRELAND

MASTA (Medical Advisory Service for Travellers Abroad) UK ☏0870 606 2782, 🖥masta-travel-health.com. Forty clinics across the UK.

Tropical Medical Bureau Republic of Ireland ☏1850 487674, 🖥tmb.ie.

IN THE US AND CANADA

Canadian Society for International Health 🖥csih.org. Extensive list of travel health centres in Canada.

CDC ☏1877 394 8747, 🖥cdc.gov. Official US government travel health site.

International Society for Travel Medicine 🖥istm.org. A full list of clinics worldwide specializing in travel health.

IN AUSTRALIA, NEW ZEALAND AND SOUTH AFRICA

Netcare Travel Clinics 🖥travelclinic.co.za. Travel clinics in South Africa.

Travellers' Medical & Vaccination Centre 🖥tmvc.com.au. Medical and vaccination centres throughout Australia and New Zealand.

Insurance

With medical cover expensive you'd be wise to have **travel insurance**. There's little opportunity for dangerous sports in Shanghai (though crossing the road might count) so a standard policy should be sufficient.

Laundry

All hotels provide a laundry service for around ¥50–100, depending on how classy the hotel is. Hostels have a self-service laundry. There are few public laundries though a hotel concierge can usually point you towards a local entrepreneur who runs a laundry service from home.

ROUGH GUIDES TRAVEL INSURANCE

Rough Guides has teamed up with WorldNomads.com to offer great travel insurance deals. Policies are available to residents of over 150 countries, with cover for a wide range of adventure sports, 24hr emergency assistance, high levels of medical and evacuation cover and a stream of travel safety information. Roughguides.com users can take advantage of their policies online 24/7, from anywhere in the world – even if you're already travelling. And since plans often change when you're on the road, you can extend your policy and even claim online. Roughguides.com users who buy travel insurance with WorldNomads.com can also leave a positive footprint and donate to a community development project. For more information, go to ⓦ roughguides.com/travel-insurance.

Living and working in Shanghai

If you want to stay on in Shanghai, first you'll need a **residence permit**, which your employer will help you sort out. You have to show your passport and Z (working) visa, health certificate, employment certificate, work permit and your employer's business licence at the main PSB (see p.30). The issued green card is then valid for a year.

Foreigners are now allowed to reside anywhere in the city, though most live in housing targeted at them. Rent in these districts is expensive, usually at least US$2000 a month, which gets you a tolerable imitation of a Western apartment. Living in ordinary neighbourhoods is cheaper: a central, furnished two-bedroom apartment costs around US$900 a month. The easiest way to find an apartment is through a real-estate agent, who will usually take a month's rent as a fee. There are plenty of agents, and many advertise in the expat magazines. When you move in you must register with the local PSB office.

Teaching and other work opportunities

Various schemes are run to place foreign teachers in Chinese educational institutions – contact your nearest Chinese embassy (see p.32) for details, or the organizations provided here (see opposite). Some employers ask for a TEFL (Teaching English as a Foreign Language) qualification, though a degree, or simply the ability to speak the language as a native, is usually enough.

Teaching at a **private school**, you'll earn about ¥12,000 a month, more than your Chinese counter-parts do, though your workload of around twenty hours a week is correspondingly heavier. The pay is less at a public school or university, but will be bolstered by on-campus accommodation. Contracts are generally for one year. Most teachers find their students keen, hardworking, curious and obedient. However, avoid talking about religion or politics in the classroom, as this could get you into trouble. Be aware, too, of the risk of being ripped off (you might be given more classes to teach than you've signed up for, for example) and check out the institution thoroughly before committing yourself.

There are plenty of jobs available for foreigners in Shanghai, with a whole section of expat society surviving as actors, cocktail barmen, "Chinglish" correctors, models, freelance writers and so on. But to really make any money here, you need to either be employed by a foreign company or start your own business.

Studying

Private schools aimed at teaching business people how to get by in **Chinese** include the Panda School (❶62376298, ⓦpandachinesetraining.com) and Mandarin House (❶62882308, ⓦmandarin house.cn). Both offer a wide range of courses and private tuition.

USEFUL RESOURCES

Chinatefl ⓦ chinatefl.com. Gives a good overview of English teaching opportunities in the Chinese public sector.

Council on International Educational Exchange ⓦ ciee.org. Exchange programmes for US students of Mandarin or Chinese studies, with placements in Shanghai.

Teach Abroad ⓦ teachabroad.com. Website on which you can post your CV.

Zhaopin ⓦ zhaopin.com. Huge jobs site, in Chinese and English.

Mail

Main **post offices** are open seven days a week between 9am and 7pm; smaller offices may close for lunch or at weekends. The International Post Office is at 276 Suzhou Bei Lu (daily 7am–10pm; ❶63936666). This is where poste restante letters end up (have letters addressed to you c/o Poste Restante, GPO, Shanghai). There are other convenient post offices inside the Shanghai Centre at 1376 Nanjing Xi Lu and on Huangpi Bei Lu at the inter-section with Jiangyin Lu.

The Chinese **postal service** is on the whole fairly reliable, with letters and parcels taking a couple of weeks to reach Europe or the US. Overseas postage rates are becoming expensive; a postcard costs ¥4.5, while a standard letter is ¥6. As well as at post offices, you can post letters in green **postboxes** or at tourist hotels, which usually have a postbox at the front desk. Envelopes can be frustratingly scarce; try the stationery sections of department stores. Stamps can be bought at post offices.

An **Express Mail Service** (EMS) operates to most countries and to most destinations within China and is available from all post offices. Besides cutting delivery times, the service ensures the letter or parcel is sent by registered delivery – though note that the DHL courier service (38 Huaxiang Lu; ☎52277770) is rather faster, and costs about the same.

To send **parcels**, turn up at any post office with the goods you want to send and the staff will sell you a box to pack them in for ¥15 or so. Once packed, but before the parcel is sealed, it must be checked at the customs window in the post office. A 1kg parcel should cost upwards of ¥70 to send surface mail, or ¥120 by airmail to Europe. If you are sending valuable goods bought in China, put the receipt or a photocopy of it in with the parcel, as it may be opened for customs inspection farther down the line.

Maps

A large foldout **map** of the city can be handy. In general, the free tourist maps – available in large hotels and printed inside tourist magazines – don't show enough detail. A wide variety of city maps are available at all transport hubs and from street vendors, hotels and bookshops, with the best selection available from the Foreign Language Bookstore on Fuzhou Lu (see p.131). With the city changing so fast, it's important to check that your map is up to date.

Money

Chinese **currency** is formally called the **yuan** (¥), more colloquially known as renminbi (RMB) or kuai; a yuan breaks down into units of ten jiao. Paper money was invented in China and is still the main form of exchange, available in ¥100, ¥50, ¥20, ¥10, ¥5 and ¥1 notes. Unlike in the rest of China, you'll receive a lot of ¥1 coins in Shanghai – this is because China's mint is here. At the time of writing, exchange rates were around ¥6 to $1, ¥10 to £1 and ¥8 to €1 – an artificially low, government-imposed

rate designed to keep Chinese exports competitive, and which is good news for visitors too.

China is suffering from a rash of **counterfeiting**. Check your change carefully, as the locals do – hold ¥50 and ¥100 notes up to the light and rub them; fakes have no watermarks and the paper feels different.

Banks and ATMs

Banks are usually open seven days a week (9am–noon & 2–5pm), though foreign exchange (there's generally a particular counter for this, marked in English) is sometimes only available Monday to Friday. All banks are closed on New Year's Day, National Day, and for the first three days of the Chinese New Year, with reduced hours for the following eleven days.

Visa and MasterCard can be used to make cash withdrawals from **ATMs** operated by the Bank of China, the Industrial and Commercial Bank of China, China Construction Bank, HSBC and Agricultural Bank of China. All ATMs with this capability have an English language option. Note that most ATMs are located inside banks or shopping centres, so close when they do; there are 24-hour ATMs in the Hong Kong Plaza on Huaihai Zhong Lu and next to Citibank on the Bund. Your bank back home will in all likelihood charge a fee on each withdrawal, with a minimum of around US$3, so it's best to get large amounts out; the maximum for each withdrawal is ¥2000. Keep your exchange receipts and when you leave you can change your renminbi into dollars or sterling at any branch of the Bank of China.

Credit cards and wiring money

China is basically a cash economy, and **credit cards**, such as Visa, American Express and MasterCard, are only accepted at big tourist hotels and the fanciest restaurants, and by some tourist-oriented shops; there is usually a four percent handling charge. It's straightforward to obtain cash advances on a Visa or MasterCard at many Chinese banks (though the commission is a steep three percent). For **lost or stolen cards**, call ☎62798082 (Amex), ☎800 110 7309 (MasterCard) or ☎63236656 (Visa).

It's possible to **wire money** to Shanghai through Western Union (ⓦwesternunion.com); funds can be collected from one of their agents in the city, in post offices and the Agricultural Bank of China.

Opening hours

Offices and **government agencies** are open Monday to Friday, usually from 8am to noon, then from 1pm to 5pm; some open on Saturday and Sunday mornings too. **Museums** are either open all week or are shut on one day, usually Monday. The best time to sightsee is during the week, as all attractions are swamped with local tourists at weekends.

Further details on opening hours can be found in the relevant sections: post offices (see p.34), banks (see p.35), restaurants (see p.100), bars (see p.114), shops (see p.124) and public holidays (see p.26).

Phones

Local calls are free from landlines, and long-distance **China-wide calls** are fairly cheap. Note that everywhere in China has an area code which must be used when phoning from outside that locality. The area code for Shanghai (❶021) has been excluded from listings in this book but must be added if you're dialling from outside the city.

A simple way to make calls is with **IC card phones**, which you'll find in every hotel lobby, and in booths on the street. IC cards (**I-C kǎ** in Mandarin) are sold at every little store and in hotels, in units of ¥20, ¥50 and ¥100, and can also be used for long-distance calls (¥0.15 per minute for domestic long-distance calls, ¥8 per minute for international calls). There's a fifty percent discount when used after 6pm and at weekends. You will be cut off when the credit left on the card drops below the amount needed for the next minute.

A cheaper option is the **IP (Internet Phone) card**, which routes calls using the web and can be used from any phone. Ask for an **I-P kǎ**. They come in ¥50 and ¥100 denominations (though the card is always discounted, and a ¥100 card can usually be had for around ¥50). You dial the number on the card, then instructions in Chinese then English ask you to dial a PIN printed beneath a silver strip on the card, which activates the account; finally you call the number you want. Check the small print – some of these can only be used for calls within China, so ask for a *guoji* (international) card if you want to make international calls. Rates can be as low as ¥2.4 per minute to the USA and Canada, ¥3.2 to Europe.

> ## CALLING MAINLAND CHINA FROM ABROAD
>
> To **call mainland China from abroad**, dial your international access code, then 86 (China's country code), then the area code, minus the initial zero of the regional code (so for Shanghai call 21, not 021), then the rest of the number.

> ## CALLING HOME FROM SHANGHAI
>
> To **call abroad from Shanghai** and the rest of mainland China dial ❶00, then the country code, then the area code, omitting the initial zero (if any), then the number.
>
> **COUNTRY CODES**
> UK ❶44
> Ireland ❶353
> US & Canada ❶1
> Australia ❶61
> New Zealand ❶64
> South Africa ❶27

Note that calling from **tourist hotels**, whether from your room or from their business centres, will attract a surcharge and may well be extortionate.

Mobile phones

Your home **cellular phone** may already be compatible with the Chinese network (visitors from North America should ensure their phones are GSM/Triband), though note that you will pay a premium to use it abroad, and that callers within China have to make an international call to reach you. Alternatively, once in Shanghai you can buy a GSM SIM card from any China Mobile shop or street kiosk, which – as long your phone is unlocked – allows you to use your phone as though it's a local mobile (you will have a new number). The SIM card costs around ¥100, with some variation in price according to how lucky the digits are – favoured sixes and eights bump up the cost, unlucky fours make it cheaper; there will already be ¥50 or so of credit on the SIM. You'll also need to buy prepaid cards to top up the credit. Making and receiving domestic calls this way costs ¥0.6 per minute; an international call will cost around ¥8 a minute.

You can also **rent mobile phones** from China Mobile, which is most conveniently arranged online at ⓦ china-mobile-phones.com. The phone can be picked up from your hotel and left there when you leave. Phones cost ¥80 for the first two days, then ¥8 a day thereafter, and all calls are at the local rate. The cheapest **phones to buy** will cost around ¥200; make sure the staff change the operating language into English for you.

Photography

The Chinese are pretty relaxed about having their picture taken, and the staff at museums and attractions surprisingly accommodating. Colour film and processing is widely available for about ¥1 a print though the quality is variable. Photographic equipment is cheaper in Shanghai than in the West (see p.130).

Time

Shanghai, like the rest of China, is eight hours ahead of GMT, thirteen hours ahead of Eastern Standard Time (North American), sixteen hours ahead of Pacific Time and two hours behind Australian Eastern Standard Time. It does not have daylight saving time.

Tourist information

The official China Tourist Service, **CITS**, at 1227 Beijing Xi Lu (Mon–Fri 9am–6pm; ☎62898899, ✆cits.net), is pretty useless at supplying information, being geared mainly towards getting you to buy one of its tours; otherwise, you'll just be handed a few leaflets. Things aren't much better at the official Tourist Information Outlets – there are a few around town, the most central being under the Bund Promenade (daily 9.30am–8pm; ☎63573718). The free 24-hour tourist hotline on ☎962288 can help with general enquiries.

There's plenty of **online information** about China in general and Shanghai specifically (see p.25), though as a general rule, avoid websites run by official agencies such as CITS as they're dry as dust.

Travellers with disabilities

In China the disabled are generally hidden away, so attitudes are not very sympathetic and little special provision is made. As it undergoes an economic boom, Shanghai resembles a building site, with uneven, obstacle-strewn paving, intense crowds and traffic, and few access ramps. Commendably, a huge effort has been made to make pavements and subway stations friendly to **the blind**.

Wheelchair users will generally find public transport inaccessible, though a few of the upmarket hotels have experience in assisting disabled visitors; in particular, Shanghai's several *Holiday Inns* (☎63538008) and *Hiltons* (☎62480000) have rooms designed for wheelchair users.

Given the situation, it may be worth considering an **organized tour**. Make sure you take spares of any specialist clothing or equipment, extra supplies of drugs (carried with you if you fly), and a prescription including the generic name – in English and Chinese characters – in case of emergency. If there's a local association representing people with your disability, contact them early on in the planning process. The official representative of the disabled in Shanghai is the Disabled Person's Federation at 189 Longyang Lu (☎58733212).

TAI JI ON THE BUND

The Bund and Nanjing Dong Lu

Shanghai's signature skyline, and the first stop for any visitor, is the Bund, a strip of grand colonial edifices on the west bank of the Huangpu River, facing the flashy skyscrapers of Pudong on the opposite shore. The product of the city's commercial frenzy at the beginning of the twentieth century, this was where the great trading houses and banks built their headquarters, each trying to outdo the last in the pomp of their edifices. Today it's the most exclusive chunk of real estate in China, with pretensions to becoming the nation's Champs-Elysées; the world's most luxurious brands have set up shop here, and there are a clutch of celebrity restaurants and some iconic hotels. Visitors can get a first taste of the frantic pace of Shanghai's modern consumerism on the roads that lead from it back towards People's Square – Nanjing Dong Lu and Fuzhou Lu.

The Bund

外滩, wàitān • Metro line #2 to Nanjing Dong Lu subway station; walk east along Nanjing Dong Lu to the Fairmont Peace Hotel

Though the row of European buildings along the Huangpu River has since 1949 been known officially as Zhongshan Dong Yi Lu, and locals know it better as Wai Tan (literally "outside beach"), it will always be **the Bund** to foreigners. The northern end starts from the confluence of the Huangpu and the Suzhou Creek, by **Waibaidu Bridge**, and runs south for 1.5km to Jinling Dong Lu, formerly Rue du Consulat.

Named after the Anglo-Indian term for the embankment of a muddy foreshore, the Bund was old Shanghai's commercial heart, with the river quays on one side, the offices of the leading banks and **trading houses** on the other. These sturdy marble-and-granite structures, built in a mongrel mix of Anglo-Oriental styles ranging from Italian Renaissance and neo-Grecian to Moorish, were both a celebration of Western commercial enterprise and a declaration of dominance. During Shanghai's riotous heyday this was also a hectic working **harbour**, where vessels from tiny sailing junks to ocean-going freighters unloaded under the watch of British (and later American and Japanese) warships. Everything arrived here, from silk and tea to heavy industrial

■ ACCOMMODATION		● RESTAURANTS AND CAFÉS		● SHOPS AND MARKETS	
24K Hotel	6	8½ Otto e Mezzo Bombana	1	Apple Store	1
Blue Mountain Bund Youth Hostel	4	Ajisen	2	Foreign Language Bookstore	3
Chai Shanghai Living	1	Lao Beijing	6	Nantai Costume Company	4
Dock Bund Hostel	2	Lao Zhenxing	3	Shanghai Antique and Curio Store	5
Jinjiang Inn	8	The Stage, Westin	4	Silk King	2
Le Royal Méridian	5	Wang Baohe	5		
Mingtown Hikers Hostel	3	Westin Bakery	4	■ NIGHTLIFE	
Westin	7			Cirque le Soir	1

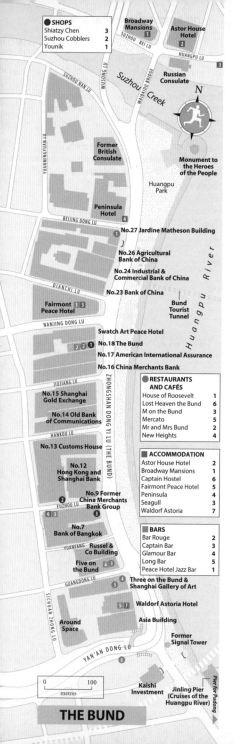

THE BUND

machinery. So too did wealthy foreigners, ready to pick their way to one of the grand hotels through crowds of beggars, hawkers, black marketeers, shoeshine boys and overladen coolies.

When the Communists took over in 1949 the buildings were mothballed, and though nothing was done to preserve these symbols of foreign imperialism, surprisingly little was destroyed. Now, as Shanghai rises, the street is once again a hub of commerce, though of the decidedly upmarket kind. As well as the city's ritziest luxury brand shops, the buildings house Shanghai's fanciest restaurants (see p.102), though if you just want to eat, rather than have a life- (and wallet-) transforming culinary experience, choice is much more limited.

Broadway Mansions

上海大厦, shànghǎi dàshà · 20 Suzhou Bei Lu
You can't miss the hulking **Broadway Mansions**, at the far north end of the Bund, though you may wish you could – this classic example of the po-faced stolidity of the Chicago School would make a good Orwellian Ministry of Truth. When it was built in 1933, it was the highest building in Asia. During World War II the building was taken over by the Japanese; it is now a half-decent hotel (see p.92). Its most illustrious resident was Jiang Qing (wife of Mao Zedong), who issued a decree during the Cultural Revolution banning barges and sampans from travelling up the Huangpu or Suzhou while she was asleep. If you're not staying here, you can appreciate the views by taking the lift to the eighteenth floor.

Russian Consulate

俄罗斯领事馆, éluósī lǐngshìguǎn · 20 Huangpu Lu
Over the road from Broadway Mansions, the **Russian Consulate** is one of the few Bund buildings that is used for its original purpose. The iron grilles over the windows came in useful on those occasions in the 1920s when this bastion of "Red" Soviet Russia was attacked by White Russians. In 1960, during one of the frostier periods of Sino-Soviet relations, it suffered the indignity of being turned into a bar for seamen; it returned to being a consulate in 1987.

1

Astor House Hotel

浦江饭店, pǔjiāng fàndiàn • 15 Huangpu Lu

The grand **Astor House Hotel**, just north of Waibaidu Bridge, was built in 1846 and enlarged in 1910, and was the city's glitziest venue until the *Peace Hotel* was built. It was also one of the few places where polite foreign and Chinese society mingled, when "tea dances" were held – with rather more whisky than tea serving as social lubricant. The original manager, a retired seaman, had the corridors painted with portholes and the rooms decorated like cabins. Today, with its endless wooden corridors, high ceilings, and slightly eccentric air of batty gentility, the hotel has something of a Victorian public school about it. It remains worth a snoop for its grand lobby, renovated ballroom and a few relics of its past glories on display (see p.92).

Shanghai Post Museum

上海邮政博物馆, shànghǎi yóuzhèng bówùguǎn • 276 Suzhou Bei Lu • Wed, Thurs, Sat & Sun 9am–4pm • Free • ☎ 63936666, Ⓦ shpost.com.cn

The Main Post Office was built in 1931, and is easily recognizable by its clocktower. It's the only Bund building that has never been used for anything but its original function. It houses the **Shanghai Post Museum** on the third floor, which is more interesting than it sounds. The collection of letters and stamps is only mildly diverting, but the new atrium is very impressive, and the view from the grassed-over roof is superb.

Waibaidu Bridge

外白渡桥, wàibáidùqiáo

Waibaidu Bridge crosses Suzhou Creek at the north end of the Bund. Built by the British in 1908, it was China's first steel truss bridge. At the outbreak of the Sino-Japanese War in 1937 it represented the frontier between the Japanese-occupied areas north of Suzhou Creek and the **International Settlement** to the south – itself a no-man's-land, guarded at each end by Japanese and British sentries. Though only built to last forty years, today it's as much a permanent feature as anything in this city. Today it's a popular spot for wedding photographs, and you'll see brides-to-be braving the traffic in order to be briefly framed by its striking girders.

Former British Consulate

英国驻上海总领事馆, yīngguó zhù shànghǎi zǒnglǐngǧ shì guǎn • 33 Zhongshan Dong Yi Lu

South of the bridge you'll come to the **former British Consulate**, set back from the road in a neat garden. Built in 1852, it is one of the oldest Bund buildings. Lavishly restored, it is today used for government functions and posh dos, so you won't get in without an invite. It was once ostentatiously guarded by magnificently dressed Sikh soldiers; nowadays, black-clad security guards will let you know where you're not allowed.

Peninsula Hotel

上海半岛酒店, shànghǎi bàndǎo jiǔdiàn • 32 Zhongshan Dong Yi Lu • ☎ 23272888, Ⓦ pensinsula.com/shanghai

The ritzy new **Peninsula Hotel** (see p.93) is the latest incarnation of the Hong Kong luxury brand. In keeping with the area, it's gone for a traditional, **Art Deco** look. Head through the doors and the windowless black marble interior is like some great emperor's tomb. The wares of the designer shops lining the gloomy space remind the visitor of grave goods – which they may as well be, for all the customers they see. The ambience improves when you get to the lobby, where a quartet plays and the local elite drink afternoon tea (see p.105).

Huangpu Park

黄浦公园, huángpǔ gōngyuán

Right on the corner of Suzhou Creek and the Huangpu River, on the east side of the road, **Huangpu Park** was another British creation, then the British Public Gardens,

1

established in 1886 on a patch of land formed when mud and silt gathered around a wrecked ship. Sikh troops here enforced the rules which forbade Chinese from entering unless they were servants accompanying their employer. After protests the regulations were relaxed in 1928 to admit "well-dressed" Chinese, who had to apply for a special entry permit. Though it's firmly established in the Chinese popular imagination as a symbol of Western racism, there's no evidence that there ever was a sign here reading "No dogs or Chinese allowed". These days the park contains a rather unattractive stone obelisk commemorating the **"Heroes of the People"**, and is also a popular spot for citizens practising *tai ji* early in the morning.

In contrast to the snooty pretensions of the buildings over the road, the riverside **promenade** remains stoutly proletarian, full of out-of-towners taking the obligatory Shanghai shot of the Oriental Pearl Tower (see p.77) – and there are plenty of vendors who will take the picture for you, or sell you a plastic copy of it (or a yapping mechanical dog). As well as affordable places to eat (including a *Costa* and a *Subway*) you'll find the entrance to the **Bund Tourist Tunnel** (外滩观光隧道, wàitān guānguāng suìdào), the psychedelic gateway to Pudong (see p.74).

Rockbund Art Museum

外滩美术馆, wàitān měishùguǎn • 20 Huqiu Lu • Tues–Sun 10am–6pm • ¥15 • ☎ 33109985, ⓦ rockbundartmusem.org

The narrow streets leading back from the Bund hold some fine Art Deco buildings, and this slim monolith, tucked behind the *Peninsula Hotel*, is one of the most striking. It dates back to the 1930s, when it was the headquarters of the Royal Asiatic Society. Now it's been skilfully restored and converted into an achingly cool four-storey gallery of contemporary art, hosting shows that usually mix China's biggest hitters with international artists. There's no permanent exhibition, so check the website for what's on, and for the programme of events and lectures.

VICTOR SASSOON

"There is only one race finer than the Jews, and that's the Derby."

More than anyone, it was **Victor Sassoon** (1881–1961), infamous tycoon and bon vivant, who shaped Shanghai's prewar character. The Sassoons were Sephardic Jews from Iraq, whose family fortune was built by trading in India. Victor, one of the fourth generation (which included the writer Siegfried Sassoon) astonished the family by moving the company assets out of India and into China – largely, it is said, to dodge the British taxman. "Sir Victor", as he liked to be known, began pouring millions of dollars into Shanghai in the 1920s, virtually single-handedly setting off a high-rise real estate boom that was to last almost a decade. His Art Deco constructions include what have become many of the city's most distinctive landmarks, among them: Hamilton House and the *Metropole Hotel* (see p.47), at the intersection of Fuzhou Lu and Jiangxi Lu; the Cathay Theatre on Huaihai Zhong Lu; the *Orient Hotel* on Xizang Zhong Lu near People's Square; the Embarkment Building on Suzhou Bei Lu; Cathay Mansions (now the *Jinjiang Hotel*; see p.65); and the enduring landmark of the Bund, the Cathay Hotel, now the *Fairmont Peace Hotel* (see p.43).

At the Cathay, Victor lived in a penthouse with a 360-degree view over the city, and indulged his tastes for the finest of everything – including women. His suite had two bathtubs because, he said, he liked to share his bed but never his bath. As described by Stella Dong in *Shanghai, the Rise and Fall of a Decadent City*, his parties sound dazzling. At his shipwreck party, guests came dressed as if they were abandoning ship; the prize for best costume was awarded to a couple who were naked except for a shower curtain. At his circus parties, guests would come as clowns or acrobats while he, of course, played ringmaster, in top hat and tails and wielding a riding crop. Victor's world came crashing down with the Japanese invasion, though he was able to spirit most of his fortune away to the Bahamas, where he died in 1961.

1

Jardine Matheson Building

外滩 27号, wàitān 27 haò • 27 Zhongshan Dong Yi Lu • ⓦ bund27.com

Heading south from the *Peninsula Hotel*, the next grand edifice is at no. 27. This was the former base of **Jardine Matheson**, founded by William Jardine – the man who did more than any other individual to precipitate the Opium Wars and open Shanghai up to foreign trade (see p.159) – the first foreign concern to buy land in Shanghai. It's seen a lot of different nationalities come and go: in 1941 the British Embassy occupied the top floor (facing the German Embassy, just across the road), shortly after which it was requisitioned by the Japanese navy, before doing service as the American consulate. Today it's known as the **House of Roosevelt**, and houses a Rolex shop, some stuffy, upscale restaurants that are worth sampling for afternoon tea (see p.150) and the city's biggest wine cellar.

Bank of China

中国银行, zhōngguó yínháng • 19 Zhongshan Dong Yi Lu

One of the Bund's more modern structures is the **Bank of China** at no. 23, built in 1937 in the Chicago style with a Chinese hat as concession to local sensibilities. No. 24, which was originally the Yokohama Bank, is rather more successful in its blend of Eastern and neo-Grecian styles. Unfortunately (but hardly surprisingly) only a couple of the Japanese martial sculptures that once ornamented the facade have survived; look above the first-floor windows.

The Fairmont Peace Hotel

和平饭店, hépíng fàndiàn • 20 Nanjing Dong Lu • ☎ 63216888, ⓦ fairmont.com/peace-hotel-shanghai

Straddling the eastern end of Nanjing Dong Lu is one of the most famous hotels in China, the **Fairmont Peace Hotel**, formerly the Cathay Hotel. The hotel's main building (on the north side of Nanjing Dong Lu) is a relic of another great trading house, **Sassoon's**, and was originally known as Sassoon House. Like Jardine's, the Sassoon business empire was built on opium trading, but by the early years of the last century the family fortune had mostly been sunk into Shanghai real estate, including the Cathay (see box opposite). Nicknamed "The Claridges of the Far East" it was the place to be seen in prewar Shanghai: Douglas Fairbanks and Charlie Chaplin were among its celebrity guests and Noël Coward is supposed to have written *Private Lives* here while laid up with flu. It boasted innovations such as telephones in the rooms before any European hotels, and had such luxuries as a private plumbing system fed by a spring on the outskirts of town, marble baths with silver taps and vitreous china lavatories imported from Britain. The *Peace* today is well worth a visit for the bar, with its legendary jazz band (see p.115), and for a walk around the lobby. On the first floor, a little museum of the hotel's history (daily 10am–7pm) displays relics such as room keys and lampshades from the Thirties, and plenty of old photographs, including one of Mao meeting Monty. There's a good view of the Bund from the balcony of the seventh-floor bar – staff will tolerate curious visitors popping in for a quick look.

The smaller wing on the south side of Nanjing Dong Lu was originally the Palace Hotel, built around 1906. It was restored – like so much of the city – in time for the 2010 expo and is now called the *Swatch Art Peace Hotel*, with a Swatch showroom and ritzy boutiques, and an extensive artists-in-residence programme.

Number 18 The Bund

外滩18号, wàitān shíbāhào • 18 Zhongshan Dong Yi Lu • ⓦ Nanjing Dong Lu

Number 18 The Bund was originally the Chartered Bank of India and Australia, but today is home to the city's most la-di-da shops, given gravitas by the building's Italian marble columns. If you want to spot Chinese celebrities (assuming you can recognize them), this is the place to go. As well as high-end stores such as Zegna and Cartier, the

1

building houses an arts space on the fourth floor; the swanky *Mr and Mrs Bund* restaurant (see p.103); and, above it, *Bar Rouge* (see p.114), which has a fantastic roof terrace with views of Pudong.

American International Assurance

外滩17号, wàitān shíqíhào • 17 Zhongshan Dong Yi Lu • ⓂNanjing Dong Lu

At no. 17, **American International Assurance** has returned to reoccupy the building it left in 1949. Back then it shared its tenancy with "the old lady of the Bund" – the English-language *North China Daily News*, whose motto is engraved over the ground-floor windows – "Journalism, Art, Science, Literature, Commerce, Truth, Printing". The Communists banned it from printing news in 1949, so the very last issue was given over to articles on the philosopher Lao Tzu and Hittite hieroglyphics.

Customs House

海关楼, hǎiguān lóu • 13 Zhongshan Dong Yi Lu

Continuing south down the Bund from no. 17, past neo-Grecian, Italian Renaissance and Art Deco edifices brings you to the magnificent **Customs House** at no. 13. The Chinese customs service was administered by foreigners, as it was discovered that this way much less money disappeared through graft. The service was headed by an Irishman, Robert Hart, who at one point was forwarding to Beijing a third of the Qing government's revenue. The clocktower was modelled on Big Ben in London, and after its completion in 1927, local legend had it that the chimes, which struck every fifteen minutes, confused the God of Fire: believing the chimes were a fire bell, the god decided Shanghai was suffering from too many conflagrations, and decided not to send any more. During the Cultural Revolution loudspeakers in the clocktower played *The East is Red* at six o'clock every morning and evening. The original clockwork was restored in time for a visit by Queen Elizabeth II in 1986. You can step into the downstairs lobby for a peek at some restored mosaics of maritime motifs on the ceiling.

Hong Kong and Shanghai Bank

汇丰中国, huìfēng zhōngguó • 12 Zhongshan Dong Yi Lu

Right next to the Customs House, and also with an easily recognizable domed roofline, the former headquarters of the **Hong Kong and Shanghai Bank**, built in 1921, has one of the most imposing of the Bund facades. It's now owned by the Pudong Development Bank, who allow visitors to poke around the entrance hall. Today, HSBC is one of Britain's biggest banks, though few of its customers can be aware of its original purpose – to finance trade between Europe and China. Each wall of the marble octagonal entrance originally boasted a mural depicting the bank's eight primary locations (Bangkok, Kolkata, Hong Kong, London, New York, Paris, Shanghai and Tokyo), and the eight words of its motto: "Within the four seas all men are brothers". The four huge marble columns in the banking hall are among the largest pieces of solid marble in the world. In the far left corner was a separate bank for Chinese customers, who entered using the entrance on Fuzhou Lu – the massive door, inscribed with the initials HSBC, still stands. The Chinese character *fu* (prosperity) can be seen on the walls and in the trim, and Chinese-style abstract designs decorate the cornices and ceilings.

It's considered lucky to rub the noses or paws of the bronze lions that stand guard outside the Corinthian columns of the entranceway. These are replacements for the two originals, which were removed by the Japanese; one stands today in the History museum (see p.77). They were officially named "Prudence" and "Security" but nicknamed "Stephen" and "Stitt", after the bank's general managers. One lion looks belligerent, the other smiles inscrutably. There are similar pairs outside the HSBC headquarters in Hong Kong and London. Locals used to joke that the lions roared when a virgin passed – so their incessant silence said something about the relaxed morals of the Shanghainese.

Five on the Bund

外滩5号, wàitān wǔhào • 5 Zhongshan Dong Yi Lu

Most of no. 5 (officially **Five on the Bund**) is home to the Huaxia Bank, but on Guangdong Lu you'll find the entrance to the building's upscale restaurant, *M the Bund* (see p.103). Opened in 1999, it kicked off the zone's present revival. The *Glamour Bar* (see p.115) above, is one of the city's most stylish bars.

Three on the Bund

外滩3号, wàitān sānhào • 3 Zhongshan Dong Yi Lu

Three on the Bund opened in 2004 and with its mix of high-end shops, swanky restaurants and a spicing of contemporary art to add cultural legitimacy, it set the tone for the new developments that followed. Check out the Armani flagship store on the ground floor, before heading to the third floor for the Shanghai Gallery of Art (see p.122).

Waldorf Astoria Hotel

华尔道夫酒店, huá'ěrdàofū jiǔdiàn • 2 Zhongshan Dong Yi Lu • ☎ 63229988, ⓦ waldorfastoriashanghai.com

When No. 2, The Bund opened in 1910, it was a private members club for well-heeled Brits, "The Shanghai Club". It closed its doors with the arrival of the Japanese in 1941, then languished for decades; in 1988 Shanghai's first *KFC* took up residence, and trashed the period fittings. Happily, it has recently been restored to its full glory as the **Waldorf Astoria Hotel**. As with the other heritage hotels in the area, it is forbiddingly expensive to stay in (see p.93), but worth a visit to check out the stylish interior – in this case, Neoclassical opulence. Don't miss the *Long Bar*, rebuilt from photos of the Club's original bar, and a fine evocation of 1930s

---

HUANGPU RIVER TOURS

Even in this age of freeway projects and a sophisticated metro system, the **Huangpu** is still a vital resource for Shanghai – one-third of all China's trade passes through here. The river is also the city's chief source of drinking water – though, thick and brown, it contains large quantities of untreated waste, including sewage and high levels of mercury and phenol. At least it no longer serves as a burial ground – until the 1930s those too poor to pay for the burial of relatives would launch the bodies into the river in boxes decked in paper flowers.

One highlight of a visit to Shanghai, and the easiest way to view the edifices of the Bund, is to take one of the **Huangpu River tours** (黄浦江旅游, huángpǔjiāng lǚyóu). These leave from Shilliupu Wharf at the south end of the Bund, opposite Jinling Dong Lu. You can buy tickets at the wharf or at the Bund Tourist Information Centre, beside the entrance to the Bund Tourist Tunnel.

On the tour, you're introduced to the vast amount of shipping that uses the port, and you'll also be able to inspect all the paraphernalia of the shipping industry, from sampans and rusty old Panamanian-registered freighters to sparkling Chinese navy vessels. You'll also get an idea of the colossal construction that is taking place on the eastern shore. Evening cruises offer spectacular views, as Shanghai is lit up like a pinball machine at night.

Cruise departure times vary depending on season and weather. Ninety-minute-long cruises (¥128) depart at least twice an hour between 11am and 9.30pm. They travel south to Yangpu Bridge, then north towards Wusongkou, then return to the wharf. Hour-long cruises (¥100) are rarer, usually hourly, and there is one daily three-hour cruise (¥150) at 2pm, which goes all the way to the mouth of the Yangzi and back. Cruises that include a buffet dinner run between 7pm and 9pm (¥200).

There are many cruise companies – one of the biggest is the Huangpu River Company (☎ 637400091, ⓦ pjrivercruise.com). You can book tickets a few days in advance over the phone and they will deliver to your hotel.

It is also possible to take half-hour cruises from Pudong. These leave from the Pearl Dock (明珠码头, míngzhū mǎtóu), every half-hour between 10am and 1.30pm (¥100).

1

Shanghai. The eastern end of the original thirty-three-metre-long bar commanded a view of the Huangpu, and only the club's elite members were allowed to sit there (see p.115).

The Bund to People's Square

Two kilometres west of the Bund lies another hotspot for tourists, People's Square (Renmin Guangchang). Connecting them is the consumer cornucopia of pedestrianized **Nanjing Dong Lu**, with its two major parallel arteries, dull Yan'an Dong Lu and quirky **Fuzhou Lu**. In the days of the foreign concessions, expatriates described Nanjing Dong Lu as a cross between New York's Broadway and London's Oxford Street. But it was also at this time that Nanjing Dong Lu and Fuzhou Lu were lined with teahouses that functioned as the city's most exclusive brothels, whose courtesans were expected, among their other duties, to be able to perform classical plays and scenes from operas, and host banquets. In a juxtaposition symbolic of prewar Shanghai's extremes, strings of the lowest form of brothel, nicknamed "nail sheds", lay just two blocks north of Nanjing Dong Lu, along Suzhou Creek. The street was dubbed "Blood Alley" for the nightly fights between sailors on leave who congregated here.

Nanjing Dong Lu
南京东路, nánjīng dōnglù

On its eastern stretch, **Nanjing Dong Lu**'s garish neon lights and window displays are iconic; come here in the evening (before things start closing up at 9pm) to appreciate the lightshow in its full tacky splendour. If you don't want to explore by foot, a daft little electric train (¥5) tootles up and down. The shopping is not what it once was, with the emphasis now firmly on cheap rather than chic, but the authorities, aware of this, have started to boot out the more low rent locals and get some international brands in.

No. 635 was once the glorious **Wing On** emporium, and diagonally opposite was the **Sincere**. These were not just stores: inside there were restaurants, rooftop gardens, cabarets and even hotels. Off the circular overhead walkway at the junction between Nanjing and Xizang Zhong Lu is the grandest of the district's department stores, the venerable **Shanghai No. 1 Department Store**; it's still a place of pilgrimage for out-of-towners, but there's nothing much of interest to a foreign visitor.

If you're looking for cheap clothes, you'll be spoilt for choice, but for something distinctly Chinese you'll have to look a bit harder. Your best bet for curiosities is to head to the **Shanghai First Food Store**, at no. 720. The Chinese often buy food as a souvenir, and this busy store sells all kinds of locally made gift-wrapped sweets, cakes and preserves, as well as tea and tasty pastries. Nearby **Taikang Foods** at no. 768 is another example, with a dried meat section at the back selling rather macabre flattened pig heads.

SCAMMERS ON NANJING DONG LU

Take note that foreign faces on Nanjing Dong Lu will be incessantly approached by pesky pimps, street vendors and "art students", but the most common **scam** is for one or two young guys or girls to befriend you, perhaps asking to practise their English or to help them take photos. They'll suggest you go to a bar for a coffee or a beer, which, when the bill comes, will cost hundreds of yuan. On a single stroll up the street, this will be tried a dozen times. There are plenty of places in Shanghai where strangers are genuine, but this is not one of them. For more on this, see Basics (p.30).

Fuzhou Lu
福州路, fúzhōu lù

Heading west from the Bund along **Fuzhou Lu**, you'll first come to the nautically themed *Captain Hostel* (see p.97), where taking the creaky lift to the sixth-floor *Captain Bar* will reward you with excellent views of Pudong. Continue west until you reach Jiangxi Nan Lu, and you'll see Shanghai at its most gloomily Gothamesque, thanks to twin Art Deco edifices, the **Metropole Hotel** and **Hamilton House**, once an apartment complex, on the south corner; both were built by British architects Palmer and Turner. In the building at the northwest corner lodged the Shanghai Municipal Council, the governing body of the International Settlement.

Fifty metres further west, the court building at no. 209 used to be the **American Club**. Georgian-style, with marble columns, it was built in 1924 with bricks shipped in from the States. After you cross Henan Zhong Lu you enter a brighter commercial area, with a medley of small stores selling art supplies, stationery, trophies, medical equipment and books, including the Foreign Language Bookstore at no. 390 (see p.131). Finally, at the end of the road, **Raffles Mall** (莱福士广场, láifúshì guǎngchǎng) is one of Shanghai's best (and busiest), with a juice bar and plenty of cheap, clean eateries in the basement, and a good mix of clothes stores above.

THE SHANGHAI MUSEUM

People's Square

People's Square (Renmin Guangchang; 人民广场, rénmín guǎngchǎng) is the modern heart of Shanghai. It functions both as a transport hub (its perimeters are defined by the city's main arteries: Xizang, Nanjing and Yan'an roads), and as home to the grand temples of culture, history and government. There's an impressive clutch of sights here, all within walking distance of each other. The pot-shaped Shanghai Museum is world class, and one of the city's highlights, while the nearby Shanghai Urban Planning Exhibition Hall looks to the future both in its design and its contents. Just north is the unexpectedly peaceful Renmin Park, with its little Museum of Contemporary Art; overall, you have one of Shanghai's most rewarding destinations. Few places in China have such a concentration of great sights, and you'll need a full day to do them justice.

In contrast to the dour totalitarianism of its Beijing counterpart at Tian'anmen, People's Square possesses a much more human feel. Instead of a concrete plain lined with po-faced edifices, Shanghai's urban centre comprises a rather haphazardly arranged park and a plaza dotted with a hotchpotch of modernist and colonial buildings (with, of course, a huge shopping mall underneath).

As People's Square is at the interchange of subway lines #1 and #2, the easiest way to get here is on the metro. A dozen exits cover a vast area, so work out which exit you want from the wall maps in the station, then navigate your way through the shopping mall – the low numbers bring you out in the southeast corner of the square near the museum, the high ones in the northwest near the park. There aren't many places to eat so if you're here for the day, you'll have to plan where you're having lunch (see p.104).

2

The Shanghai Museum

上海博物馆, shànghǎi bówùguǎn • 201 Renmin Avenue • Daily 9am–5pm, no entry after 4pm • Free; audio-guide ¥40, with ¥400 deposit • ☎ 63723500, ⓦ shanghaimuseum.net/en • Ⓜ People's Square

People's Square metro station can get fearsomely busy but fortunately as you head west onto Renmin Dadao the crowds thin out dramatically. On the south side of this giant boulevard, Renmin Square is a pleasant plaza with a fountain where you might catch a few skateboarders, and tourists feeding the pigeons. At the back stands the unmistakeable showpiece **Shanghai Museum**.

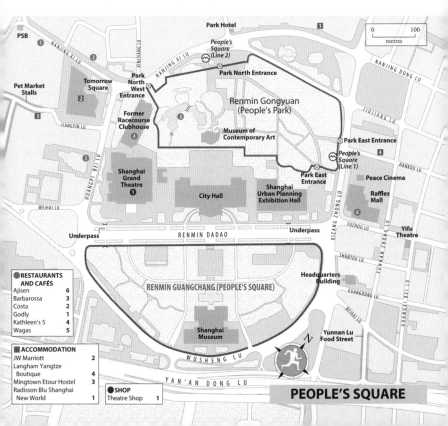

● RESTAURANTS AND CAFÉS	
Ajisen	6
Barbarossa	3
Costa	2
Godly	1
Kathleen's 5	4
Wagas	5

■ ACCOMMODATION	
JW Marriott	2
Langham Yangtze Boutique	4
Mingtown Etour Hostel	3
Radisson Blu Shanghai New World	1

● SHOP	
Theatre Shop	1

PEOPLE'S SQUARE

The building's form is based on a *ding*, an ancient Chinese pot, and its layout, like many Chinese buildings, is inspired by traditional cosmogony, with a square base to represent Earth and a rounded roof to represent Heaven. Inside, there are eleven galleries, with well-displayed pieces and plenty of explanation in English. You'll need several hours for a comprehensive tour, though some galleries can be safely skipped; the best stuff, on the whole, is on the ground and top floors. Informative leaflets are available at an information desk on the ground floor.

The ground floor

One of the museum's major highlights is its ground-floor gallery of **bronzes**, most of which are more than two thousand years old yet appear strikingly modern in their simple lines and bold imagery. The cooking vessels, containers and weapons on display were used for ritual rather than everyday purposes, and are beautifully made. Many are covered with intricate geometrical designs that reference animal shapes, while others reveal startlingly naturalistic touches – check out the cowrie container from the western Han dynasty, with handles shaped like stalking tigers and lid surmounted by eight bronze yaks. There's also a charming wine urn with a dragon spout and another shaped like an ox. A display near the entrance shows how these were made, using an early form of the "lost wax" method – the original is made in wax, then covered in plaster, after which the wax is heated and poured away to create a mould.

A crowd-pleasing pottery dog guards the entrance to the **sculpture** gallery next door. Most of the exhibits are religious figures – boggle-eyed temple guardians, serene Buddhas and the like. Look out for the row of huge, fearsome Tang-dynasty heads and the figurines of dancers in flowing robes, which resemble Brancusi sculptures in their simplicity.

The first floor

The Tang dynasty steals the show once again in the **ceramics** gallery, which takes over the first floor. The spiky, multicoloured tomb guardians, in the shape of imaginary beasties, make the delicate glazed pots look reserved in comparison. The accompanying text reminds you that the delicate art of porcelain was invented in China; some fine examples from the Song and Ming dynasties are on display.

The second floor

On the second floor, skip the calligraphy and carved seals unless you have a special interest and check out the **painting** gallery instead. The winning dynasty here has to be the Ming, as the amazingly naturalistic images of animals from this time are much easier to respond to than the interminable idealized landscapes. Look out in particular for Bian Wenzhi's lively images of birds.

The top floor

The top floor contains the most colourful gallery, dedicated to the many **Chinese minority peoples**. To anyone who thinks of China as a monoculture, this striking assembly of the weird and wonderful will come as a shock. One wall is lined with spooky lacquered masks from Tibet and Guizhou (in southwest China), while nearby are colourfully decorated boats from the Taiwanese minority, the Gaoshan. The silver ceremonial headdresses of southwest China's Miao people are breathtaking for their intricacy, if rather impractical to wear; elsewhere, elaborate abstract designs turn the Dai lacquered tableware into art. In the section on traditional costumes, look out for the fish-skin suit made by the Hezhen people of Dongbei, in the far north. The explanation might insist on the "Chineseness" of all this but it's quite clear from their artefacts that these civilizations at the furthest edges of the Chinese Empire, many of them animist in their beliefs, are culturally very distant from the Han mainstream, and those from southwest China have more in common with their Thai or Laotian coreligionists.

The Ming- and Qing-dynasty **furniture** next door is more interesting than it sounds. The Ming pieces are elegant and reserved while those from the Qing, as illustrated in the diorama of a study room, swarm with intricate detail. They may look a little old-fashioned compared to, say, the bronzes downstairs, but there is a similar aesthetic on display – everyday objects raised to high art.

Along Renmin Dadao

人民大道, rénmín dàdào

2

Head from the Shanghai Museum to the north side of **Renmin Dadao**, and you are faced with some fine modern buildings, all worthy of exploration. Keep going north and you'll find some lovely old ones too, notably the **Former Racecourse Clubhouse** and the *Park Hotel* (see p.162).

Former Racecourse Clubhouse

You'll spot this building by its distinctive clocktower (see box below), modelled on Big Ben. It was until recently an art museum, and its new role is uncertain. Inside, you'll see hints of its former role in the equestrian detailing on the balustrades. Head up to the top-floor restaurant, *Kathleen's 5* (see p.105 and p.104) for afternoon tea and fantastic views over the square.

Shanghai Urban Planning Exhibition Hall

城市规划展示馆, chéngshì guīhuà zhǎnshìguǎn • 100 Renmin Avenue • Tues–Sun 9am–5pm, last entry 4pm • ¥30 • ☎ 63184477, ⓦ supec.org • Ⓜ People's Square

It's surely revealing that one of Shanghai's grandest museums is dedicated not to the past but the future: the **Shanghai Urban Planning Exhibition Hall** is interesting for its insight into the grand ambitions and the vision of the city planners, though if you're not keen on slick propaganda presentations it can be safely skipped. Most worthy of note is the tennis court-sized model on the second floor, showing what the city will (if all goes to plan) look like in 2020. No room in this brave new world for shabby little alleyways: it's a parade ground of skyscrapers and apartment blocks in which, according to this model, the whole of the Old City (see p.53) is doomed. In a video room next door you get taken on a virtual helicopter trip around this plan, which is liable to make you giddy. Back on the first floor, there's a collection of old photographs of Shanghai from colonial times – most interesting if you've already grown somewhat familiar with the new look of these streets. Avoid the tacky "olde-worlde" cafés in the basement.

Shanghai Grand Theatre

上海大剧院, shànghǎi dàjùyuàn • 300 Renmin Dadao • ☎ 63273094, ⓦ shgtheatre.com

Head west past the frumpy City Hall, and you come to the impressive **Shanghai Grand Theatre**, distinguished by its convex roof and transparent walls and pillars – a different take

---

THE SHANGHAI RACECOURSE

The area of People's Square was originally the site of the Shanghai racecourse, built by the British in 1862. The races became so popular among the foreign population that most businesses closed for the ten-day periods of the twice-yearly meets. They soon caught on with the Chinese too, so that by the 1920s the **Shanghai Race Club** was the third wealthiest foreign corporation in China. When not used for racing the course was the venue for polo and cricket matches. During World War II it served as a holding camp for prisoners and as a temporary mortuary; afterwards most of it was levelled, and while the north part was landscaped to create Renmin Park, the rest was paved to form a dusty concrete parade ground for political rallies. The former paved area has now been turned over to green grass, bamboo groves and fountains, while the bomb shelters beneath have become shopping malls.

on the same cosmological principles that influenced the Shanghai Museum's designers. Created by the architectural agency responsible for the Bastille Opera House in Paris, it has ambitions of being a truly world-class theatre (see p.119). If you're just passing, there's a café on site and a good shop sells reasonably priced DVDs and CDs (see p.131).

Renmin Park

人民公园, rénmín gōngyuán · Open 24hr (but only the north gate is open after 7pm) · Free

Just east of the Former Racecourse Clubhouse is the north gate to lovely **Renmin Park**. It's surprisingly quiet, with rocky paths winding between shady groves and alongside ponds – the only sign that you are in the heart of a modern city are the skyscrapers looming above the treetops. In the morning, the park is host to *tai ji* practitioners and joggers, and old folk arrive to camp out all day playing cards.

Bearing left brings you to a small square. On weekends, this is the venue for an extraordinary **marriage market**. Hundreds of middle-aged parents mill round with printouts displaying the statistics of their children – height, education, salary – and arrange dates. Interestingly, few display photos – these folks know what attributes they want for their little darling's partner, and looks aren't top of the list.

Head through bamboo groves to the lotus pond and a quintessential Shanghai view will open out in front of you. It's a shocking architectural mash-up: from left to right, elegant modernism (MoCA), then Arabian fantasy *Barbarossa* (see p.104), followed by the colonial edifice of the old racecourse clubhouse, and looming over that the corporate brutalism of Tomorrow Square (see p.52).

Museum of Contemporary Art

上海当代艺术馆, shànghǎi dāngdài yìshùguǎn · Daily 10am–6pm · ¥20, students free · ☎ 021 63279000, Ⓦ mocashanghai.org · Ⓜ People's Square

Crossing the zigzag bridge, a minute's walk to the south of *Barbarossa* brings you to the attractive, glass-walled **Museum of Contemporary Art** (**MoCA**). This privately funded museum has no permanent collection but its shows are always interesting and imaginatively curated, and its three storeys make an excellent exhibition space. There's a lot of video and installation art, with a roughly equal balance between Chinese and foreign artists, and the museum holds regular talks and tours; check the website for details.

Tomorrow Square

明天广场, míngtiān guǎngchǎng

Come out of the north entrance of Renmin Park, turn left and cross back over Huangpi Bei Lu and that scary, claw-roofed monolith towering over you, with a striking resemblance to Saruman's castle out of the *Lord of the Rings* films, is **Tomorrow Square**. The top floors house the *JW Marriott* hotel; head to the lobby on the 38th floor for great views over People's Square – you can see how much prettier it would be without City Hall in the middle. If you want to linger here you'll have to buy a drink (the cheapest cocktails are around ¥70).

Jiangyin Lu

江阴路, jiāngyīn lù

Just behind Tomorrow Square, and in stark contrast to its corporate sheen, is an area of ramshackle low rise, **Jiangyin Lu**. Heading west along here for a hundred metres or so, past the excellent *Mingtown Hostel*, where the bar is a good place for a cheap drink (see p.97), brings you to a little pet market, where you can buy a cricket in a bamboo cage for ¥5 or a snake for a little more.

YUYUAN BAZAAR

The Old City and around

The Old City (老城, lǎochéng) is that strange oval on the map, circumscribed by two roads, Renmin Lu and Zhonghua Lu, which follow the old path of the city walls. This district never formed part of the International Settlement and was known by the foreigners who lived in Shanghai, rather patronizingly, as the Chinese City. Based on the original walled city of Shanghai, which dated back to the eleventh century, the area was reserved in the nineteenth and early twentieth centuries as a ghetto for vast numbers of Chinese who lived in conditions of appalling squalor, while the foreigners carved out their living space around them. It's an area of about four square kilometres, and at its northern edge is not half a kilometre from the Bund – though a great distance in spirit.

Although tree-lined ring roads replaced the original walls and moats as early as 1912, and sanitation has obviously improved vastly since, to cross the boundaries into the Old City is still to enter a different world. The twisting alleyways are a haven of free enterprise, bursting with makeshift markets selling fish, vegetables, cheap trinkets, clothing and food. Ironically, for a tourist entering the area, the feeling is like entering a Chinatown in a Western city. It probably won't stay that way for long though; as prime real-estate, the area is squarely in the sights of developers and city planners and many of the lanes have already been demolished.

In modern times the area has been slashed down the middle by the main north–south artery, Henan Nan Lu (河南南路, hénán nán lù). The easiest approach from Nanjing Dong Lu is to walk due south along Henan Lu or Sichuan Zhong Lu; or just take the metro to Yu Yuan.

Visitor activity centres on the tourist **Yuyuan Bazaar** and the attached **Yu Gardens**, but there are also a few charming **temples** sunk into the **alleyways**. Heading west, you abruptly re-enter the modern city when you hit **Renmin Lu**. Not far from here you'll find the shabby but intriguing **Dongtai Lu Antique Market**, worth a mooch even if you're not into buying. From here you can walk to swanky Huaihai Zhong Lu (淮海中路, huáihǎi zhōng lù), Xintiandi and Tianzifang, all covered in the next chapter.

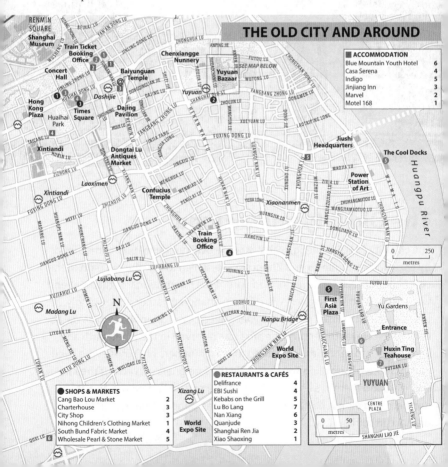

Yuyuan Bazaar

豫园商城, yùyuán shāngchéng

Surrounding the Yu Gardens is the touristy **Yuyuan Bazaar**, a tangle of narrow lanes lined with souvenir shops, all new but built in a style of architectural chinoiserie. Some might complain that it looks like Disneyland but it's very popular with Chinese tourists, and it gets fearsomely busy. If you need to get some souvenir **shopping** done in a hurry, this is the place to come, though watch out for tea scam artists (see p.30). You'll have to bargain hard, except at the large jewellery shops, where gold and platinum pieces are sold by weight, and the price per gram – lower than in the West – is marked on the wall. Wooden signs point to the more famous shops (see p.124).

Yu Gardens

豫园, yùyuán · Daily 8.30am–5.30pm · ¥40 · ☎ 63260830 · Ⓜ Yu Yuan

A classical Chinese garden featuring pools, walkways, bridges and rockeries, the **Yu Gardens** (Yu Yuan or Jade Garden) were created in the sixteenth century by a high-ranking official in the imperial court in honour of his father. Despite fluctuating fortunes, the gardens have surprisingly survived the passage of the centuries. They were spared from their greatest crisis – the Cultural Revolution – apparently because the anti-imperialist "Little Sword Society" had used them as their headquarters in 1853 during the Taiping Uprising (see p.160). The Yu Gardens are less impressive than the gardens of nearby Suzhou (see p.137), but given that they predate the relics of the International Settlement by some three centuries, the Shanghainese are understandably proud of them. During the lantern festival on the fifteenth day of the traditional New Year, the gardens are brightened up by thousands of lanterns and an even larger number of spectators.

Garden connoisseurs will appreciate the whitewashed walls topped by undulating dragons made of tiles, the lotus ponds full of koi and the paths winding round hillocks. The first building you come to is the **Cuixiu Hall** (Hall of Gathering Grace), built as a venue for the appreciation of an impressive twelve-metre-high **rockery**; Chinese gardens are meant to be landscapes in miniature, so the rockery is something of a mini-Himalaya. The **Yuhua Tang** (Hall of Jade Magnificence) behind it has some lovely wooden screens on the doors and inside is full of Ming-dynasty rosewood furniture. The huge, craggy, indented rock in front of the hall was intended for the Summer Palace in Beijing, but the boat carrying it sank in the Huangpu, so it was recovered and installed here. Chinese guides demonstrate that a coin dropped in the hole at the top can emerge from several different exits – according, so they say, to your astrological sign. The southeast section of the gardens is a self-contained **miniature garden** within a garden and tends to be rather less busy, so it's a good place to head for a sit down.

Huxin Ting Teahouse

湖心亭茶馆, húxīntíng cháguǎn · 257 Yuyuan Lu · Daily 8am–9pm · ☎ 63736950

After visiting the Yu Gardens, check out the charming (if touristy) **Huxin Ting** (Heart of Lake Pavilion), a two-storey teahouse on an island at the centre of an ornamental lake, reached by a zigzagging bridge. The Queen of England and Bill Clinton, among other illustrious guests, have dropped in for tea. These days it's a bit pricey at ¥60 for a cup of tea (albeit limitless). Rely on the waiter's recommendation and you'll be given the most expensive option, so insist on seeing the menu. Vendors on the bridge sell fish food for ¥5 so you can feed the carp.

3

Chenxiangge Nunnery

沉香阁, chénxiāng gé · 29 Chenxiangge Lu · Daily 8am–4pm · ¥10

A short walk west from the Yu Gardens, the **Chenxiangge Nunnery** is one of the more active of Shanghai's temples. This tranquil complex is enlivened by the presence of a few dozen resident nuns, who gather twice daily to pray and chant in the Daxiongbao Hall, under the gaze of the Sakyamuni Buddha. His gilded statue is flanked by images of 384 disciples, all supposedly the work of a single recent, still living, craftsman.

The alleyways

If you head west out of the Yuyuan Bazaar (past all the construction work) you will soon find yourself in some gritty alleyways – the real old town, if you like. It's being torn down at a fearsome rate, but hopefully there will still be a few streets left by the time you read this.

Dajing Lu

大镜路, dàjìng lù

Crossing Henan Nan Lu brings you to the most interestingly ramshackle street, **Dajing Lu**, where you'll likely come across ducks being killed and plucked, laundry and cured meat hung up on the same lines, and plenty of hole-in-the-wall restaurants with their fare – crabs, toads, shrimps and the like – crawling around plastic tubs outside. Look behind you for a great Shanghai snapshot, the Jinmao Tower rising over the shabby street like a mirage – very *Blade Runner*.

Baiyunguan Temple

白云观, báiyún guān · 239 Dajing Lu · Daily 9am–5pm · ¥5 · ☎ 63287236

At the end of Dajing Lu is the pretty Taoist **Baiyunguan Temple**. Worshippers light incense and burn "silver ingots" made of paper in the central courtyard – some burn paper cars and houses too. Taoist priests wander round in yellow robes with their long hair tied in a bun. In the main hall there's a huge effigy of the Jade Emperor looking judgemental. Taoism is the most esoteric of China's three big religions, and there are some weird figures of Taoist Immortals on display at the side of the hall – look for the fellow with arms coming out of his eyes.

Dajing Pavilion

大镜阁, dàjìng gé · 237 Dajing Lu · Daily 9am–4pm · ¥5

Next door to the Baiyunguan Temple, the **Dajing Pavilion** is a new structure built over the last surviving slice of a Ming-dynasty wall. Brick markings on the wall bear the names of the two emperors, Tongzhi and Xianfeng, who commissioned it as protection against Japanese pirates. The pavilion today contains a rather threadbare exhibition on the history of the Old City.

Confucius Temple

文庙, wén miào · Wenmiao Lu · Daily 9am–5pm · ¥10

Sunk deep into the southwestern corner of the Old City on Wenmiao Lu is the **Confucius Temple**. Confucius was a philosopher who, around 500 BC, lectured on ethics and statecraft, emphasizing the importance of study and obedience. He was deified after his death and his theories provided the ideological underpinnings to the feudal Chinese state. Though Confucianism is no longer an active religion, its ideological influence on Chinese culture is obvious in the general Chinese respect for education and patriarchal authority.

Like most such temples across China, the Confucius Temple has become a park and museum. Shanghai has had a temple dedicated to Confucius since the Yuan dynasty but most of the present buildings date back to 1855, when the Small Swords Society (see p.160) made the temple a base. The only original Yuan building left is the elegant three-storey **Kuixing Pavilion**, near the entrance, which is dedicated to the god of artistic and intellectual endeavour. An appealing atmosphere of scholarly introspection infuses the complex – students wishing for good exam results tie red ribbons to the branches of the pine trees, and there's a statue of Confucius himself looking professorial (though it's not the recently approved "official" likeness).

In the **study hall** is an exhibition of teapots, more interesting than it sounds, as some display a great deal of effort and ingenuity. One, appropriately for the venue, is in the shape of a scholar, with the spout being his book, while another is nearly a metre high – it must have been hell to pour.

The temple is never busy except on Sundays, when there is a secondhand book fair in the main courtyard. Outside, vendors sell kitschy trinkets and street food.

Fuyou Lu antique market

福佑路, fúyòu lù • 457 Fangbang Zhong Lu • Ⓜ Yu Yuan

3

If you're in the Chenghuang Miao area early on Sunday morning (8–11am is the best time, though trade continues into mid-afternoon), you can visit a great indoor **market** on Fuyou Lu, the small street running east–west along the northern edge of Yu Yuan. The market has a raw, entrepreneurial feel about it; all sorts of curios and antiques – mostly fakes – ranging from jade trinkets to *Little Red Books* can be found here, though you'll have to bargain fiercely if you want to buy.

Dongtai Lu antique market

东台路, dōngtái lù/liuhekou Lu • Ⓜ Laoximen

On the outskirts of the Old City, in a small alley called Dongtai Lu leading west off Xizang Nan Lu, is the largest permanent **antique market** (daily 10am–4pm) in Shanghai. Even if you're not interested in buying, this is a fascinating area to walk around. The range is vast, from old Buddhas, coins, vases and teapots to mah jong sets, renovated furniture and Cultural Revolution badges. As with all antique markets in China, the vast majority of goods are fake.

Power Station of Art

上海当代艺术博物馆, shànghǎi dāngdài yìshù bówùguǎn • 200 Huayuangang Lu, near Miaojiang Lu • Daily 9am–5pm • Free • ☎ 31278535, ⓦ powerstationofart.org • Ⓜ Xizang Lu, then a fifteen-minute walk

A long way south of the Old City, on the site of the 2010 Expo, you'll find this huge new **art space**. It might seem strange that a city so dedicated to material pleasures should suddenly boast so many art galleries – but then Chinese art is big business these days, and the city fathers are well aware that nothing confers prestige like a bright new gallery. This is a state-run contemporary art museum in a renovated old power station – perhaps an attempt to replicate the success of London's Tate Modern. The building, with its sturdy industrial lines and fittings, is certainly striking; it's huge too, and thus far it seems to have been rather a struggle to fill. There's no permanent show; it is the new home of the Shanghai Biennale (see p.27) and hosts international touring exhibitions.

The Old French Concession

Shanghai might be changing furiously but one thing always stays the same: the Old French Concession (法租界, fǎzūjiè) is its most charming area. More than anywhere else in the city it has retained its historic feel; when people call Shanghai the Paris of the East, this is the part they're thinking of. The area is predominantly low rise, thanks to a colonial ruling that no building be more than one and a half times taller than the road is wide, and lined with glorious old mansions – many of which have become restaurants, boutiques, embassies and galleries. Certain French characteristics linger here, in the local chic and in a taste for bread and sweet cakes, and in the many old plane trees providing shade. The district invites leisurely strolling, with a little shopping, people-watching, a good meal and lots of coffee the order of the day.

Less crowded than Nanjing Dong Lu and more upmarket, **Huaihai Zhong Lu** is the main street running through the heart of the area. The most interesting streets are the quieter ones leading off it. To the east you'll find the **Xintiandi** development, a zone of rebuilt traditional houses (*shikumen*) that even critics of its yuppie ambience admit has great architectural charm, and, just south of here, the quaint **Tianzifang** area, where alleys of *shikumen* have been converted to artsy boutiques and coffee shops; both are well worth exploring. Heading west from here, there are plenty of former residences and boutiques to poke around in the area of Ruijin Er Lu, Maoming Nan Lu and Fenyang Lu (汾阳路, fēnyáng lù). As the street heads towards Hengshan Lu (衡山路, héngshān lù), embassies, bars and restaurants start to predominate.

A great way to explore is by **bike** (see p.23), though note that bikes are not allowed on Huaihai Zhong Lu (淮海中路, huáihǎi zhōng lù). Otherwise, take the metro to Huangpi Nan Lu (黄陂南路, huángpí nán lù), Shaanxi Nan Lu or Changshu Lu (常熟路, chángshú lù) and walk.

Brief history

Established in the mid-nineteenth century, the former French Concession lay to the south and west of the International Settlement, abutting the Chinese City (see p.53). Despite its name, its population was never particularly French. Before 1949, in fact, it was a shabby district mainly inhabited by Chinese and White Russians – what is now Huaihai Zhong Lu was then Avenue Joffre, after the French general, but it was nicknamed "Little Moscow". Other Westerners looked down on the White Russians as they were obliged to take jobs that, it was felt, should have been left to the Chinese (see box, p.65).

It's hard to imagine it now, but the French Concession was notorious for being low rent, for its lawlessness and for the ease with which police and French officials could be bribed – in contrast to the well-governed areas dominated by the British. This made it ideal territory for gangsters, including the king of all Shanghai mobsters, Du Yuesheng. For similar reasons, political activists also operated in this sector – the first meeting of the Chinese Communist Party took place here in 1921, and both Zhou Enlai and Sun Yatsen, the first provisional president of the Republic of China after the overthrow of the Qing dynasty, lived here. The preserved former homes of these two in particular (see p.63 & p.64) are worth visiting simply because, better than anywhere else in modern Shanghai, they give a sense of how the Westerners, and the Westernized, used to live.

4

Xintiandi

新天地, xīntiāndì • Ⓜ Huangpi Nan Lu, then walk south for five minutes; alternatively, walk east from Ⓜ Xintiandi

Although it might seem like an obvious idea, the **Xintiandi** development, which comprises two blocks of renovated and rebuilt *shikumen* (see box, p.63) converted into a genteel open-air mall, was the first of its kind in China. It has met with such success that town planners all over the country are now studying its winning formula. Detractors may call it a working-class neighbourhood reimagined as a yuppie playground, but architecturally the area is a triumph – its stone buildings have retained their charm without being chintzy and the attention to detail is fantastic. Paved and pedestrianized, with *longtang* opening out onto a central plaza, Xintiandi is a great place to wind down or linger over a coffee, with upscale restaurants and shops and plenty of outside seating for people-watching. Access is subtly but strictly controlled, with security guards keeping the riffraff out, so there aren't even any art students to hassle you.

North Block

Heading into the **North Block**, you'll first have to pass the city's most popular *Starbucks*. The branch of the popular Shanghai Tang boutique on the left is lovely, with a great tiled floor, but the prices for their distinctive clothes and accessories are mind-boggling;

THE OLD FRENCH CONCESSION

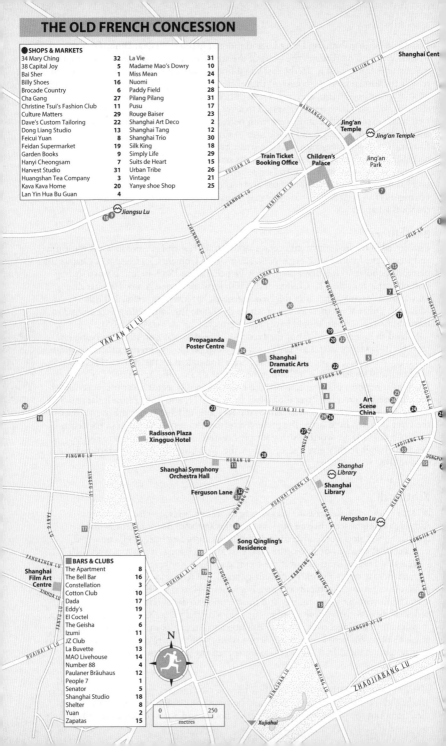

Shanghai Cent

Beijing Xi Lu

Wanhangdou Lu

Jing'an Temple

Jing'an Temple

Jing'an Park

Train Ticket Booking Office

Children's Palace

Yuyuan Lu

Xuanhua Lu

Nanjing Xi Lu

Jiangsu Lu

Zhenning Lu

Julu Lu

Changshu Lu

Huaihai Lu

Yan'an Xi Lu

Huashan Lu

Changle Lu

Anfu Lu

Wulumuqi Zhong Lu

Propaganda Poster Centre

Shanghai Dramatic Arts Centre

Wuyuan Lu

Art Scene China

Baoqing Lu

Fuxing Xi Lu

Radisson Plaza Xingguo Hotel

Yongfu Lu

Taojiang Lu

Dongping Lu

Pingwu Lu

Hunan Lu

Shanghai Symphony Orchestra Hall

Huaihai Zhong Lu

Shanghai Library

Shanghai Library

Gao'an Lu

Hengshan Lu

Hengshan Lu

Ferguson Lane

Wukang Lu

Song Qingling's Residence

Tianping Lu

Xingfu Lu

Fanyu Lu

Huashan Lu

Wanping Lu

Kangping Lu

Wuxing Lu

Yongjia Lu

Wulumuqi Nan Lu

Fahuazhen Lu

Shanghai Film Art Centre

Xinhua Lu

Huaihai Xi Lu

Huaihai Xi Lu

Tianlin Lu

Hengshan Lu

Wanping Lu

Jianguo Xi Lu

Zhaojiabang Lu

Xujiahui

N

0   250
metres

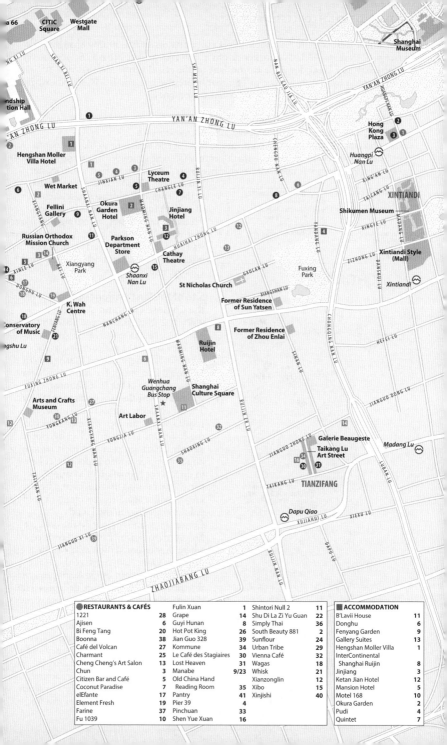

RESTAURANTS & CAFÉS

1221	28
Ajisen	6
Bi Feng Tang	20
Boonna	38
Café del Volcan	27
Charmant	25
Cheng Cheng's Art Salon	13
Chun	3
Citizen Bar and Café	5
Coconut Paradise	7
elEfante	17
Element Fresh	19
Farine	37
Fu 1039	10
Fulin Xuan	1
Grape	14
Guyi Hunan	8
Hot Pot King	26
Jian Guo 328	39
Kommune	34
Le Café des Stagiaires	30
Lost Heaven	31
Manabe	9/23
Old China Hand Reading Room	35
Pantry	41
Pier 39	4
Pinchuan	33
Shen Yue Xuan	16
Shintori Null 2	11
Shu Di La Zi Yu Guan	22
Simply Thai	36
South Beauty 881	2
Sunflour	24
Urban Tribe	29
Vienna Café	32
Wagas	18
Whisk	21
Xianzonglin	12
Xibo	15
Xinjishi	40

ACCOMMODATION

B'Lavii House	11
Donghu	6
Fenyang Garden	9
Gallery Suites	13
Hengshan Moller Villa	1
InterContinental Shanghai Ruijin	8
Jinjiang	3
Ketan Jian Hotel	12
Mansion Hotel	5
Motel 168	10
Okura Garden	2
Pudi	4
Quintet	7

for similar stuff at more reasonable prices visit imitators such as nearby Shanghai Trio (see p.124), or you'll find crude knock-offs at any fake market (see p.126). It's also worth having a jaunt down the narrow lane on the east side (the one that runs north–south from Annabel Lee to T8): that impressive mansion is 1 Xintiandi, where its Hong Kong owners hang out and count their money.

Shikumen Open House Museum

石库门民居陈列馆, shíkùmén mínjū chénlièguǎn • Daily 10am–10pm • ¥20

The **Shikumen Open House Museum**, at the bottom end of the north block, does an excellent job of evoking early twentieth-century Chinese gentility. This reconstruction of a typical *shikumen* is filled with everyday objects – typewriters, toys, a four-poster bed and the like so it doesn't look as bare as the "Former Residences" elsewhere in the city. A top-floor display details how Xintiandi came about, admitting that most of it was built from scratch. A quote on the wall is perhaps more revealing than was intended: "Foreigners find it Chinese and Chinese find it foreign."

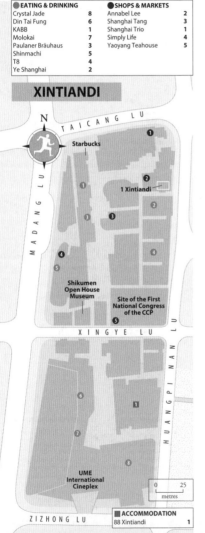

● EATING & DRINKING		● SHOPS & MARKETS	
Crystal Jade	8	Annabel Lee	2
Din Tai Fung	6	Shanghai Tang	3
KABB	1	Shanghai Trio	1
Molokai	7	Simply Life	4
Paulaner Bräuhaus	3	Yaoyang Teahouse	5
Shinmachi	5		
T8	4		
Ye Shanghai	2		

XINTIANDI

N

TAICANG LU

Starbucks

MADANG LU

1 Xintiandi

Shikumen Open House Museum

Site of the First National Congress of the CCP

XINGYE LU

HUANGPI NAN LU

UME International Cineplex

0   25
metres

ZIZHONG LU

■ **ACCOMMODATION**
88 Xintiandi   1

Site of the First National Congress of the Chinese Communist Party

中国一大会址纪念馆, zhōngguó yīdàhuìzhǐ jìniànguǎn • Daily 9am–5pm, last admission 4pm • Free

On the east side of the complex, at the junction of Xingye Lu and Huangpi Nan Lu, you'll find one of the shrines of Maoist China, the **Site of the First National Congress of the Chinese Communist Party**. The official story of this house is that on July 23, 1921, thirteen representatives of the communist cells which had developed all over China, including its most famous junior participant **Mao Zedong**, met here to discuss the formation of a national party. The meeting was discovered by a French police agent (it was illegal to hold political meetings in the French Concession), and on July 30 the delegates fled north to nearby Zhejiang Province, where they resumed their talks in a boat on Nan Hu. Quite how much of this really happened is unclear, but it seems probable that there were in fact more delegates than the record remembers – the missing names would have been expunged according to subsequent political circumstances. There's a little **exhibition hall** downstairs, whose period relics – such as maps, money and a British policeman's uniform and truncheon – are more interesting than the comically outdated propaganda rants. The last room has a waxwork diorama of Mao and his fellow delegates.

SHIKUMEN

The *shikumen*, or stone-gated house, was developed in the late nineteenth century as an adaption of Western-style terrace housing to Chinese conditions. By the 1930s, such houses were ubiquitous across Shanghai, and housed eighty percent of the population. Crammed together in south-facing rows, with a narrow alley or *longtang* in between, they were all built to a similar design, with a stone gate at the front leading into a small walled yard. Some were very salubrious, others little more than slum dwellings. Those aimed at the middle classes had five rooms upstairs, five down. The least desirable room was the north-facing *tingzijian*, at the bend in the staircase; these were generally let to poor lodgers such as students and writers. Many classics of Chinese literature were composed in these pokey spaces.

As the city's population mushroomed in the twentieth century, *shikumen* were partitioned into four or five houses. In the rush to develop, most *shikumen* neighbourhoods have been demolished; those that remain are cramped and badly maintained, with archaic plumbing. Xintiandi is the single example of stylish renovation, though perhaps pastiche would be a more accurate word, as there's not much left in the area of the original houses. The *longtangs* at Taikang Lu (see p.64) and Duolun Lu (see p.82) have, however, been well preserved.

South Block

Xintiandi's **South Block** is rather anticlimactic, with a modern glass mall at the end rather spoiling the olde-worlde effect. Inside you'll find Xintiandi's best restaurant, *Crystal Jade* (see p.106), as well as the UME International Cineplex (see p.122) and a host of luxury brands.

4

Fuxing Park

复兴公园, Fùxīnggōngyuán • 105 Fuxing Zhong Lu • Daily 6am–6pm • Free • ⓜ Xintiandi

This park was laid out by the French in 1909, and remains rather European in feel, so the bronze statue of Marx and Engels in the northwest corner looks rather incongruous. Come in the morning or at dusk and you'll see groups of middle-aged locals performing *tai ji*, ballroom dancing and opera singing. Later in the evening, the area is the haunt of a younger crowd, attracted by the restaurants and clubs on the park's edges.

Former Residence of Sun Yatsen

孙中山故居, sūnzhōngshān gùjū • 7 Xiangshan Lu • Daily 9am–4.30pm • ¥20 • ☎ 64372954

Just outside the western exit of Fuxing Park stands the **Former Residence of Sun Yatsen**, the first president of the Chinese Republic, and his wife, Song Qingling. The first building you enter is a rather dry museum, with an exhibition of the man's books and artefacts, and not much in English. Much more interesting is the building next door, his actual house, which, just as an example of an elegantly furnished period house, is worth a wander round.

St Nicholas Church

圣尼古拉斯教堂, shěngní gǔlā sījiào táng • 16 Gaolan Lu

This lovely Russian Orthodox church was built in 1933, by White Russian exiles. It was abandoned in 1941, and then did service as a laundry and a washing-machine factory. An image of Mao was hung from the roof during the Cultural Revolution, to prevent it being sacked. In recent years, it has been used as a restaurant and nightclub; these closed when the Russians complained that was sacrilegious. During the 2010 Expo it was reconsecrated to allow services. It is presently empty and though there are plans afoot to return it to its original purpose the government is wary, aware that it would set an awkward precedent for the many other old religious buildings in Shanghai.

Former Residence of Zhou Enlai

周恩来故居, zhōuēnlái gùjū · 73 Sinan Lu · Daily 9am–4pm · Free · ☎ 021 64730420 · Ⓜ Xintiandi

Tucked away in a very smart neighbourhood of old houses lies the **Former Residence of Zhou Enlai**. Zhou was Mao's right-hand man, but he has always been looked on with rather more affection than the Chairman, as he was rather less harsh and not so barmy. When he lived here he was head of the Shanghai Communist Party, and as such was kept under surveillance from a secret outpost over the road. There's not, in truth, a great deal to see, beyond a lot of hard beds in bare rooms, but the garden, with hedges and ivy-covered walls, could easily be a part of 1930s suburban London.

Tianzifang

田子坊, tiánzifāng · Main entrance 210 Taikang Lu · ☎ 021 54657531 · Ⓜ Dapuqiao Lu

This is the latest fashionably artsy shopping and lunching quarter. You'll have to look hard to find the unassuming entrance, an arch over Lane 210, which stretches north off Taikang Lu. This leads onto **Taikang Lu Art Street** (泰康路田子坊, tàikānglù tiánzifāng), a narrow north–south alleyway that is the central artery for a web of alleys filling up with trendy boutiques, coffee shops, handmade jewellery stores, art galleries, interior design consultancies and the like, all housed in converted *shikumen* houses. At its northern end it comes out at Sinan Lu, but don't even try to come in from there, the entrance is really tough to find.

Inevitably, the place gets compared with Xintiandi; but whereas the architecture there is modern pastiche, this is a set of real, warts-and-all *longtangs*, with the result that it's quainter, shabbier and more charming. There are still plenty of local families around, who continue, boutiques or no boutiques, to hang their woolly underwear out to dry, and old folk shuffle round in their pyjamas, studiously ignored by the chic ladies who lunch. There are several hundred little shops here now, and if you're looking for an artsy knick-knack or accessory, quirky souvenir, tasteful homeware or a designer original, this is the place to come. Sadly most of the newer arrivals are selling tourist tat, but they haven't yet pushed out the better stores.

The emphasis on local design and creativity rather than brands still makes this the best shopping experience in the city. There's a map just inside the entrance – take careful note, though you'll likely get lost anyway as the alleys are something of a warren. And if you can, avoid the weekend, when the narrow lanes get fearsomely busy.

For gorgeous clothes by local designers, head to La Vie (see p.127), or Nuomi (see p.127). More affordable are the witty T-shirt designs offered by Plastered and Shirtflag (see p.127). For a coffee stop, the centrally located *Kommune* (see p.110) is a local institution, while for food, there are a plethora of tiny but pricey restaurants.

Ruijin Hotel

瑞金宾馆, ruìjīn bīnguǎn · 118 Ruijin Er Lu, main entrance on Fuxing Lu · ☎ 64725222, ⊕ ruijinhotelsh.com

The south section of **Ruijin Er Lu** (瑞金二路, ruìjīn èr lù) is busy and cramped, but there's a wonderful escape in the form of the stately **Ruijin Hotel**, just south of Fuxing Zhong Lu. This Tudor-style country manor was home in the early twentieth century to the Morris family, owners of the *North China Daily News*; Mr Morris raised greyhounds for the Shanghai Race Club and the former Canidrome dog track across the street. The house, having miraculously escaped severe damage during the Cultural Revolution because certain high-ranking officials used it as their private residence, has now been turned into an exclusive guesthouse by the Intercontinental Group (see p.94). Even if you're not a guest, you're free to walk around the spacious, quiet grounds, where it's hard to believe you're in the middle of one of the world's most hectic cities.

Maoming Nan Lu

茂名南路, màomíng nánlù

This street is the artery for one of the city's most prestigious districts. There are a plethora of boutiques, and it's a good place to pick up a tailored suit or *qipao* (see p.127). Two plush hotels, the *Okura Garden* (see p.95) and the *Jinjiang* (see p.95), are both worth a visit for glimpses of former luxuries.

Lyceum Theatre

兰心大戏院, lánxīn dàxìyuàn • 57 Maoming Nan Lu • ☎ 62565544

Exit from the *Ruijin Hotel* and head north and you'll come to the Art Deco **Lyceum Theatre**, built in 1931 and once home to the British Amateur Dramatic Club. It now hosts nightly acrobatic shows (see p.120).

Okura Garden Hotel

上海花园饭店, shànghǎi huāyuán fàndiàn • 58 Maoming Nan Lu • ☎ 64151111, ⓦ gardenhotelshanghai.com

The *Okura*, originally the French Club, or Cercle Sportif Français, was taken over by the Americans during World War II and converted by the egalitarian Communists into the People's Cultural Palace. Anyone can wander round the lovely gardens and go in to look at the sumptuous ceiling design of stained glass in the ballroom.

Jinjiang Hotel

锦江之星, jǐnjiāngzhīxīng • 59 Maoming Nan Lu • ☎ 62582582, ⓦ jinjianghotels.com

The *Jinjiang* compound includes the former **Grosvenor Residence** complex, the most fashionable and pricey address in pre-World War II Shanghai. The hotel has been modernized, but the *VIP Club* still retains much of its 1920s architecture and Great Gatsby ambience. Non-guests might be able to sneak a peek by taking the lift to the top floor of the old wing of the *Jinjiang*, where the club is located, although gaining entrance to one of the twenty astonishingly beautiful, refurbished Art Deco VIP mansion rooms on the floors directly below (a snip at US$850 per night) might prove slightly more difficult.

4

WHITE RUSSIANS

After the **Bolsheviks** took power in 1917, loyalists of the czar, known as **White Russians** to distinguish themselves from the Red Communists, first fought, then, when defeated, fled into exile. Many came to Shanghai. As stateless peoples without extraterritorial protection they were subject to Chinese laws, and suffered harsh Chinese punishments. Some had brought their family jewels and heirlooms, but most arrived with little.

The girls, ex-ballerinas and opera singers among them, could at least rely on their feminine charms; many became "taxi girls", dancing for a small gratuity at nightclubs, or the mistresses of established Westerners – the divorce rates shot up as a result, particularly among the British. Other girls (as many as one in four, according to a League of Nations report), drifted into prostitution.

The lives of the men were even more precarious. Destitution forced many to earn their living in ways no other foreigner would consider, as rickshaw pullers or beggars. Ex-soldiers found work as bodyguards for Chinese gangsters. This was all terribly embarrassing to other foreigners, as it punctured a carefully constructed facade of superiority, and a scheme was mooted to have them all packed off to Australia, though it came to naught.

But the influence of the Russians was by no means all negative; as well as a certain élan, they brought a wealth of skills. Cultivated sophisticates became teachers, exposing the children of boorish merchants to cultured pastimes such as fencing and horseriding, and it was Russian musicians, ballerinas and singers who, more than anyone, created the city's unique cultural scene.

Around Shaanxi Nan Lu

陕西南路, shǎnxī nánlù

This area is rather busier with traffic than elsewhere in the French Concession, but it's still good for walking, with shade provided by the plane trees, and plenty of quirky little shops to explore.

Hengshan Moller Villa

衡山马勒别墅饭店, héngshān mǎlèbiéshù fàndiàn · 30 Shaanxi Nan Lu · ☎ 62478881

The **Hengshan Moller Villa** is a Gothic fantasy of turrets and crenellations so incongruous that if you glimpse it from a moving vehicle it's easy to think you had imagined it. It was built in 1936 by Eric Moller, and – rumour has it – designed by his twelve-year-old daughter. There's certainly something appealingly childlike about the tapering spires and striped brickwork. It's like a castle made of cake – perhaps she should have been allowed a hand in more of Shanghai's buildings. These days it's a pricey hotel (see p.94).

Russian Orthodox Mission Church

圣母大堂, shèngmǔ dàtáng · 55 Xinle Lu

The **Russian Orthodox Mission Church**, unmistakeable with its proud blue dome, is more evidence of the area's strong Russian connection. It's been used as a factory, a disco and a teahouse, but today it's empty. You can poke around outside but the interior is not open to the public.

Arts and Crafts Museum

工艺美术博物馆, gōngyì měishù bówùguǎn · 79 Fenyang Lu · Daily 9am–4pm · ¥8 · ☎ 021 64314074 · Ⓜ Changshu Lu

This grand French mansion from 1905 has been rather haphazardly converted into a museum. Visitors are first confronted with a gamut of overpriced craft shops; ignore these and head upstairs, and you will find an intriguing collection of jade, ivory, wood and embroidery pieces. A lot of the objects are very well made but seem fussy. The most striking exhibits are the ivories, carved in the Sixties, that depict communist subjects, political meetings and the like; they're brilliantly done but look very kitsch now. You'll also see craftspeople practising their trades – jade being worked at a lathe, a seamstress embroidering and so on.

West of Changshu Lu

West of **Changshu Lu** metro station you really get a good idea of what the French Concession is all about. Many of the villas here have been converted to embassy properties (the more sensitive are guarded by soldiers with fixed bayonets) and there are also plenty of upmarket, expat-oriented restaurants and cafés, a fair few beauty salons but, oddly, not that many shops. It's more the place to soak up atmosphere on a sunny day or people-watch over a cappuccino than to take in sights.

The Propaganda Poster Centre

宣传画年画艺术中心, xuānchuánhuàniánhuà yìshùzhōngxīn · Daily 9.30am–4.30pm · ¥25 · ☎ 62111845, Ⓦ shanghaipropagandaart.com

A pleasant ten-minute stroll northwest of Changshu Lu metro station on Huashan Lu, the **Propaganda Poster Centre** is an abrupt change of tone, providing a fascinating glimpse into communist China – you will not come across a more vivid evocation of the bad old days of Marx and Mao. To find the place, present yourself to the security guard at the entrance to 868 Huashan Lu. He will give you a name card with a map on the back showing you which building in the complex beyond to head for – the centre is a basement flat in building 4. The walls are covered with Chinese socialist realist posters, over three thousand examples arranged chronologically from the 1950s to the 1970s, which the curator will talk you round, whether or not you understand his Chinese. There are, fortunately, English captions. With slogans like "The Soviet Union is the stronghold of world peace" and "Hail the over-fulfilment of steel production by ten million tons" and images of sturdy, lantern-jawed peasants and soldiers defeating big-nosed, green-skinned imperialists or riding tractors into a glorious future, the black-and-white world view of communism is dramatically realized. Note how the Soviet Union flips from friend to enemy and back again – it's all very *1984*. A few posters celebrate real achievements, such as the new freedom of girls to choose their husbands, but they are outnumbered by the grotesque lies, such as a picture of Tibetans welcoming the Chinese army. Never mind; it might be only a few decades ago but China has moved on so far it feels like centuries.

The style of this dry communist art owes much to images with a very different message – popular prewar calendar posters – and the exhibition concludes with a room of these. The popular adverts show fetching Chinese girls in fashionable dress and make-up, surrounded by the accoutrements of modernity. They served once to introduce the Chinese to the delights of consumer culture, such as cigarettes and hair curlers, and daring new fashions such as the slim-cut *qipao* and bobbed hair.

Take a look at the knick-knacks in the gift shop, such as an image of an ack-ack gunner on a teapot. Don't be tempted by these or by the posters on sale, priced at thousands of yuan; they're bound to be fakes. Only buy the postcards, at ¥10 each. The particular artistic style, influenced by Soviet socialist realism, advertising images and folk art, is not without merit, and many contemporary artists like to pastiche it, but with an ironic twist – peasants waving iPods instead of Mao's *Little Red Book*, say. It's even got a name: **McStruggle**. If that's your thing, you'll find examples in the galleries and boutiques at Moganshan (see p.72).

4

Song Qingling's Residence

宋庆龄故居, sòngqìnglíng gùju • 1843 Huaihai Xi Lu • Daily 9–11am & 1–4.30pm • ¥20 • ☎ 021 64747183 • ⓜ Hengshan Lu

As the wife of Sun Yatsen, **Song Qingling** was part of a bizarre family coterie – her sister Song Meiling was married to Chiang Kai-shek and her brother, known as T.V. Soong, was finance minister to Chiang. She lived in Shanghai on and off from 1948 until her death in 1981. Today, her house serves as a charming step back into a residential Shanghai of the recent past. The trappings on display – including her enormous official limousines parked in the garage – are largely post-1949. Inside, note the lovely wood panelling and lacquerwork.

JING'AN TEMPLE

Jing'an

Jing'an (静安, jìngān), west of People's Square, has always been one of the smartest areas in the city; in the colonial era, it was a popular place for the "Shanghailanders" – Europeans who settled here – to build their mock-Tudor mansions behind high walls. Today the area is notable for its grand, exclusive hotels and ultramodern malls. Unexpectedly, and in counterpoint to the rampant commercialism that surrounds them, Jing'an is also host to two of the city's few notable places of worship: Jing'an and Yufo temples, both surprisingly busy with devotees. And lastly, in the north of the area close to Suzhou Creek, is the Moganshan Art District, an outpost of bohemianism – with dozens of art galleries and boutiques to explore, you'll certainly find something to like.

Nanjing Xi Lu

南京西路, nánjīng xī lù • Bus #20 runs the length of the road and there are a couple of metro stops: Nanjing Xi Lu and Jing'an Temple, both on line #2

The main artery of Jing'an, **Nanjing Xi Lu** was once known as Bubbling Well Road after a spring that used to gush at the far end of the street. It's now one of Shanghai's busiest shopping boulevards, though with a parade of giant malls it's rather less intimate than some of the city's other shopping areas; after all the unrelenting materialism you may be ready for the attractive temple at the street's western end.

Han City

风翔服饰礼品广场, fēngxiáng fúshìlǐpǐn guǎngchǎng • 580 Nanjing Xi Lu • Daily 9am–8pm

Starting from Renmin Square and heading west along Nanjing Xi Lu, first stop for most visitors is **Han City** on the north side of the street, where you can gauge China's true level of commitment to protecting intellectual property. The entire mall, all three storeys, is devoted to stalls selling fake goods – clothes, watches, software, bags and shoes (see p.126). Remember to bargain hard.

Upscale malls

Further west from Han City, the north side of the street is given over to a string of malls – **Westgate** (梅龙镇广场, méilóngzhèn guǎngchǎng), **CITIC Square** (中信泰富广场, zhōngxìntàifù guǎngchǎng) and **Plaza 66** (恒隆广场, hénglóng guǎngchǎng) – kitschy buildings arranged in a row like souvenirs on a mantelpiece. They're all rather too heavily weighted towards luxury brands, with the result that there are generally more staff than shoppers. The last of the giants is the **Shanghai Centre** (上海商城, shànghǎi shāngchéng), which despite an underwhelming entrance through a car park, is one of the more interesting luxury places, host to the decent *Element Fresh* café (see p.101) and the five-star *Portman Ritz-Carlton* hotel (see p.95). The Shanghai Centre Theatre here has nightly acrobatics shows (see p.120).

Shanghai Friendship Exhibition Hall

展览馆, zhǎnlǎnguǎn • 1000 Yan'an Zhong Lu • ☎ 62790279

This Stalinist wedding cake built to celebrate communism must surely be in a permanent sulk at the behemoths of capitalism that hem it in. It's worth examining for its colossal ornate entrance, decorated with columns patterned with red stars and capped by a gilded spire. Constructed by the Russians in 1954, it was originally known as the Palace of Sino-Soviet Friendship and housed a permanent exhibition of industrial machinery from the Shanghai area – proof of the advances achieved after 1949. These days it's used as a vast and vulgar hall for trade fairs and art shows. In the ultimate affront to its origins, it once hosted the Shanghai Millionaires Fair.

Jing'an Temple

静安寺, jìng'ān sì • 1686 Nanjing Xi Lu • Daily 7.30am–5pm • ¥10

The **Jing'an Temple** is another building hemmed in by skyscrapers, that doesn't seem quite comfortable in itself (perhaps aware that Shanghai's true places of worship are up the road, with names like Plaza 66). Building work first began on the temple in the third century, and its apparent obscurity today belies its past as the richest Buddhist foundation in the city. In the late nineteenth century it was headed by legendary abbot Khi Vehdu, who combined his religious duties with a gangster lifestyle; the abbot and his seven concubines were shadowed by White Russian bodyguards, each carrying a leather briefcase lined with bulletproof steel, to be used as a shield in case of attack. Today, having been comprehensively rebuilt for the 2010 Expo, it all looks a little too new, though the main hall, with its ornate roof of flying eaves, is undeniably impressive. Inside you'll find a golden statue of the Laughing Buddha and figures of eighteen *arhats*. Just as much effort seems to have gone into creating the shop in the west wall, which sells religious trinkets.

JING'AN

0 — 250 metres

N

ZHONGSHAN BEI LU

♨ Zhenping Lu

2

MOGANSHAN LU

CHANGHUA LU

Mogan
Arts Di
1

AOMEN LU

Suzhou Creek

GUANGFU XI LU

YICHANG LU

AOMEN LU

Changshou
Park

SHANXI BEI LU

Yufo Temple

JIANENING LU

XIKANG LU

CHANGSHOU LU

XINHUI LU

3

ANYUAN LU

2

JIAOZHOU LU

ANYUAN LU

HAIFANG LU

♨ Changshou Lu

CHANGDE LU

Wet Market

CHANGPING LU

SHANXI

WUNING LU

ANYUAN LU

4

The New Factories
1
4

3

CHANGNING LU

♨ Changping Lu

4

KANDING LU

XIKANG LU

YUYAO LU

YANGPING LU

WUDING LU

WUNING NAN LU

KANGDING LU

5

WANHANG LU

ZHAOZHOU LU

XINZHA LU

WUDING LU

6
10

BEIJING LU

Shanghai Cer
3

CHANGDE LU

Train
Booking
Office

WANHANGDU LU

11

NANJING XI LU

Jing'an
Temple

♨ Jing'an Temple

WUDING BEI LU

Children's
Palace

4

Jing'an
Park

YUYUAN LU

12

▼ Jiangsu Lu ♨

YAN'AN ZHONG LU

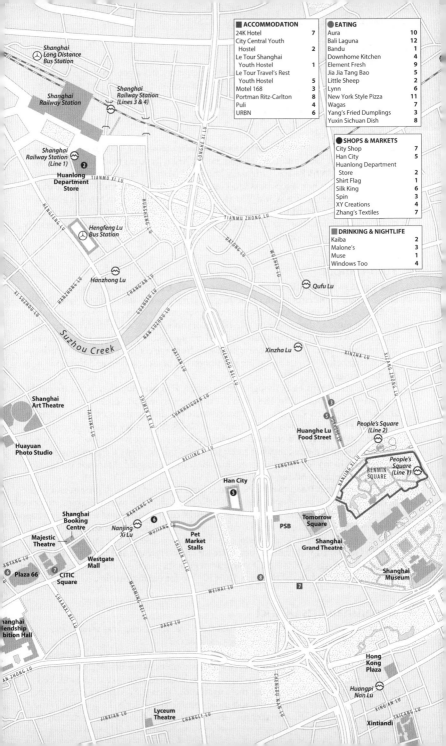

ACCOMMODATION
24K Hotel	7
City Central Youth Hostel	2
Le Tour Shanghai Youth Hostel	1
Le Tour Travel's Rest Youth Hostel	5
Motel 168	3
Portman Ritz-Carlton	8
Puli	4
URBN	6

EATING
Aura	10
Bali Laguna	12
Bandu	1
Downhome Kitchen	4
Element Fresh	9
Jia Jia Tang Bao	5
Little Sheep	2
Lynn	6
New York Style Pizza	11
Wagas	7
Yang's Fried Dumplings	3
Yuxin Sichuan Dish	8

SHOPS & MARKETS
City Shop	7
Han City	5
Huanlong Department Store	2
Shirt Flag	1
Silk King	6
Spin	3
XY Creations	4
Zhang's Textiles	7

DRINKING & NIGHTLIFE
Kaiba	2
Malone's	3
Muse	1
Windows Too	4

5

Jing'an Park

静安公园, jìngān gōngyuán

Attractive **Jing'an Park**, once Bubbling Well cemetery, has a good pit-stop in the form of the *Bali Laguna* restaurant (see p.111). It's a welcome oasis in a part of the city where peace and quiet are rarely found. A pleasant walled garden (¥3) has a small photo exhibition on the history of the area.

Children's Palace

上海市少年宫, shànghǎishì shìshàoniángōng • 1799 Nanjing Xi Lu • Wed–Fri 4–6.30pm, Sat & Sun 9am–6.30pm • ¥20

At the corner of Wulumuqi Bei Lu and Yan'an Xi Lu lies the grandiose yet slightly run-down **Children's Palace**. Originally known as Marble Hall, the sprawling estate was built in 1918 as a home for the Kadoories, a Sephardic Jewish family and one of the principal investors in pre-World War II Shanghai. The drab, worn exterior gives no clue to the chandeliered ballrooms of the mansion's grand interior. It now serves as a children's art centre, hosting frequent singing and dancing performances on weekday afternoons and at weekends.

Yufo Temple

玉佛寺, yùfó sì • 999 Jiangnin Lu, near Anyuan Lu • Daily 8am–5pm • ¥15 • ☎ 62663668, ⓦ yufotemple.com

Some 1.5km kilometres north of the Jing'an Temple is the **Yufo Temple** (Jade Buddha Temple), a much more interesting and attractive complex. The pretty temple buildings feel much more authentically temple-like than those at Jing'an, with flying eaves, complicated brackets and intricate roof and ceiling decorations. It's a lively place of worship, with great gusts of incense billowing from the central burner and worshippers kowtowing before effigies and tying red ribbons to branches, bells and the stone lions on the railings.

The star attractions here, though, are the relics. Two **jade Buddhas** were brought here from Myanmar (Burma) in 1882 and the temple was built to house them. The larger, at nearly two metres tall, sits in its own separate building in the north of the temple, and costs ¥10 to see. It was carved from a single block of milky white jade and is encrusted with agate and emerald. The second statue, in the western hall, is a little smaller, around a metre long, but easier to respond to. It shows a recumbent Buddha at the point of dying (or rather entering nirvana), with a languid expression on his face, like a man dropping off for a nap.

The central **Great Treasure Hall** holds three huge figures of the past, present and future Buddhas, as well as the temple drum and bell. The gods of the twenty heavens, decorated with gold leaf, line the hall like guests at a celestial cocktail party, and a curvaceous copper Guanyin stands at the back. It's all something of a retreat from the material obsessions outside, but it's still Shanghai: religious trinkets, such as fake money for burning and Buddhas festooned with flashing lights, are for sale everywhere and the monks do a roaring trade flogging blessings. If you're at all peckish, check out the attached vegetarian restaurant, where a bowl of noodles costs ¥10 – go for the mushrooms.

Moganshan Arts District

莫干山路50号, mògānshānlù wǔshíhào • 50 Moganshan Lu • Most galleries, though not all, are closed Mondays • Nearest metro stop is Shanghai Station, a twenty-minute walk away; it's best to take a taxi

A kilometre northeast of the Yufo Temple, in a former industrial zone beside Suzhou Creek, the **Moganshan Arts District** (M50) is a complex of studios and galleries. In the early 1990s, attracted by cheap rents, artists began to take over the abandoned warehouse buildings here and use them as studios. Then the art galleries moved in. Now the design studios and cafés and more commercial galleries are arriving as the district is gentrified. What makes the area interesting for the moment is the way it is both shabby and sophisticated, jumbling together paint-spattered artists, slick dealers, pretentious fashionistas and baffled locals. Most of the smaller galleries double as studios and there's something for all tastes, from cutting-edge video installations to chintzy kitsch. It's a good place to dip your toe into the thriving Shanghai art scene though it's not comprehensive – nothing like Beijing's 798.

Entrance is through a gate signed **50 Moganshan Lu** (there's a map on the wall near here). There are dozens of galleries but most are small concerns selling work that's frankly rather derivative – lots of McStruggle (see p.67) and brightly coloured caricature figures. You'll need to seek out the good ones (some are listed below). When you are arted out, *Bandu* (see p.112) is a good place for a coffee.

Island 6 Art Centre

六岛艺术中心, liùdǎo yìshù zhōngxīn • Building 6, first floor • Daily 10am–7pm • ☎ 021 62277856, ⓦ island6.org

This arts collective with noble, not-for-profit motives prides itself on its technological nous, and puts together varied multi-media and cross-cultural shows. The space doubles as a high tech studio so it's possible to meet the artists themselves.

M97

M97画 廊, M jiǔ shí qì huà lá ng • 97 Moganshan Lu, near Aomen Lu, second floor • Tues–Sun 10am–6pm • ☎ 021 62661597, ⓦ m97gallery.com

Of the numerous **photography galleries**, half seem to show images of buildings in states of demolition – Shanghai's relentless development offers plenty of material to those heirs of romanticism who find ruins picturesque. This photography gallery, over the road from the main M50 complex, is by far the most professionally run. American owner Steve Harris puts on imaginative shows.

Art Scene Warehouse

艺术景仓库, yìshùjǐng cāngkù • Building 4, first floor • Tues–Sun 10.30am–6.30pm • ☎ 62774940, ⓦ artscenewarehouse.com

To see the best of Chinese art, you need to seek out the big hitters, who represent some true innovators. The best place to start is the cavernous **Art Scene Warehouse**, on the first floor of building 4, just beyond the main gate and on the left. Not only will you find a representative selection of contemporary paintings, but the work is sympathetically displayed (which you can't say about all the galleries) in a minimalist white space. Look out for Xue Jiye's comically straining naked men and Shao Yinong's melancholy images of empty halls.

ShangART

香格纳画廊, xiānggénà huàláng • Buildings 16 & 18 • Daily 10am–6pm • ☎ 63593923, ⓦ shangartgallery.com

Though the work is not well displayed here – it tends to be propped against the walls – the artists represented include big names such as Yang Fudong (see box, p.122) and Zhao Bandi, whose satirical photographs of himself with his toy panda captured the public imagination when they were used in an advertising campaign.

Bizart Centre

比翼艺术中心, bǐyì yìshù zhōngxīn • Building 7, fourth floor • Mon–Sat 11am–6pm • ☎ 62775358

The **Bizart Centre** scores highest for credibility; it's a not-for-profit operation that promotes Chinese and foreign contemporary art, with an artist-in-residence programme. It doesn't represent artists, but works with them, putting on themed shows, and is always worth checking out.

CENTURY PARK

Pudong

Pudong (浦东, pǔdōng), the eastern bank of the Huangpu River, opposite the Bund, has been transformed in just a couple of decades from paddy fields into a glittering cityscape of giant boulevards and architectural showpieces. The maze of skyscrapers now stretches east as far as the eye can see. In fact there may be too many: the weight of all those buildings is causing Pudong to sink at the rate of 2cm a year. Critics also say that the iconic skyline is only interesting from a distance. The bustling street life that so animates the rest of the city is striking for its absence – in between those fancy monoliths there are too many empty, windy boulevards – and it's the only part of the city that does not reward aimless wandering. That said, if you know where you're going, a visit to Pudong can be very worthwhile.

Historically, the area was known as the wrong side of the Huangpu. Before 1949, it was populated by unemployed migrants and prostitutes, and characterized by murders and the most appalling living conditions in the city. It was here that bankrupt gamblers would *tiao huangpu*, commit suicide by drowning themselves in the river. Shanghai's top gangster, Du Yuesheng, more commonly known as "Big-eared Du", learned his trade growing up in this rough section of town. Under communist rule it continued its slide into shabby decay until in 1990, fifteen years after China's economic reforms started, it was finally decided to grant Pudong the status of Special Economic Zone (SEZ). This decision, more than any other, is fuelling Shanghai's dizzying economic advance.

There are two areas that reward exploration. First is **Lujiazui**, the battery of skyscrapers just across the water from the Bund, which is home to the giant World Financial Centre and Jinmao and Pearl Orient towers (come for the views from their observation decks), as well as a decent museum. The second rewarding area to explore is spacious **Century Park**, 4km away; the successful architectural experiments here include the Science and Technology Museum and the Oriental Arts Centre.

In 2010 the south end of Pudong was the site of the **World Expo**, which was a great fillip for the city, the spur for dozens of infrastructure, renovation and regeneration projects. Today, few of the Expo structures remain, except for the huge China pavilion, which has been converted into Asia's biggest art museum, the China Art Palace.

ARRIVAL AND DEPARTURE   PUDONG

By Bund Tourist Tunnel The most entertaining way to cross from the west bank of the Huangpu to Pudong is to take the Bund Tourist Tunnel (外滩观光隧道, wàitān guānguāng suìdào). Capsules (departures every minute; daily 8am–10.30pm; ¥50 one way, ¥70 return) take a couple of minutes to chug creakily past psychedelic light displays, which have names such as "Heaven" and "Meteor Shower". It's something of a kitsch throwback and not what you'd expect in sophisticated Shanghai. The entrance is in the underpass at the north end of the Bund, opposite Beijing Dong Lu.

By ferry A cheaper alternative to the Bund Tourist Tunnel is to take the ferry (every 15min daily 7am–10pm; ¥2) from

a jetty at the south end of the Bund opposite Yan'an Dong Lu (not to be confused with Jinling Pier, the jetty for river cruises, further south). Ferries arrive at the south end of Binjiang Dadao (see p.76), a fifteen-minute walk from the Jinmao Tower.

By metro From west of the river, the metro is the quickest way to travel, whooshing passengers from People's Square to Lujiazui in less than three minutes, and all the way to the Science and Technology Museum in ten.

By bus Bus #3 runs from in front of the Shanghai Museum to the Jinmao Tower, but beware rush hour as the traffic in the tunnel gets badly snarled up.

Lujiazui

陆家嘴, lùjiāzuǐ

In Lujiazui you'll find not just Shanghai's daftest edifice, the bulbous **Oriental Pearl Tower**, but also its most elegant, the **Jinmao Tower**, and its highest, the **World Financial Centre**; all offer sublime views across the city (so pick a clear day to visit). Pretty soon you'll also find the Shanghai Tower, set to be the tallest building in China at 632 metres – it is projected to be open in 2015 (and will no doubt boast an observation platform to trump all others). In order to take advantage of the crowds of tourists who flock to the Pearl Tower, a couple of **attractions** have opened nearby, including the decent History Museum, and a fun aquarium (though avoid the tacky Natural Wild Insect Kingdom, where the animals are kept in unpleasant conditions).

This is an area where it helps to plan where you're going to eat, as there aren't too many options. For cheap eats head to the Superbrand Mall (正大广场, zhèngdà guǎngchǎng), the Jinmao Tower's basement food court or the *Element Fresh* café in the World Financial Centre (see p.77); for something pricey and memorable you can't beat the *Pudong Shangri-La* (see p.112).

The riverside promenade

滨江大道, bīnjiāng dàdào

The riverside promenade, **Binjiang Dadao**, is a pleasant place for a stroll, close enough to the river to hear the slap of the water and much less crowded than the other side. There is outside seating at each of the name-brand **bars and cafés** (*Starbucks, Paulaner Bräuhaus, Häagen-Dazs*) along the strip, from which you can appreciate the glorious views of the full length of the Bund.

It's a short walk from here to the **Pearl Dock** (明珠码头, míngzhū mǎtóu) where you can get a half-hour boat tour down the Huangpu (see p.45).

Shanghai Aquarium

上海海洋水族馆, shànghǎi hǎiyáng shuǐzúguǎn • 1388 Liujiazui Lu • Daily 9am–6pm • ¥160, children ¥110 • ☏ 58779988, Ⓦ aquarium.sh.cn

The surprisingly decent **Shanghai Aquarium** is a stone's throw from the Pearl Tower. On display are sharks, penguins and seals as well as endemic species such as the Chinese alligator. Particularly impressive is the aquarium's one-hundred-and-fifty-metre-long viewing tunnel. There's not much English, just the species names. If you speak Chinese, you'll likely overhear local visitors debating how tasty the exhibits might be.

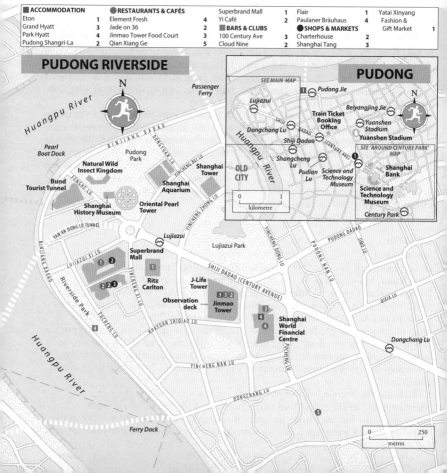

◼ ACCOMMODATION		●RESTAURANTS & CAFÉS		Superbrand Mall	1	Flair	1	Yatai Xinying
Eton	1	Element Fresh	4	Yi Café	2	Paulaner Bräuhaus	4	Fashion &
Grand Hyatt	3	Jade on 36	2	◼ BARS & CLUBS		●SHOPS & MARKETS		Gift Market	1
Park Hyatt	4	Jinmao Tower Food Court	3	100 Century Ave	3	Charterhouse	2	
Pudong Shangri-La	2	Qian Xiang Ge	5	Cloud Nine	2	Shanghai Tang	3	

The Oriental Pearl Tower

东方明珠广播电视塔, dōngfāngmíngzhū guǎngbō diànshìtǎ · 1 Century Avenue · Daily 9am–9.30pm · ¥150 for access to highest level · ☎ 58791888, ⓦ opg.cn

Like it or loathe it, the 457-metre-high **Oriental Pearl Tower** has come to symbolize Shanghai, and its **viewing platforms** are now a required destination for every Chinese tourist. As a result, there's often a very long queue to get in: don't even bother trying to come here on the weekend or during a holiday. In fact, the observation platforms in the Jinmao and World Financial Centre towers (see below) are less busy, higher and classier – though of course, viewing the city from inside the Pearl Tower does have one major advantage: for once, you can't see the gaudy thing. There are fifteen viewing platforms in all, and the pricing system is ridiculously complex. The highest bauble is the "Space Module" at 350 metres; it costs ¥150 – but this has the longest queues and the windows are dirty. Better is the smaller bauble underneath (¥100) which has a reinforced glass floor for proper, all-round views, though it's not for the faint-hearted. There is a revolving restaurant in the middle globe but it's best avoided, as is the "space show" exhibition.

Shanghai History Museum

上海城市历史发展馆, shànghǎi chéngshì lìshǐ fāzhǎnguǎn · Daily 8am–9.30pm · ¥35

The **Shanghai History Museum** at the base of the Oriental Pearl Tower is far better than you might expect. On display is a fraction of a huge collection (the museum is still looking for a dedicated, permanent home). The majority of exhibits, which focus on the nineteenth century onwards, do a good job of evoking the old glory days, with waxwork figures in dioramas of pharmacies, teahouses and the like. One of the old bronze lions from outside the HSBC building (see p.44) is on display, as well as a boundary stone from the International Settlement, and there's a detailed model of the Bund as it would have looked in the 1930s.

Jinmao Tower

金茂大厦, jīnmào dàshà · 88 Century Avenue · Observation deck (金茂大厦88层观光厅, jīnmào dàshà bāshíbācéng guānguāngtīng) daily 8.30am–10pm · ¥120 · ☎ 50476688, ⓦ jinmao88.com · Ⓜ Lujiazui

Shanghai's most attractive modern building, the **Jinmao Tower**, is an elegantly tapering postmodern take on Art Deco, built by the Chicago office of Skidmore, Owings and Merrill. All the proportions are based on the lucky number 8 – the 88 floors are divided into sixteen segments, each of which is one-eighth shorter than the sixteen-storey base – but never mind the mathematics, the harmony is obvious at first glance. The roof wittily references a pagoda and, for once, doesn't look like a tacked-on afterthought. What look from a distance like filigree are actually decorative metal struts – they make the building appear eminently possible to climb, and indeed in 2001 it was scaled, apparently on a whim, by a visiting shoe salesman; hence the "no climbing" signs around the base. The tower's first 53 floors are offices; from there on up is the spectacular *Grand Hyatt* hotel (see p.96).

The **observation deck** on the 88th floor is accessible from the basement, via an entrance on the building's north side. An ear-popping lift whisks you up 340m in a matter of seconds. The spectacle before you is of course sublime, but turn round for a giddying view down the building's glorious galleried atrium. Alternatively, for great views for free, go in the front door (on the eastern side) and up to the hotel lobby on the 54th floor where you can take advantage of the *Hyatt*'s comfy, window-side chairs.

The **J-Life annexe** on the northern side of the tower is a high-end shopping mall – all very pricey but it's good to know about the juice bar near the bottom of the escalators.

The Shanghai World Financial Centre

环球金融中心, huánqiú jīnróng zhōngxīn · 100 Century Avenue · Observation decks daily 8am–11pm, last admission 10pm · Floor 94 (423m) ¥100, floor 94 & 97 (439m) ¥120, floor 94, 97 & the top deck (474m) ¥150; ticket office is in the southwest side · ☎ 68777878, ⓦ swfc-observatory.com

> ### BARS WITH A VIEW
>
> As an alternative to the observation decks at the Jinmao and World Financial Centre towers, consider heading up to the two **hotel bars**: *Cloud Nine* on the 87th floor of the Jinmao (see p.116), and *100 Century Avenue* on floors 91–93 of the World Financial Centre (see p.116). You won't be quite as high, but there won't be a queue to get in, and the surroundings are very refined. A cocktail is pricey but still less than a ticket for the Observation Platform.

6

At 492m, the **Shanghai World Financial Centre** is the tallest building in China, and the third tallest in the world. In contrast to its elegant neighbour, the Jinmao Tower, its lines are simple: just a tapering slab whose most distinctive feature is the hole in the top. Locals call it "the bottle opener". That hole was originally meant to be circular, but was redesigned as an oblong when the mayor complained that it would look like the Japanese flag hovering over the city.

Of the hundred and one floors, most house offices, but the *Park Hyatt* hotel, the highest in the world (see p.96), takes up floors 79 to 93. Of most interest to visitors are the **observation decks** above that, the world's highest, which offer, on a clear day, fantastic views of the city. There are three ticket prices, depending on how high up you want to go. The top level is by far the most impressive and now you're here you may as well bite the pricey bullet and go all the way. Polite, well-groomed and unnecessary button-pressing staff escort you into a lift. The floors flicker past, lights glow softly, and the whole experience is rather more *2001* than the usual *Blade Runner*. At the top level, the strip above the hole, you'll be greeted by a magnificent 360-degree view across the city – swaths of bright-roofed housing developments to the east and the sights of Puxi and the Huangpu to the west. Hardened glass tiles in the floor even allow you to look right down between your feet; a sign nearby asks you not to jump on them – as it seems to imply there's a chance they'll break, it's pretty unnerving. Landmarks are pointed out in the booklet that comes with your ticket, and you can get a photo printed for ¥50. Note that the view is at least as impressive at night. Heading back down, you'll pass an *Element Fresh* café and a *Costa Coffee* on the second floor.

Century Park and around

From Lujiazui, the eight-lane Shiji Dadao (Century Avenue; 世纪大道, shìjì dàdào) zooms west for 4km to one of the city's largest and newest green expanses, **Century Park**. The area was spruced up heavily for the 2010 Expo, which is perhaps why there's

AROUND CENTURY PARK

Science and Technology Museum — PSB
Oriental Arts Centre
Shanghai Bank
Science and Technology Museum
Century Park
N
Century Park
0 250 metres

an odd feeling here of being on a stage set that's waiting for its actors. It is, however, a very pleasant place to pass some time, with wide pavements and priority given to pedestrians over traffic, stretches of unbroken lawn and low-rise buildings conferring a great sense of space – and making you realize how cramped the rest of the city is. Skaters and kite-flyers congregate here, as both activities are banned in the city centre.

There are also some striking new buildings – not high-rises for once – foremost among which are the **Science and Technology Museum** and the **Oriental Arts Centre**. There's no shopping to speak of, apart from a giant fake market (see p.126), and not many places to eat – the cheap canteen in the Science and Technology Museum subway stop is one option.

Century Park

世纪公园, shìjì gōngyuán • Huama Lu • Daily 7am–6pm • ¥10 • Tandem bike rental ¥50/hr, pedalo rental ¥60/hr • Ⓜ Century Park

The park, designed by a British firm, is spacious, the air is clean (well, cleaner) and it's possible to feel that you have escaped the city, at least on weekdays when it's not too crowded. You can rent a tandem bike – sadly you're not allowed to ride your own bicycle – and pedalos are available to rent on the big central lake.

Science and Technology Museum

上海科技馆, shànghǎi kējìguǎn • Tues–Sun 9am–5pm • ¥60, students ¥45 • Space theatre screenings every 40min; ¥40 • IMAX screenings hourly 10.30am–4.30pm; ¥30/¥40 • IWERKS screenings every 40min; ¥30 • Ⓦ sstm.org.cn • Ⓜ Science and Technology Museum

The **Science and Technology Museum** is an absolutely enormous gleaming new building. There are two wings; you can safely ignore the one on nature, which is mostly stuffed animals, in favour of the diverting science wing, which scores well for interactivity and has lots of English captions. The section on space exploration is great – a big topic in China right now, with the nation fully intending to get to the moon as soon as possible – featuring real spacesuits, models of spacecraft and the like, and a gyroscope to make you queasy. In the section on robots you can take on a robotic arm at archery and play a computer at Go, then watch a virtual endoscopy (a different way to make you queasy).

The **cinemas** provide the most interest: the space theatre shows astronomical films; the two IMAX domes in the basement show cartoons; while the IWERKS dome on the first floor is an attempt to take the concept of immersive realism even further. The seats move, and there are water and wind effects – no Smell-O-Vision yet, but surely it's only a matter of time. The only distinctly Chinese example of science on display is a fantastic Ming-dynasty azimuth in the courtyard. Held up by sculptured dragons, it's a more successful blend of science and aesthetics than anything inside.

Oriental Arts Centre

上海东方艺术中心, shànghǎi dōngfāng yìshù zhōngxīn • 425 Dingxiang Lu • ☎ 68547759, Ⓦ shoac.com.cn • Ⓜ Science and Technology Museum

Just north of the Science and Technology Museum, the **Oriental Arts Centre** is a magnificent, glass-faced, flower-shaped building that houses a concert hall, opera theatre, exhibition space and performance hall – they form the petals. It was designed by French architect Paul Andreu, who also created the new opera house in Beijing. If you happen to be in the area, it's worth a visit just to appreciate the elegant curves, puzzle at why they made the interior walls look like snakeskin, and check out the charming fourth-floor exhibition of European music boxes (daily 10am–5pm; ¥50), which includes automata able to blink, draw and sing.

Further afield in Pudong

The **2010 World Expo** was held on both banks of the Huangpu, either side of Nanpu Bridge. The majority of weird and wonderful national pavilions were dismantled after the show; now that the government has got its hands on these swaths of valuable land, expect them to rapidly fill with glitzy new developments. A couple of buildings have been left on the Pudong site as a legacy – the eighteen thousand-seat Mercedes Benz Arena (1200 Expo Avenue; Ⓦ mercedes-benzarena.com; see p.120) and the **China Art Palace**, which makes the long trip down here worthwhile.

Another long trip, deep into Pudong's suburbs, will take you to the **Long Museum**; a new private museum with big ambitions, it's an essential destination for the artily inclined.

China Art Palace

中华艺术宫, zhōnghuá yìshù zhúgōng • 161 Shangnan Lu, near Guozhen Lu • Tues–Sun 9am–5pm • Free; audio-guide ¥20, ¥200 deposit • ☎ 63272425, ⓦ sh-artmuseum.org.cn • Ⓜ China Art Museum

It's a long way from anything else, but this huge art museum is worth a diversion to see – and it's right on the subway. The enormous red crown-like building was the home of the China pavilion at the 2010 Expo site. It's meant to look like a *dougong*, or roof bracket, with four legs like a *ding* pot.

There are five floors; the lift starts you at the top and you work your way down. First you'll find an exhibition of early Chinese twentieth-century art, which shows Chinese artists who returned from abroad grappling with exciting foreign ideas such as Impressionism. The intricate animation based on the classic scroll painting, *Along the River During Qingming Festival*, which was the most popular exhibit at the Expo, is displayed here, though you have to pay ¥60 to see it.

The fourth floor is dedicated to the Shanghai Film Animation studio, which churned out children's stories from the 50s to the 80s. There are plenty of cells and cut-outs, and it might make you want to dig up more about the underappreciated art of Chinese animation (which was a big influence on rather more famous Japanese tradition).

The third and second floor hold temporary shows, usually big names from abroad. The ground floor is feeble, with dull works by academic artists and socialist realist pictures that celebrate achievements like the Chinese conquering Mount Everest and the opening of the Mag-Lev – interesting only to show how bad Chinese official art remains.

Long Museum

龙美术馆, lóngměi shùguǎn • 210 Luoshan Lu • Daily 9.30am–5pm • ¥50 • ☎ 68778787, ⓦ thelongmuseum.org/en • Ⓜ Huamu Lu, then a fifteen-minute walk

This odd, rather forbidding building – a minimalist brick with tiny windows – is China's biggest private museum, holding treasures from the collection of billionaires, Wang Wei and Liu Yiqian. It's a long way out, 45 minutes on the subway then a fifteen-minute walk, but is worth the trip; it's a tremendously ambitious attempt to introduce the entire span of Chinese art. All exhibits are well captioned and displayed, with lights that brighten as you approach.

There are three floors and the exhibits are arranged chronologically, with the oldest art on the top floor, so it is best to start here. Avoid the interminable calligraphy in the painting gallery and seek out the meticulous yet lively animal and bird studies, most from the Ming dynasty. The furniture gallery has some lovely wooden screens. The gallery on revolutionary art is full of Soviet realism-influenced official painting, images of Mao inspecting factories and the like – and not without interest, simply as you'll rarely see this kind of achingly unfashionable image on show anywhere else. The ground-floor show of twentieth-century and contemporary art is a very mixed bag, but you'll likely find something to respond to, perhaps the gaudy satires of postmodernists Fang Lijun or Zhou Chunya.

Hongkou

North from the Bund, you enter Hongkou, an area that, before World War II, was the Japanese quarter of the International Settlement. Since 1949 it has been largely taken over by housing developments, but though it may seem undistinguished – you certainly won't find any celebrity restaurants – it's a charming, rather homely neighbourhood. The two obvious focuses of interest are the pretty Duolun Culture Street and Lu Xun Park, around which are scattered several memorials dedicated to the political novelist Lu Xun. Both areas are within easy walking distance of each other, so it's a good place to come on a sunny afternoon for a stroll, a mooch around the shops and a coffee. Tourists don't get out here much, but it's popular with locals and lively at weekends. As ever, if you like your scenic spots uncrowded, come during the week.

Duolun Culture Street

多伦文化名人街, duōlún wénhuà míngrén jiē • ⑩ Dongaoxing subway station, then a five-minute walk; or take Bus #21 from Sichuan Zhong Lu, behind the Bund

Duolun Culture Street is a pedestrianized strip lined with *shikumen* houses (see p.63) that have been converted to shops selling antiques, curios and art equipment, and genteel teahouses. The street was once home to some of China's greatest writers, including Mao Dun, Guo Moruo, and Lu Xun (see box, p.84), to whom so many statues have been dedicated that he seems practically to have been deified. One bronze effigy has Lu in static conversation with Guo; beside them is an empty seat for you to join the debate, which has inevitably become a favourite photo spot.

At the southern end of the street, where it makes a right angle, you'll find shops catering to the Chinese hobbyist's appreciation for oddly shaped or coloured rocks. Stalls here sell more pebbles and crystals than (it is safe to say) a person could possibly need. Pebbles valued for their colours are best viewed in a bowl of water – apparently all to do with balance, shape and harmony.

Mao Museum

毛泽东像章馆, máozédōng xiàngzhāngguǎn • 183 Duolun Lu • Daily 9am–5pm • ¥2

The *shikumen* at 183 Duolun Lu functions as a private **Mao Museum**. Badges make up the bulk of the display – during the cult of personality, it was practically obligatory to wear your devotion in the form of a tin badge, and they came in a great variety of shapes and sizes. The rarest, now worth thousands of yuan, are those produced in homage by communist African states. The owner's pampered lapdog commonly sleeps at the feet of a porcelain Mao, which makes for an amusing photo. A couple of minutes south you'll reach the *Old Film Café*, charmingly decorated with film posters (see p.112).

Museum to the League of Left-wing Writers

中国左翼作家联盟会址纪念馆, zhōngguó zuǒyìzuòjiā liánméng huìzhǐ jìniànguǎn • 201, Lane 2, Duolun Lu • Tues–Sun 9am–4pm • ¥5

Head down Lane 2 and you'll find the small **Museum to the League of Left-wing Writers**, which was set up in 1930. Writers, sadly, don't make for compelling museums and the collection of oddments, books and photos is less interesting than the building itself, a fine example of a well-preserved *shikumen* house.

Former Residence of H.H. Kong

孔祥熙公寓, kǒngxiángxī gōngyù • 250 Duolun Lu

The grand Former Residence of Guomindang politician **H.H. Kong**, built

7

JEWISH SHANGHAI

Many of the founders of international Shanghai were **Sephardic Jews** who fled the Middle East in the nineteenth century, with families such as the Kadoories and the Sassoons (see p.42) amassing vast fortunes and empires. The Jewish presence increased during World War II, when more than twenty thousand refugees from Europe arrived. As stateless persons, they were forced to live in a special enclosure in Hongkou, centred on Huoshan Park and nicknamed Little Vienna, where they lived cheek by jowl with the local Chinese.

After the war, most Jews left Shanghai, and the only record of their presence today are touches only the sharpest observer will pick up: a Star of David on an old window grille or nail holes where the *mezuzoth* hung. In the middle of Huoshan Park is a small memorial in Chinese, Hebrew and English, and just to its north a plaque marks the site of the American Jewish Joint Distribution Committee, which cared for the refugees.

Regular, four-hour-long tours of Jewish Shanghai are run by Dvir Bar-Gal (☎ 1300 2146706, ⓦ shanghai-jews.com; ¥400).

in 1924, is the grandest example of Spanish-style architecture in the city. Unfortunately it's been mauled in a cack-handed recent restoration, but you can still see the stained glass windows and the columns copied from the Alhambra.

Duolun Museum of Modern Art

多伦现代美术馆, duōlún xiàndài měishùguǎn • 27 Duolun Lu • Tues–Sun 10am–6pm • ¥10 • ☎ 65872530, ⓦ duolunmoma.org • ⓜ Dongbaoxing

The **Duolun Museum of Modern Art** is an unattractive seven-storey monolith that broods at the end of Duolun Lu. As a state-run gallery, you won't see anything remotely contentious here, and privately run galleries are better (see p.122); still, the place does pull in some big-name shows, often of visiting foreigners. Artists in residence have studios on the fifth floor, and visitors are welcome to come and chat. There's a good, if pricey, bookshop and a schedule of performances and lectures.

Ohel Moishe Synagogue

摩西会堂, móxī huìtáng • 62 Changyang Lu • Daily 9am–5pm • ¥50 • ☎ 65415008 • ⓜ Dalian Lu

The **Ohel Moishe Synagogue**, just east of Huashan Park (华山公园, huáshān gōngyuán), was built in 1927. Today it has been heavily restored – only the wooden floors are original. It is no longer used as a place of worship but as a Jewish Refugee Museum, concerning the lives of the twenty-odd thousand Jews who fled to Shanghai in World War II. There are plenty of old photos and images of Sassoon's many buildings (see p.42), though not many exhibits. The curator will show a short film of archive footage.

Lu Xun Park

鲁迅公园, lǔxùn gōngyuán • 146 Jiangwan Dong Lu • Daily 6am–7pm • ¥2 • ⓜ Hongkou Stadium

Lu Xun Park is one of the best places for observing Shanghainese at their most leisured. In the morning, the masses undergo their daily *tai ji* workout, while later in the day, amorous couples frolic on paddle boats in the park lagoon, old men teach their grandkids how to fly kites, and middle-aged ladies while away their time with games of badminton and cards. You might also catch some open-air ballroom dancing or an impromptu performance by amateur musicians.

Tomb of Lu Xun

The park is home to the pompous **Tomb of Lu Xun**, complete with a seated statue and an inscription in Mao's calligraphy, which was erected here in 1956 to commemorate the fact that Lu Xun had spent the last ten years of his life in this part of Shanghai. The

LU XUN

Lu Xun (1881–1936) is regarded as the father of modern Chinese literature. Coming from humble origins in the nearby city of Shaoxing, he gave up a promising career in medicine to write books with the intention, he claimed, of curing the social ills of the nation. He used the demotic of the day, eschewing the sophisticated and obscure language of the literati so that ordinary people could read his books. His stories are short and punchy, something that can't be said about all Chinese classics.

Lu Xun's first significant work was *Diary of a Madman*, published in 1918. Taking its name from Gogol's short story of the same name, it was a satire of Confucian society. Three years later followed his most appealing and accessible book, *The True Story of Ah Q*, a tragicomic tale of a peasant who stumbles from disaster to disaster and justifies each to himself as a triumph – an allegory for the Confucian state. Ah Q ends up taking up the cause of revolution and is executed, as ignorant at the end as he was at the beginning.

Lu Xun's writing earned him the wrath of the ruling Guomindang and in 1926 he took refuge in Shanghai's International Settlement. The last ten years of his life were spent in his simple quarters in Hongkou. Since his death, the fact that he never joined the Communist Party has not stopped them from glorifying him as an icon of the Revolution.

building of the tomb went against Lu Xun's own wishes to be buried simply in a small grave in a western Shanghai cemetery.

Lu Xun Memorial Hall
鲁迅纪念馆, lǔxùn jìniànguǎn • Daily 9–11am & 1.30–4pm • Free

The novelist is further commemorated in the **Lu Xun Memorial Hall**, to the right of the main entrance to the park. Exhibits include original correspondence, among them letters and photographs from George Bernard Shaw.

Lu Xun's Former Residence
鲁迅故居, lǔxùn gùjū • Lane 132, House 9, Shanyin Lu • Daily 9am–4pm • ¥8

A block southeast of Lu Xun Park on Shanyin Lu, **Lu Xun's Former Residence** is worth going to see if you are in the area. The humble and sparsely furnished house, where Lu Xun and his wife and son lived from 1933 until his death in 1936, offers an intriguing glimpse into typical Japanese-influenced housing of the period – small, neat and tasteful.

Hongkou Stadium
虹口足球场, hóngkǒu zúqiúchǎng • Ⓜ Hongkou Stadium

You can't miss the hulking **Hongkou Stadium** on the west side of Lu Xun Park, which has its own line #3 metro stop. Shanghai Shenhua football team play here, with matches on Sundays between March and November (see p.27).

Xujiahui and beyond

Shanghai stretches westward for miles and miles, but it's not a zone that need bother the sightseer particularly. Xujiahui, on the western edge of the Old French Concession, and Hongqiao, further south, are modern residential areas where the most talked-about landmark is the IKEA superstore. There are plenty of shopping opportunities here, but as well as malls, freeways and gated communities, there are a few places to visit. Sedate St Ignatius of what is actually Shanghai's oldest foreign community. Not too far away is the city's most active Buddhist temple, the Longhua Temple, and close by you can learn something of the city's intriguing and tumultuous history as the Longhua Cemetery of Matyrs. Venturing further afield, you'll find that rare thing in Shanghai – a sense of space – at the Botanical Gardens and the Zoo.

Xujiahui and Longhua

徐家汇, xújiāhuì

The **Xujiahui** subway pitches you right into the thick of things. You come out into the five-storey Grand Gateway mega-mall, then when you've found your way out, emerge at the giant intersection of Hongqiao Lu, Hengshan Lu, Zhaojiabang Lu and Caoxi Lu, where you're confronted with another five giant malls (see box, p.124). It's easy to feel overwhelmed by a surfeit of neon and concrete, but fortunately just around the corner there's a rather nice cathedral, **St Ignatius**, a pleasant interruption to any

■ ACCOMMODATION		■ BARS & CLUBS	
Rock and Wood		390 Bar	2
International Hostel	1	Yuyintang	1

shopping trip. Afterwards, hop into a taxi (or take a bus) a couple of kilometres south to **Longhua Temple** and the **Cemetery of Martyrs** – actually a rather charming park.

St Ignatius Cathedral

圣依纳爵主教坐堂, shèngyīnàjué zhǔjiào zuòtáng • 158 Puxi Lu • Weekday services start at 6.30am; Sunday services begin at 8am • ☎ 64382595

It may be hard to imagine today, but Xujiahui is actually the site of Shanghai's oldest Western settlement: the Jesuits set up shop here in the seventeenth century. The only

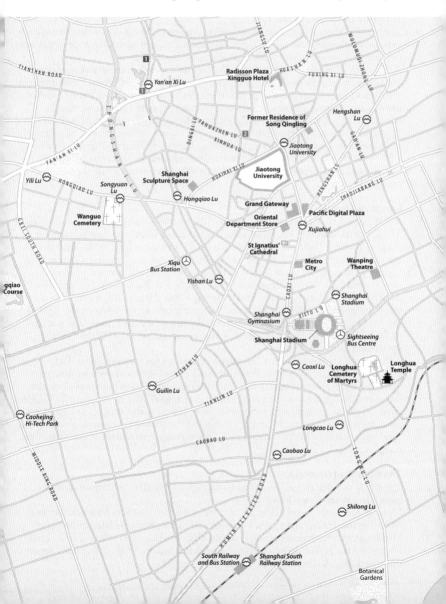

significant remnant from their sojourn is the red-brick, Gothic-style Catholic cathedral, **St Ignatius**, built in 1910 on the grave of Paul Xu Guangqi, Matteo Ricci's personal assistant and first Jesuit convert. The cathedral was vandalized during the Cultural Revolution, its stained-glass windows smashed, and used as a granary. It reopened in 1979, when the spires were renovated; now the windows have been replaced with some that marry Christian and Chinese motifs. St Ignatius is one of the many places of public worship to have received a new lease of life as China's Christian population has boomed.

Longhua Cemetery of Martyrs

龙华烈士陵园, lónghuá lièshì língyuán · 18 Longhua Xi Lu · **Cemetery** Daily 6.30am–4pm · ¥1 · ☎ 64685995, ⊛ slmmm .cn **Exhibition hall** Tues–Sun 6.30am–4pm · Free · Bus #41 from Huaihai Zhong Lu (close to Shaanxi Nan Lu), or from near the Shanghai Centre on Nanjing Xi Lu to terminus, then short walk; or subway to Longcao Lu, then 20min walk east

A couple of kilometres southeast of the St Ignatius Cathedral, **Longhua Cemetery of Martyrs** memorializes those who died fighting for the cause of Chinese communism in the decades leading up to the final victory of 1949. Commemorative stone sculptures, most in a bombastic, Soviet style and many bearing a photo and a name, dot the park. The fresh flowers brought daily testify to the resonance these events maintain. Particularly remembered are those workers, activists and students massacred on this site in Shanghai by Chiang Kaishek in the 1920s. There's a chilling underground hallway which leads from the old prison to the execution ground. In the centre of the park is a glass-windowed, pyramid-shaped **exhibition hall** with a rather random show of paintings and relics.

Longhua Temple

龙华寺, lónghuá sì · 2853 Longhua Lu · Daily 5.30am–4pm · ¥10 · ☎ 64566085 · Ⓜ Longcao Lu, then walk east for fifteen minutes

The **Longhua Temple** is the most active Buddhist site in the city and a centre for training monks. There has been a temple on the site (or at least in the area) since the third century, and though the present buildings are only around a century old, the design and layout are true to the original, comprising a complex of elegant multi-eaved halls. Pleasantly laidback, the temple sees many more devotees than day-trippers. Visiting is a must during Spring Festival (see p.26), when it hosts a huge and boisterous fair. At this time, the temple bell, in the tower to the right of the entrance, is banged 108 times, supposedly to ease the 108 "mundane worries" of Buddhist thought. You can whack it yourself, anytime, for ¥10; three hits is considered most auspicious.

The temple's standout feature is its tenth-century pagoda, an octagonal, forty-metre-high structure with seven brick storeys that are embellished with wooden balconies and red-lacquer pillars. Until the feverish construction of bank buildings along the Bund in the 1910s, it was the tallest edifice in Shanghai. After a long period of neglect (Red Guards saw it as a convenient structure to plaster with banners), an ambitious rezoning project has spruced up the pagoda and created the tea gardens, greenery and shop stalls that now huddle around it. A little vegetarian restaurant at the back of the complex serves simple "blessing" noodles (¥10).

The Botanical Gardens

上海植物园, shànghǎi zhíwùyuán · 111 Longwu Lu · Daily 7am–4pm · ¥40 · ☎ 54363369, ⊛ shbg.org · Bus #56 down Longwu Lu just to the west of Longhua Temple

More than nine thousand plants are on view in the vast, 240-acre **Botanical Gardens**, including two pomegranate trees which are said to date from the reign of Emperor Qianlong in the eighteenth century; despite their antiquity they still bear fruit. Look out too for the orchid chamber, where more than a hundred different varieties are on show, and the aviary where you can feed the doves (¥1).

The western outskirts

Most visitors only head west of Xujiahui to get to Hongqiao Airport, but if you have time it's worth a trip out to Hongqiao Lu subway stop and a nose around the **Wanguo Cemetery** and **Shanghai Zoo**, particularly if you have kids in tow, though pick a fine day. It's a long way out, but if you want a different kind of city view, head to **Lupu Bridge**.

Wanguo Cemetery

万国烈士陵园, wànguó lièshì língyuán • Songyuan Lu • Ⓜ Hongqiao Lu, then a 10min walk

There were once ten cemeteries for foreigners in Shanghai, but most of the tombstones of those interred in the city suffered ignoble fates – destroyed, used as foundation stones for buildings or sold in antique stores – and those that remain have been collected here, the only foreigners' cemetery left. There are over six hundred people buried here, from nearly thirty nations, though many of the tombstones have been removed. The great Jewish families, the Kadoories and the Sassoons, are memorialized, as is "Friend of China" Talitha Gerlach, whose tomb stands out, as it bears her photograph. Gerlach worked to improve the conditions of Chinese labourers and set up a night school for women. In 1987, she was awarded the first green card given by the Communists to a foreigner in Shanghai. The cemetery's most celebrated occupant is Song Qingling (see p.67), who has her own mausoleum and, next to it, a small exhibition on her life.

Shanghai Zoo

上海动物园, shànghǎi dòngwùyuán • 2381 Hongqiao Lu • Daily: April–Sept 6.30am–5.30pm; Oct–March 7am–5pm • ¥40 • ☎ 62687775, Ⓦ shanghaizoo.cn • Ⓜ Shanghai Zoo

A couple of kilometres west of Wanguo Cemetery along Hongqiao Lu, shortly before the airport, is **Shanghai Zoo**, the grounds of which were one of Shanghai's most exclusive golf courses until 1949. The zoo is a massive affair with more than two thousand animals and birds caged in conditions rather better than most Chinese zoos, though that is not saying much. The stars, inevitably, are the ten giant pandas. Children will enjoy the petting zoo and the twice-hourly elephant show. Check out the animal-shaped topiary in the lovely grounds. It's overrun at weekends so try to come during the week.

Lupu Bridge

卢浦大桥, lúpǔdàqiáo • 909 Luban Lu • Daily 9am–4pm (closed if winds are high) • ¥80 • Ⓜ Luban Lu

One of Shanghai's more unusual views is from the top of **Lupu Bridge**, the world's second-longest steel-arch bridge, in the south of the city, a short walk from Lupu Bridge subway stop. Head to the west side of the bridge and you can buy a ticket to climb up to the open-air viewing platform at the apex of the bridge's arch, about one hundred metres above the river. There are over three hundred steps, so it's bracing exercise, and when you're at the top it's a great place to watch boats passing.

8

Accommodation

Accommodation in Shanghai is plentiful, and often stylish, with prices that are higher than elsewhere in China but still much cheaper than you'll find in a large Western city. A double room in one of the grand old-world hotels that form so integral a part of Shanghai's history will cost at least US$150 per night these days; they might not quite offer the comfort and elegance of newer arrivals but make up for it with character. The concept of chic boutique hotels has only just taken hold, but has been enthusiastically embraced. As yet though, there are not quite enough small, affordable places – honourable exceptions are listed here.

9

WHICH AREA?

If you want to be near the centre of the action, go for somewhere between People's Square and the Bund, where there are options for all budgets. It might be noisy but as soon as you walk out the front door you'll know you're in the real Shanghai. For style and panache, head to the more genteel **Old French Concession**, where there are a number of mid-range hotels, housed in attractive buildings and grounds and close to upmarket dining and nightlife. To the north, the upscale accommodation in the commercial district of **Jing'an** puts you at the heart of modern, international Shanghai, with plenty of places to eat, drink and shop nearby. For the latest in corporate chic, **Pudong** has the fanciest options, but really, the area is rather dull.

ESSENTIALS

BOOKING AND RATES

Booking websites Trip Advisor (Ⓦ tripadvisor.com), a huge compendium of hotels, has useful user reviews and photos, but take note of when the review was written, as places can change rapidly. There's no booking fee at Asia Hotels (Ⓦ asiahotels.com), though they do require that you pay a percentage of the fee up front by credit card. Ⓦ trivago.com also has plenty of choices. The most useful websites for the budget places, with lots of reviews, are Ⓦ hostelbookers.com and Ⓦ hostelworld.com, both of which require a ten percent deposit on the booking.

Rates Room rates vary considerably, according to the time of year; the rates listed below are for a double room in summer peak season. Off season, in winter, you'll find rooms at least a third cheaper; but during Chinese national holidays, they might be twice as much (see p.26). The biggest discounts are available online, and if you don't have a reservation, it's quite possible that you'll end up paying less for your room on the internet than by going to reception.

Checking in Reception staff will always speak passable English except at the cheap business hotels, which don't see much foreign custom. Checking in involves filling in a form and paying a deposit. Remember to grab a few hotel business cards – these are vital when you want to let taxi drivers know where you're staying. And don't just show them the matchbox from the hotel bar – an apocryphal American tourist did that and found himself taken to a suburban match factory.

HOTELS

Upmarket There are plenty of upmarket places and more are being thrown up all the time. They're comparable to their counterparts elsewhere in the world, offering all the facilities you might expect, with gyms, saunas and swimming pools, and lavish buffet breakfasts with plenty of choice. The choice in this bracket comes down to whether you want to be right in the heart of the neon jungle or if you want views of it from your window – few places manage both. You may find the finer nuances of service lacking, particularly in older places – the Chinese hospitality industry is experiencing a steep learning curve, which means that the staff and services in newer places are much better. An annoyance at this level is

the high extra charges for services that are free in cheaper places, such as wi-fi (sometimes as much as ¥100 a day); hoick your laptop to a nearby café instead. Even if a room in one of these establishments is beyond your budget, you can still avail yourself of their lavish facilities, including restaurants that are often pretty good and, by Western standards, not expensive.

Mid-range The 2010 Expo left Shanghai with a decent selection of mid-range hotels (those priced less than ¥1000). All are well equipped and comfortable, though they tend to be rather anonymous. An exception are those housed in converted French Concession mansions. You can expect an en-suite bathroom, a business centre, wi-fi (for which you may have to pay a small surcharge), a booking service for onward transport, and the larger ones will have a gym and sauna. Meals are better eaten out than in the hotel restaurant as hotel food at this level is never much good. Breakfast will likely be included, and there will be a choice of Chinese or Western breakfast, but it won't be anything to write home about.

Budget chains An alternative budget option is the hotel chains, presently blasting the much-loathed dingy two-star Chinese hotel into deserved oblivion – at last, you don't have to tolerate cigarette burns on the carpets and mould on the walls. Not much English will be spoken, the hotel restaurant won't be up to much and you'll have to go out for breakfast, and there are no extras such as health centres or pools. Rooms though are clean and bright, with wi-fi, and represent good value at less than ¥250 a night (see p.96).

HOSTELS

A host of good, cheap accommodation options have opened in Shanghai in the last few years. In the youth hostels you can expect free internet, some degree of free wi-fi (perhaps only in the lounge), a self-service kitchen and laundry, air-conditioning in the room, a cheap bar that does a Western breakfast – and a hostel cat. Though you might find some aspects of your stay a little rough around the edges, standards are higher than anywhere else in China and if the staff aren't always completely professional they usually make up for it with friendliness. Anywhere calling itself a hostel will offer a discount (¥10 or so) with a Hostelling International

9

card; you can also pick up a card on the premises (¥50). The hostels we list offer more rooms than dorms so even if you don't identify with the backpacking hordes they're still worth considering. Note that dorm beds have recently become comparatively expensive; you'd generally be better off finding someone to share a twin with.

HOTELS

THE BUND AND NANJING DONG LU

★**Astor House Hotel** 浦江饭店 pǔjiāng fàndiàn 15 Huangpu Lu ☎63246388, ⓦpujianghotel.com; ⓜNanjing Dong Lu; map p.40. Formerly the Astor Hotel and dating back to 1846, this charming old-fashioned place, just north of the Bund across Waibaidu Bridge, has the feel of a Victorian school, with creaky wooden floors, enormous rooms, rambling corridors, and chunky brass fixtures. Portraits of past guests such as Einstein and Charlie Chaplin line the walls; they too may have wondered why the lift was so slow – never mind, the staircase is magnificent. Rooms vary so ask to see a few – basically it's a choice between the atmospheric old rooms or new and better-appointed executive suites. As with all government-owned Chinese businesses, the finer points of service are lacking – the views aren't great and the restaurant should be avoided – but overall this is one of the best of Shanghai's historic hotels: reasonably priced, and with heritage that has been preserved rather than reinvented. Think of it as a batty maiden aunt with some good stories and forgive its eccentricities. **¥640**

Broadway Mansions 上海大厦 shànghǎi dàshà 20 Suzhou Bei Lu ☎63246260, ⓦbroadwaymansions .com; ⓜNanjing Dong Lu; map p.40. This hulking bruiser of a 1930s building, on the north bank of the Suzhou Creek, was originally a residential block. Today it seems aimed at Chinese business travellers, but it does offer superb views along the length of the Bund (room rates increase the

---

APARTMENTS

If you plan to stay for an extended period, you'll need to make special arrangements and probably employ an agent to help you find a place to rent, unless your employer has sorted everything out for you (see p.34).

higher you go). Some rooms are drab, others have been newly renovated, so check out a few, and ask for a river view. It can leave something to be desired in terms of style and service, and the breakfast isn't up to much, but recent improvements mean this is one to consider. **¥880**

★**CHAI Shanghai Living** 上海灿客栈 shànghǎicàn kèzhàn 400 Suzhou Bei Lu ☎63561812, ⓦchailiving.com; ⓜTiantong Lu; map p.39. One of the city's more unusual accommodation options, but well worth seeking out. Basically, it's luxury serviced apartments in an Art Deco apartment block that's seen better days. There's no lobby or reception to speak of – you'll be met on arrival and shown around. Your neighbours will be locals who hang their washing and practise *tai ji* in the corridors. The apartments are wonderful, though. Each is thoughtfully and quirkily designed, with wooden floors, underfloor heating and fully equipped kitchens – go for one with a view of Pudong. Obviously there's no gym or business centre, but you do get free wi-fi. It's a little far from the action, just north of Suzhou Creek, though only a few minutes' walk from the subway. **¥1210**

Fairmont Peace Hotel 和平饭店 hépíng fàndiàn Junction of the Bund and Nanjing Dong Lu ☎63216888, ⓦfairmont.com/peacehotel; ⓜNanjing Dong Lu; map p.40. As the Cathay Hotel, this was the most famous hotel in Shanghai, with a list of illustrious guests including Charlie Chaplin and Noël Coward (see p.43). Its star faded in the modern era thanks to bad management, but its fortunes have been turned around by the Fairmont group, who bought the place in 2007, and refurbished it completely. The place certainly looks grand, and the famous Art Deco lobby and *Jazz Bar* have been restored to their former glory. A new low-rise extension at the rear contains modern luxuries such as a spa and sky-lit swimming pool. **¥1880**

Hotel Indigo 外滩英迪格酒店 waìtān yīngdígē jiǔdiàn 585 Zhongshan Dong Er Lu ☎33029999, ⓦshanghai.hotelindigo.com; ⓜYuyuan Garden; map p.54. The city's newest luxury hotel is next to the Shiliupu Docks, at the south end of the Bund right on the river – the best rooms have fantastic views. The design is high end and really stands out, with fresh and funky detailing everywhere – in the lobby a pod for relaxing sits next to a fire-engine-red rickshaw, and in the bathrooms you'll find Japanese-style electric toilets and rubber ducks. Rooms are big and comfortable and service is extremely attentive. The steakhouse restaurant gets great reviews and don't miss the thirtieth-floor *Sky Bar* for the views. **¥2130**

Le Royale Méridien 世贸皇家艾美酒店 shìmào huángjiā àiměi jiǔdiàn 789 Nanjing Dong Lu ☎33189999, ⓦstarwoodhotels.com; ⓜPeople's Square; map p.39. With its excellent location, five-star services and discreet style, this high-end venue at the People's Park end of Nanjing Dong Lu holds its own. The building is one of the city centre's landmarks, with 66 floors and what look like antennae on the roof. The rather cavernous reception, which has something of a Bond villain's secret base about it, is on the 11th floor. Ask for a room as high up as possible to take full advantage of the views from the floor-to-ceiling windows. **¥1670**

Peninsula 上海半岛酒店 shànghǎi bàndǎo jiǔdiàn 32 Zhongshan Dong Yi Lu ☎23272888, ⓦpeninsula.com /shanghai; ⓜNanjing Dong Lu; map p.40. The latest incarnation of the exclusive Hong Kong brand. In keeping with the area, it's gone for a traditional, Art Deco look, and the tone is set nicely by the white-columned lobby, where a quartet plays and the local elite drink afternoon tea. Most rooms have a Bund view, and all feature TVs in the bathroom, walk-in closets and phones that offer free international calls. **¥2460**

Seagull 海鸥饭店 hǎiōu fàndiàn 60 Huangpu Lu ☎63251500, ⓦseagull-hotel.com; ⓜTiantong Lu; map p.40. Gull statuary, pink-uniformed staff and a chintzy lobby give this place a camp air, though there's sadly nothing flamboyant about the tired-looking rooms. It's very popular for Chinese weddings, which means it's geared around banquets and the restaurant is best avoided. The only reason to stay is for the fantastic river view – specify that clearly when you reserve – which costs less than you'd pay elsewhere. The area isn't very exciting but you're only a 5min walk across the bridge to the Bund. **¥680**

Waldorf Astoria 外滩华尔道夫酒店 wàitān huàér dàofū jiǔdiàn 2 Zhongshan Dong Yi Lu ☎63229988, ⓦwaldorfastoria3.hilton.com; ⓜNanjing Dong Lu; map p.39. Shanghai's grandest old gentlemen's club (see p.45) has been restored to its former Baroque-Revival glory, with a glut of crystal chandeliers, marble floors and columns, and wrought iron and brass fittings. There are attractive period details throughout, from the antique lift to the Art Deco-style sofas, but the highlight for heritage fans has to be the famous Long Bar (see p.115). The original 1910 building has the classiest suites, which boast Bund-view balconies. Most rooms though are in the New Tower just behind, where the emphasis is on understated luxury; the spacious suites have internet-enabled flatscreen TVs, sunken baths and dressing rooms. **¥2740**

Westin 威斯汀大酒店 wēisītīng dàfàndiàn 88 Henan Zhong Lu ☎63351888, ⓦwestin.com /shanghai; ⓜNanjing Dong Lu; map p.39. Chinese luxury hotels usually try to impress with either a water feature or palm trees in the lobby; the over-the-top *Westin* goes for both. So is it the best? Well no, but it's not bad. It scores for having good on-site restaurants such as the *Stage* (see p.104) and a nice little bakery (see p.104), for the Banyan Tree spa (see p.28), and for its location behind the Bund, but loses a few points for the Vegas ambience and the lack of views from most of the rooms. Decor is modern with a few flash touches such as rainforest showerheads and mood lighting. **¥1270**

PEOPLE'S SQUARE

JW Marriott 明天广场JW万怡酒店 míngtiān guǎngchǎng JW wànyí jiǔdiàn Tomorrow Square, 399 Nanjing Xi Lu ☎53594969, ⓦmarriott.com; ⓜPeople's Square; map p.39. Housed in the top floors of one of Shanghai's most uncompromising landmarks (something like an upraised claw), this swanky venue boasts more than 200 serviced apartments for stressed executives, who will at least always be able to find their way home. With its excellent location and magnificent views it's one of the best of the top-end destinations, though not if you suffer vertigo or dislike ear-popping lifts – the lobby is on the 38th floor. Request an east-facing room for views of the liveliest scenes. Windows are huge and have deep sills for sitting and gazing. **¥1880**

Langham Yangtze Boutique 上海朗廷扬子精品酒店 shànghǎi lǎngtíngyángzǐ jīngpǐn jiǔdiàn 740 Hankou Lu ☎60800800, ⓦyangtzeboutique .langhamhotels.com; ⓜPeople's Square; map p.39. This new hotel, conveniently located off People's Square, is not quite as "boutique" as it bills itself – it's too big and corporate – but it is given a heritage feel by the Art Deco building and retro styling. Rooms are spacious, with TVs in the bathroom; many have balconies. **¥1201**

Marvel 商悦青年会大酒店 shāngyuè qīngniánhuì dàjiǔdiàn 123 Xizang Nan Lu ☎63261040, ⓦmarvelhotelsshanghai.com; ⓜDashijie; map p.39. You won't get excited by the rather anonymous decor, but this place is worth considering for its great location, in the thick of the action just off People's Square, and reasonable price. The building is newly renovated and rooms are clean, spacious and well soundproofed (as they need to be, on such a busy road). Free wi-fi throughout. Ask for an upper floor, for the views. **¥830**

Radisson Blu Shanghai New World 新世界丽笙大酒店 xīnshìjiè lìshēng dàjiǔdiàn 88 Nanjing Xi Lu ☎63599999, ⓦradisson.com; ⓜPeople's Square; map p.39. This swish business hotel offers a slick and upscale experience, though the lobby, with its gold lighting, is a bit too much. Has all the facilities you could expect, including spa, gym and pool, and a great location at the end of Nanjing Xi Lu, though eclectic design features give the impression that it hasn't yet worked out an identity. That

9

UFO on the roof is actually a revolving restaurant; the view is more distinguished than the food. **¥1210**

THE OLD FRENCH CONCESSION

★ **88 Xintiandi** 88 新天地 bāshíbā xīntiāndì 380 Huangpi Nan Lu ☎ 53838833, ⓦ 88xintiandi.com; Ⓜ Huangpi Nan Lu; map pp.60–61. Handily close to the metro, this fifty-room boutique hotel is at the edge of the yuppie fantasyland that is the Xintiandi complex. With so many restaurants on your doorstep you won't have to go far to eat, though each room has a little kitchen attached so you can do your own cooking if you (rather perversely) want to. Carved wood, screens and curtains jazz up a design that isn't quite far enough away from the standard business hotel model – still, it's got a lot more character than most Shanghai hotels. The best rooms have a view of the small lake to the east and the no-smoking floors are a nice touch. There's also a pool and guests can use the adjacent spa and fitness centre. Note that it can get noisy outside at weekends. Pricey, but worth it. **¥1830**

B'Lavii House 宝丽会馆 bǎolì huìguǎn 285 Hunan Lu ☎ 64677171, ⓦ blavii.com; Ⓜ Huangpi Nan Lu; map pp.60–61. This elegant, well-appointed French Concession mansion has fourteen sleek rooms arranged around a courtyard, all individually decorated, though a common theme is dark wood furniture and red lacquer. The area is quiet and civilized, and there are plenty of dining options nearby, though it's no trial eating in, as on-site restaurant *Lapis Thai* is very good. Booking is essential. **¥1076**

Casa Serena 巴越风大酒店 bāyuèfēng dàjiǔdiàn 68 Taicang Lu ☎ 53821600, ⓦ casaserenahotel.com; Ⓜ Huangpi Nan Lu; map pp.60–61. Whether you'll like this place depends on how keen you are on imitation period furniture – the stuff is everywhere – while incense in the corridors, big wooden doors and lots of pale stone give the place an oddly monastic feel. There are only 18 rooms; ask to see a few as all are different and some are rather on the chintzy side, though all have appealing glass-walled bathrooms with big tubs. Though it might not be as stylish as it thinks it is, it's still more personal than the chains and is well located right next to Xintiandi for plenty of dining options – though the on-site *Bellagio's* is well regarded. **¥960**

Donghu 东湖宾馆 dōnghú bīnguǎn 70 Donghu Lu, one block north of Huaihai Zhong Lu ☎ 64158158, ⓦ donghuhotel.com; Ⓜ Changshu Lu; map pp.60–61. Seven buildings in total make up the *Donghu*, in a sprawling complex separated by Donghu Lu. The villas on the south side have a chequered past; they served as an opium warehouse and the centre of gangland operations in the 1920s and 1930s. Today, rooms in this section are sedate and spacious with big bathrooms – the best are in Building One, where all the furniture is in traditional Chinese style. The rooms in the annexe on the north side of

the street are much less interesting, a bit run down too, but cheaper. Unusually for a hotel in this range, there's a good-sized indoor pool. Food is mediocre so eat out, even for breakfast; there are plenty of great places in the area. Overall, its good location, smattering of heritage and pleasant gardens make this one worth considering. **¥550**

Fenyang Garden 汾阳花园酒店官方网站 fényáng huāyuán jiǔdiàn guānfāng wǎngzhàn 45 Fenyang Lu ☎ 54569888, ⓦ fenyanggardenhotel .com; Ⓜ Changhsu Lu; map pp.60–61. This elegant and discrete converted villa is set back from the road in well-maintained grounds. It's grand, featuring a fine clutch of chandeliers, and rooms are spacious and refined, though perhaps the place is not as slick as it could be – there's no business centre and wi-fi is patchy, and breakfast is a little too Chinese for most foreign tastes. Still, it's a good, civilized option for the French Concession, and there are plenty of great places to eat in the area. **¥980**

Gallery Suites 联艺 凯文公寓 liányì kǎiwén gōngyù 525 Hengshan Lu ☎ 51795000, ⓦ artgallery hotels.com; Ⓜ Hengshan Lu; map pp.60–61. This artsy, forty-room hotel is well located a short walk from Hengshan Lu subway station. There isn't much to the lobby, but the Art Deco-styled rooms are spacious, with big desks, and elegant fittings. There are freestanding baths in the bathrooms – though, weirdly, there's no door, only a bead curtain. There isn't a restaurant but it's no problem finding a good place to eat in the area. Ask for a room away from the busy road – ideally, get one overlooking the courtyard. The whole place is non-smoking. A good pick for its price range. **¥932**

Hengshan Moller Villa 衡山马勒别墅饭店 héngshān mǎlèbiéshù fàndiàn 30 Shaanxi Nan Lu ☎ 62478881, ⓦ mollervilla.com; Ⓜ Shaanxi Nan Lu; map pp.60–61. Describing itself as a "boutique heritage hotel", the main villa here is a gorgeous Scandinavian-Gothic fantasy (see p.66), built in the 1930s and set in lovely, quiet grounds. The main villa's rooms have balconies, wood panelling and fireplaces, but they're pricey, and there are only a couple of singles, which you'll have to book way in advance. Rooms in the new three-storey block just behind are clean and modern, of much less interest but considerably cheaper. Stay for the building only; service is so-so and the restaurant is to be avoided. **¥1214**

InterContinental Shanghai Ruijin 瑞金宾馆 ruìjīn bīnguǎn 118 Ruijin Er Lu (main entrance on Fuxing Lu) ☎ 64725222, ⓦ ihg.com; Ⓜ Shaanxi Nan Lu; map pp.60–61. This Tudor-style villa complex, a couple of blocks south of Huaihai Zhong Lu, is set in manicured gardens, complete with lawn tennis courts. In the 1920s, it was home to the editor of the *North China Daily News*; in the 60s and 70s, the hotel hosted both Ho Chi Minh and Nixon. The villas, none higher than four storeys, are cosy and exclusive; Mao used to stay in Building One, which has the finest Art Deco touches in the lampshades, balustrades and window decorations. Today, the largest and best-appointed rooms, with the best facilities, are in the new club building. **¥1430**

Jinjiang 锦江之星 jǐnjiāngzhīxīng 59 Maoming Nan Lu ☎ 62582582, ⓦ jinjianghotels.com; ⓜ Shaanxi Nan Lu; map pp.60–61. This vast place with many wings, built in the 1930s, is one of Shanghai's most historic addresses (see p.65). Perhaps it's a trifle old-fashioned, and has been overtaken by slick new competitors, but it's well located in sedate gardens, just north of Shaanxi Nan Lu subway, off busy Huaihai Zhong Lu. Try to get a room in the newly renovated Georgian-style Cathay Building at the north end of the complex. **¥1212**

Ketang Jian Hotel 客堂间璞 堤克酒 店 kètáng jiānpú dīkè jiǔdiàn 335 Yongjia Lu ☎ 54666335, ⓦ ketangjian.com; ⓜ Shaanxi Nan Lu; map pp.60–61. The kind of hotel there aren't enough of in Shanghai – small, well located, characterful, not too pricey. The half dozen or so guestrooms are spacious and charming and given an appealingly vintage look by the mix of old and new furniture and decor, plus you're right at the heart of the French Concession. But, there are no facilities, the free breakfast is terrible (don't even bother), the attached restaurant can be noisy (go for a high room) and the service could sometimes be friendlier – you're pretty much left to your own devices. Overall though, it's still decent value. **¥850**

Mansion Hotel 上海首席公馆酒店 shànghǎi shǒuxí gōngguǎn jiǔdiàn 82 Xinle Lu ☎ 54039888, ⓦ chinamansionhotel.com; ⓜ Shaanxi Nan Lu; map pp.60–61. This painstakingly reconstructed 1920s mansion, discreetly tucked away from the street among manicured gardens, has the feel of an elite private members club – in fact it was once home to notorious gangster Du Yuesheng (see p.161). The building is magnificent but they've tried a little too hard with the lobby and corridor furnishings, cramming repro antiques and memorabilia into every corner. Still, the thirty guestrooms are impressive – light and airy, despite the dark wooden furnishings – and all rooms have two-person jacuzzi tubs. The rooftop terrace is a great venue for a drink. A downside though is the lack of facilities – no gym or lounge. **¥1610**

Okura Garden 上海花园饭店 shànghǎi huāyuán fàndiàn 58 Maoming Nan Lu ☎ 64151111, ⓦ garden hotelshanghai.com; ⓜ Shaanxi Nan Lu; map pp.60–61. The grounds are lovely at this Japanese-run mansion, and the lobby, which used to be the Cercle Sportif French Club, has some great Art Deco detailing. Rooms, though, are in a nondescript monolith looming at the back, and they are rather outdated and kitschy. Still, cleanliness is at Japanese levels, and bathrooms boast that staple of Japanese luxury, the multi-function toilet with bidet attachment and seat warmer. There's also an *onsen* for those into communal bathing. Wi-fi only in the lobby, and be sure to ask for a

nonsmoking room. Large discounts sometimes available online make this oldie worth considering. **¥1190**

Pudi 璞邸精品酒店 púdǐ jīngpǐn jiǔdiàn 99 Yandang Lu ☎ 51585888, ⓦ boutiquehotel.cc; ⓜ Huangpi Nan Lu; map pp.60–61. This small boutique hotel has stylish and unusual touches, such as aquaria in the lobby, and copper sinks, kitchenettes and big desks in the rooms, not to mention what is supposedly the only hotel room in China for pets. For some though it's all a little too fashionably dark. Well located right next to Fuxing Park in the French Concession, but as it's built over a nightclub you might want to avoid the lower floors. Note that the entrance is round the side of the building, and not too easy to spot first time. **¥1605**

★ **Quintet Bed & Breakfast** 五重奏旅店 wǔchóngzòu lǚdiàn 808 Changle Lu, near Changshu Lu ☎ 6249 9088, ⓦ quintet-shanghai.com; ⓜ Changshu Lu; map pp.60–61. A three-storey courtyard house converted into a snug guesthouse, *Quintet* scores for style, with each of the six split-level rooms designed around a theme. It's small and intimate, staff are knowledgeable, and the whole place is nonsmoking. Not many business facilities, but ideal for tourists looking for something a little different. Reservations essential – check out the suites on the website. **¥850**

JING'AN

Portman Ritz-Carlton 波特曼丽嘉酒店 bōtèmàn-lìjiā jiǔdiàn 1376 Nanjing Xi Lu ☎ 62798888, ⓦ ritzcarlton.com; ⓜ Nanjing Xi Lu; map pp.70–71. With 600 rooms on fifty floors, this is the mother ship of business hotels. The underwhelming entrance resembles an underground car park but leads to a luxurious foyer. Rooms are crisply modern with Chinese motifs in the fittings and wooden sliding-panel doors. There's a health club, two swimming pools, tennis and squash courts and a gym, and the Shanghai Centre expat complex next door has good cafés (including a branch of *Element Fresh*; see p.101), bars and restaurants. It's a reliable staple if you want to be at the centre of the action and don't need a view, but is in danger of being superseded by newer, hungrier rivals. Big discounts off the rack rate are sometimes available. **¥2050**

Puli 璞丽酒店 púlì jiǔdiàn 1 Changde Lu ☎ 32039999, ⓦ thepuli.com; ⓜ Jing'an Temple; map pp.70–71. This elegant and attractive hotel is coolly minimal; "designer" without being too gimmicky or hip. The tone is set by the multipurpose 32-metre-long bar in the lobby, where reception staff use MacBooks. Rooms have wooden floors and grey slate walls and stylish if rather impractical sinks. The *Puli* has a reputation for smart service, and staff speak good English. Ask for a view of Jing'an Park. **¥1886**

★ **URBN Hotel** 雅悦酒店 yǎyuè jiǔdiàn 183 Jiaozhou Lu ☎ 51534600, ⓦ urbnhotels.com; ⓜ Jing'an

9

Temple; map pp.70–71. Though it doesn't quite live up to the hype it has generated, this hip little hotel is still pretty good value for an upmarket place. The typical Shanghai idea of stylishness – low lighting and rough grey brick – is leavened with quirky touches, such as a wall made of leather suitcases behind reception. Rooms are elegant with sunken baths, flat-screen TV and a view of the garden, and none of that chintzy furniture that clutters up similar places. On the downside, supposed eco-credentials are just a marketing gimmick, and the area is a little anonymous, though it's only a 10min walk to the subway. Breakfast is not included and is rather pricey – so pop to one of the many cafés nearby. **¥1510**

PUDONG

Eton 裕景大饭店 yùjǐng dàfàndiàn 69 Dongfang Lu ☎38789888, ⓦtheetonhotel.com; ⓜPudong Avenue; map p.76. Perhaps a little far out in Pudong, but right next to the subway. This luxury Singaporean venue is stylish (think corporate boutique chic) and offers lavish facilities – like a flat-screen TV in the bathroom – at cheaper rates than its competitors. Ask for a room with a view of the Huangpu. Note that breakfast is not included and is a little pricey, so eat elsewhere. **¥970**

Grand Hyatt 上海金茂凯悦大酒店 shànghǎi jīnmào kǎiyuè dàjiǔdiàn Jinmao Tower, 88 Shiji Dadao ☎50491234, ⓦshanghai.hyatt.com; ⓜLujiazui; map p.76. Taking up the top floors of the magnificent Jinmao Tower, the *Hyatt* is one of the world's highest hotels. Rooms are undistinguished but, with floor-to-ceiling windows, are all about the view, so pay a little extra to go as high as you can (get one overlooking the Bund, preferably on a corner) and reserve long in advance. Spacious bathrooms, all glass and mirrors, are designed so that you can even get your fix on the clouds from the tub. Great design, lots of lucky numbers (see p.76) as well as awesome views – but, it has to be said, the area is hardly interesting. Never mind, you might not want to leave the hotel anyway. **¥2180**

Park Hyatt 柏悦酒店 bóyuè jiǔdiàn 100 Century Avenue ☎68881234, ⓦshanghai.park.hyatt.com; ⓜLujiazui; map p.76. This stylish, ultramodern business hotel, located in the World Financial Centre from floor 79 up, has stolen the "highest hotel in the world" crown from its sister establishment, the *Grand Hyatt* in the Jinmao Tower, and just might edge it for service too. Surprisingly large, high-ceilinged rooms have great views, and on-site attractions include an infinity pool and a spa. **¥2410**

Pudong Shangri-La 浦东香格里拉大酒店 pǔdōng xiānggélǐlā dàjiǔdiàn 33 Fucheng Lu ☎68828888, ⓦshangri-la.com/shanghai; ⓜLujiazui; map p.76. The other monster hotel in Pudong, with almost a thousand rooms, the *Shangri-La* is popular with upscale business travellers for comfort, convenience and, of course, the views through its huge windows. Classy, with discreet Chinese motifs in the decor, it's not overly corporate, which makes up for the time it takes to get across the river. It's worth upgrading for a Bund view. The restaurant is excellent (see p.112). **¥2430**

BUDGET CHAINS

24K Hotel 24K国际连锁酒店 24k guójì liánsuǒ jiǔdiàn 155 Weihai Lu ☎51181222, ⓜNanjing Xi Lu, map pp.70–71; 555 Fuzhou Lu ☎5150358, ⓜPeople's Square, map p.39; ⓦ24khotels.com. This business hotel chain has a winning formula: chirpy design, spacious no-frills rooms and prices which are much cheaper than the competition. Most branches are a little too far out to be convenient, but these two are very central, both located on busy roads not far from People's Square, and walkable from the metro. Little English is spoken. It's wise to pay a little extra for a window and a bathroom. You should go out to eat, but if you're just looking for somewhere comfortable to crash, this is one to consider. **¥248**

Jinjiang Inn 锦江饭店 jǐnjiāng fàndiàn 33 Fujian Lu ☎65979188, ⓜYuyuan Garden, map p.54; 293 Yunnan Lu ☎63262200, ⓜDashijie, map p.59; reservations ☎4008299999, ⓦjinjianginns.com. This sober, no-frills budget business-hotel chain has dozens of branches in Shanghai; we've listed the two most central, both of which can be booked from their website (you'll have to register, but you also then get a small discount) or from the reservation hotline. They certainly do the job if all you need is a comfortable, clean room and free wi-fi, and they also offer no-smoking rooms and cable TV. **¥340**

Motel 168 莫泰连锁旅店 mòtài liánsuǒ lǚdiàn 531 Jingling Dong Lu, ⓜDashijie, map pp.70–71; 1119 Yan'an Xi Lu, by Fanyu Lu, 5min walk from ⓜJiangsu Lu, map p.54; ☎63168168, ⓦmotel168.com. There are two dozen or so branches of this functional American-style business hotel all over Shanghai – we've listed the two most convenient. Services are basic but the rooms are cheap and clean, with bright, breezy decor, and staff speak some English. **¥268**

YOUTH HOSTELS

THE BUND AND NANJING DONG LU

Blue Mountain Bund Youth Hostel 蓝山外滩 国际 青年旅舍 lánshān wàitān guójì qīngnián lǚshè 6th floor, 350 Shanxi Nan Lu ☎33661561, ⓦbmhostel .com; ⓜNanjing Dong Lu; map p.39. This hostel is clean, friendly and well located – just south of Suzhou Creek, ten minutes' walk from the Bund. Note that it occupies the sixth floor of an office building, and the lifts are slow. It can feel a bit crowded, as communal areas are small, and there's only wi-fi in the bar (which kills the atmosphere there). Dorms are same-sex. Dorm ¥80, en-suite double ¥200

Captain Hostel 船长青年酒店 chuánzhǎng qīngnián jiǔdiàn 37 Fuzhou Lu ☎63235053; Ⓦcaptainhostel.com.cn; ⓂNanjing Dong Lu; map p.40. This well-located hostel, right on the Bund, has a nautical theme, which is carried through with admirable thoroughness – rooms are made up to look like cabins, with portholes for windows, and staff are dressed in sailor suits (though it hasn't made them any jollier). It also has a very good bar – the *Captain Bar* (see p.114) – on the sixth floor, with great views of Pudong – though two beers will cost as much as a bed for the night. On the downside, communal areas are a bit grotty. Dorms are same-sex, and Chinese and foreign guests are billeted together. Be warned that the cleaning staff will barge in and get on with it whether you're out of bed or not. Wi-fi in the lobby. Bike rental is ¥2/hr (guests only), and there's free use of a washing machine. Eight-bed dorm ¥80, double ¥358

Dock Bund Hostel 外滩源青年旅舍 wàitānyuán qīngnián lǚshè 55 Xianggang Lu ☎53500077; ⓂTiantong Lu; see map p.39. This little cheapie is just behind the Bund – you could pretty much throw rocks at the Peninsula. There's virtually no lobby, communal areas are small, and corridors are shabby, but the rooms are clean and spacious, though those overlooking the street are a bit noisy. Patchy wi-fi. Dorm ¥55, double ¥180

Mingtown Hikers Hostel 明堂上海旅行者国际青年旅馆 míngtáng shànghǎi lǚxíngzhě guójì qīngnián lǚguǎn 450 Jiangxi Zhong Lu ☎63297889; ⓂNanjing Dong Lu (line 2 & 10); map p.39. Very well located just west of the Bund, this cheap and cheerful hostel books up quickly. It's sociable, so can be noisy, and the rooms with bathrooms are not a good deal as they're rather dark, but the other options are good for the price. Free wi-fi and internet. Four- or six-bed dorm ¥45, double ¥180, en-suite double ¥240

PEOPLE'S SQUARE

★ **Mingtown Etour Hostel** 上海明堂新易途国际青年旅馆 shànghǎi míngtáng xīnyìtú guójì qīngnián lǚguǎn 55 Jiangyin Lu ☎63277766; ⓂPeople's Square; map p.49. This is the best of the cheapies, being very well located – tucked in the alleyway behind Tomorrow Square, right beside People's Park – yet quiet and surprisingly affordable. A dark corridor opens into a relaxing courtyard featuring a pond with goldfish and a cat. The cheap bar-restaurant here has a free pool table and shows films at night, and there's also a self-service laundry and kitchen, free internet, and

free wi-fi throughout. Rooms, in an old Shanghai building, vary in size, so ask to see a few – one or two have balconies – and bathrooms are shared between two or three rooms. Head to Tomorrow Square and look for the blue hostel sign in the alley immediately south. Six-bed dorm ¥80, double ¥220

JING'AN

★ **Le Tour Travel's Rest Youth Hostel** 乐途国际青年旅舍 lètú guójì qīngnián lǚshè Lane 36, 319 Jiaozhou Lu ☎62671912, Ⓦletourshanghai.com; ⓂJing'an Temple; map pp.70–71. This huge hostel was once a textile factory and though it's been livened up with a lick of green paint and quirky stencils, the concrete floors in the hallways and ceiling ducts reveal its industrial origins. Though rooms are comparatively pricey, dorms are good value and this place boasts the most facilities of any hostel – as well as a rooftop bar, bike hire, and free wi-fi in the lobby, there's a DVD room, a mini-gym and a ping-pong table, which is perhaps why it's so popular with European school groups. No kitchen though. It's a 10min walk north from Jing'an Temple subway stop, and can be hard to find first time, as it's located down a narrow alley just off busy Bai Lan Lu. Look out for the big green building; if you reach Wuding Lu you've gone too far. Dorm ¥90, double ¥300

SOUTH OF THE CENTRE

Blue Mountain Youth Hostel 蓝山国际青年旅舍 lánshān guójì qīngnián lǚshè Building 1, 1072 Nong, Quxi Lu ☎63043938, Ⓦbmhostel.com; ⓂLuban Lu; map p.54. Though it's a long way from the centre, in the southwest of the city, the *Blue Mountain Hostel* is right next to Luban Lu subway stop – you'll see the triangular YH sign as soon as you exit. Offering good value for money in its price range, this large and well-run place is deservedly popular with young Chinese backpackers. Rooms are spotless, with wooden floors and beds, but ask to see a few, as some don't have windows (although they're no cheaper than those that do). It's well equipped, with free wi-fi, bike rental, a kitchen and a washer and dryer (¥15), as well as the hostel staples of bar, pool table and skinny cat. Eight-bed dorm ¥60, double ¥180, en-suite double ¥220

WEST OF THE CENTRE

City Central Youth Hostel 万里路国际青年旅舍 wànlǐlù guójì qīngnián lǚshè 300 Wuning Lu, near Zhongshan Bei Lu ☎52905577; ⓂCaoyang Lu; map pp.70–71. This giant, no-nonsense hostel, painted a striking blue and orange, boasts some of the city's cheapest rooms and dorms. It's clean, and staff are efficient, though don't bother with the bar-cum-restaurant. Offers DVD rental and wi-fi in the lobby. Despite the name, it's rather far out, but it's only about 300m north of Caoyang Lu metro station, in the west of town. It's tricky to find the first time:

9

follow the subway line north until you reach the crossroads with Wuning Lu, cross over and on your right you'll see an archway. Walk through it and you'll see the hostel sign. Dorms are mixed or female only. Four-bed dorm ¥80, double ¥190

Le Tour Shanghai Youth Hostel 乐途上海国际青年旅舍 lètú shànghǎi guójì qīngnián lǔshè 136 Bailan Lu, near Kaixuan Bei Lu ☎52510800, ⓦletourshanghai.com; ⓜCaoyang Lu; map pp.70–71. Friendly staff and good facilities make this brightly painted place worth considering despite its rather peripheral location a few minutes' walk from Caoyang Lu subway station, in the northwest of the city. The rooms with shared bathrooms are some of the cheapest in the city. Facilities include lockers and laundry, wi-fi in the lounge and a DVD room. Use of the hostel computers is free. Dorms are same-sex. Four- or six-bed dorm ¥80, double ¥160, en-suite double ¥220

Rock and Wood International Hostel 老木国际青年旅舍 lǎomù guóyì qīngnián lǔshè Lane 615, 278 Zhaohua Lu ☎33602361, ⓦrockwood.hostel .com; ⓜZhongshan Park; see map pp.86–87. One of those places that, being a little far from the centre, tries a lot harder than its competitors. Scores highly for being clean, spacious and attractive with big, comfortable communal areas – home to a few pets and a lot of potted plants and bamboo. The light and well-designed en-suite rooms are more expensive than usual in a hostel, so you get two different types of clientele. Dorms are mixed. It's a ten-minute walk to the nearest metro, Zhongshan Park. Dorm ¥60, double ¥450

M ON THE BUND

Eating

Food is one of the true attractions of China; eating might not be the reason you came, but it will be one thing you remember. And Shanghai can make a convincing claim to be China's culinary hotspot. Upmarket restaurants starring celebrity chefs are opening every few months – and they're great for splashing out – but what any visitor here can really appreciate is the diversity and superb quality of everyday, white-collar eateries. It's all a little more expensive than in the rest of China, but still a bargain – it's not difficult to get a good meal for around ¥60 a head.

10

You'll be able to find all of China's many regional **cuisines** somewhere – Sichuan and Cantonese are perennially popular. Japanese and Korean food are widely available and Thai and Indian are growing in popularity. If you're looking for Western food, you've come to the right Chinese city, with a great number of restaurants catering for expats; all the big internationals are here too. Note that a lot of the best places are chains, with several locations, many of them inside plazas and malls.

Finally, remember that **street food** is generally okay as long as you avoid seafood or anything that's fried (the oil can be dodgy), and try to avoid drinking tap **water**, as it's laced with heavy metals.

ESSENTIALS

REVIEWS

For the latest in dining – and bitchy user reviews of over-hyped restaurants – check the following sites:

ⓦ **smartshanghai.com** Expat-oriented listings site with reviews that include Chinese addresses and maps.

ⓦ **cityweekend.com.cn/shanghai** A useful, if rather arbitrary, ranking system. Lots of user reviews.

RESTAURANTS

Cost Restaurants are more expensive in Shanghai than elsewhere in China, although prices remain reasonable by international standards; most dishes at Chinese restaurants are priced at around ¥50, and even many upmarket Western restaurants have meal specials that come to less than ¥90 (¥88 is a popular set-menu price, 8s being lucky). Prices per head, given in the reviews, cover a couple of dishes and tea. Tipping is never expected, but some of the

pricier places, and most hotel restaurants, add a 15 percent service charge.

Meal times The Chinese like to eat early, sitting down for lunch at noon and dinner at 6pm; you'll find the popular Chinese places packed in the early evening then empty at 9 and closed by 10. Anywhere with a bar, or any expat-oriented place, will usually be open much later. Shanghai has a plethora of stylish destination restaurants, and it's worth splashing out at least once. Many have reasonably priced lunch or late-night deals.

CAFÉS AND QUICK BITES

Fast food For fast food, *McDonald's*, *KFC* and their ilk are everywhere like a rash; rather better – and certainly healthier – is the Asian fast-food noodle chain *Ajisen* (see p.101). Every mall and shopping centre has a cluster of fast-food restaurants, either in the basement or on the top

---

DINING ETIQUETTE

Most places will have a **menu** in English, though it might be a handwritten scrap of greasy paper – anyway, just about everywhere has picture menus these days. Cold appetizers are served first, main courses arrive a few minutes later, then the meal is finished off with soup and perhaps some fruit. Note that rice generally arrives about halfway through the meal, and is eaten to fill you up rather than be mixed with your dishes. If you want it brought earlier, you have to ask for it – say **mǐ fàn**. Tea is free except at more upscale places; if you want your teapot refilled, upend the lid. It's common at **business banquets** to drink **báijiǔ**, the pungent Chinese booze that tastes like lighter fluid, in toasts, during which you are expected to **gān bēi** – swallow it all in one ghastly, throat-searing gulp. You won't get away with saying that you just like a little in moderation, so it might be a good idea on such occasions to pretend that you don't drink at all.

As for **table manners**, well, earthy peasant values are out of fashion, so don't spit on the floor; apart from that, pretty much anything goes. It's impolite to show your teeth, so if you want to use a toothpick, cover your mouth with the other hand. Slurping your soup is normal, even rather polite. You don't have to eat with chopsticks; all restaurants have knives (**dāozi**) and forks (**chāzi**). Tofu dishes are eaten with a spoon.

Service standards often leave something to be desired, and you'll have to be a little more forward than you might expect to get what you want from the staff. To get the waitress's attention, wave and call **fúwùyuán**, and if you want the bill ask for the **mǎidán**.

In restaurants, the Chinese don't usually share the **bill**, so offering to pay your share may cause embarrassment to your hosts. Instead, diners contest for the honour of paying it, with the most respected winning. You should make some effort to stake your claim but, as a visiting guest, you can pretty much guarantee that you won't get to pay a jiao. If it makes you uncomfortable, insist that next time dinner is on you. Equally, if you were the most senior or respected figure – or a guy taking a girl on a date – you'd be stumping up for everything.

floor, and the one in Raffles' basement is particularly good. Street food is not as prevalent here as elsewhere in China, but there are a few places worth trying (see box, p.107).

Pastry shops Unlike many other Chinese, the Shanghainese are famous for their sweet tooth, a tradition that dates back to the period of the International Settlement. They are indulged by bakeries and pastry shops across the city; try Nanjing Dong Lu, the *Pantry* (see p.111) or the bakery at the *Westin* (see p.104).

Cafés Café culture has really taken off in Shanghai, and every mall and shopping street now boasts a *Starbucks*, the British *Costa* (see below) or the Japanese *Manabe* (see below). As any tourist itinerary here involves lots of fairly unstructured wandering around, visitors might find themselves spending more time than they thought people-watching over a cappuccino. All cafés have wi-fi unless otherwise noted. If you're looking for a pitstop in the afternoon, many of the best restaurants and hotels now serve afternoon tea (see box, p.105).

Breakfast places The typical Chinese breakfast of glutinous rice and fried dough sticks appeals to few foreigners; steamed buns and dumplings are a tastier local alternative (see p.102). Fortunately, there are plenty of places for a good Western breakfast – best are *Wagas* (see below) and *Element Fresh* (see below).

DELIVERY

Scooter-borne delivery is relatively new for China but catching on fast, especially for busy workers at lunchtimes. Note that restaurants *Element Fresh* (see below) and *Pier 39* (see p.110) will deliver for free.

Sherpa's ☎62096209, ⓦsherpa.com.cn. You can forgo the whole tiresome business of leaving your room altogether. For a delivery fee of ¥15 to ¥35, Sherpa's will deliver from a host of different restaurants around town, though expect a wait of up to an hour.

SUPERMARKETS

With so many affordable restaurants around, self-catering is hardly necessary, but if you do want to give the kitchen a workout you'll find it easy to get ingredients. Every neighbourhood has a wet market, but for Western goods you'll have to head to an international supermarket.

City Shop Basement, Times Square, 93 Huaihai Zhong Lu; map p.54; 1st Floor, Shanghai Centre, 1376 Nanjing Xi Lu; map pp.70–71. If you're self-catering, it's worth knowing about City Shop, which sells Western and Chinese groceries. Daily 10am–10pm.

Feidan 158 Anfu Lu, map pp.60–61; 382 Dagu Lu, map pp.60–61; ⓦfeidan.cn. This deli has an impressive range of imported food and deli items; the Anfu Lu branch is popular with expats as you can buy beers inside then drink them on the patio. Daily 9.30am–10pm.

Parkson Supermarket In the basement at 918 Huaihai Zhong Lu; map pp.60–61. A good selection of imported Western products at a hefty mark-up. Daily 10am–10pm.

10

CITY-WIDE

Ajisen 味千拉面 wèi qiān lā miàn 327 Nanjing Dong Lu ☎63607194; map p.39; 518 Huaihai Zhong Lu ☎63725547; map pp.60–61; Basement, Raffles Mall, Fuzhou Lu ☎63366500; map p.39. This casual Japanese chain offers set meals for less than ¥50. A good range of ramen noodles, and the curry pork chop is pretty good too. All meals come with miso soup. Daily 10am–11pm.

Costa 品质咖啡 pǐnzhì kāfēi 388 Nanjing Xi Lu ☎35051958; map p.39; Grand Gateway Mall, 1 Hongqiao Lu ☎64795633; map pp.86–87. The latest coffee colonizers are from the UK, and they're spreading fast, with eighty branches in Shanghai already. Hard to get excited about but at least it's better than *Starbucks*. The Nanjing Xi Lu branch is handy, as there aren't too many cafés in the area. Daily 9am–10pm.

Element Fresh 新元素 xīnyuánsù Shanghai Centre (east side), 1376 Nanjing Xi Lu ☎62798682; map pp.70–71; 4th Floor, K. Wah Centre, 1028 Huaihai Zhong Lu ☎54038865; map pp.60–61; 2nd Floor, World Financial Centre, 100 Century Avenue ☎68774001; map p.76; ⓦelementfresh.com. This airy, informal bistro is the best place in town for a Western breakfast (note that most are open early) – there are plenty of options both hearty and healthy. ¥80 for breakfast which includes limitless coffee. It's also well

liked for its deli-style sandwiches, smoothies, and health drinks. The one at the World Financial Centre is particularly useful, as affordable options are few and far between in Pudong. Free delivery. Shanghai Centre daily 7am–11pm; K. Wah Centre Sun–Thurs 8am–11pm, Fri & Sat 8am–midnight; World Financial Centre 10am–10pm daily.

Manabe 真锅咖啡厅 zhēnguō kāfēitīng 85 Huating Lu, just off Huaihai Zhong Lu ☎54040608; map pp.70–71; 100 Haining Lu ☎00590213; map pp.60–61; 1037 Yuyuan Lu ☎52390920; map pp.70–71. The Japanese-style food at this coffee-shop chain is so-so, but their breakfast deal – ¥28 for pancakes and a coffee – is worthy of note, and there is an extensive range of teas. Daily 10am–1am.

Wagas 沃歌斯 wògēsī 7 Donghu Lu, near Xinle Lu ☎54661488; map pp.60–61; 277 Huangpi Bei Lu, near Weihai Lu ☎53752758; map pp.60–61; Lower Ground Floor 11A, CITIC Square, 1168 Nanjing Xi Lu ☎52925228; map pp.70–71. Good-looking yet wholesome food, decor and staff at this New York-style deli. Order the Western breakfast before 10am and it's half-price – only ¥32 – with coffee an extra ¥10. There are also smoothies and frappés for ¥38, and wraps and sandwiches for a little more. At lunchtimes though, it's rather too busy. Daily 7.30am–10pm.

THE BUND AND NANJING DONG LU

The strip of real estate along the Bund must contain some of the world's most hyped restaurants. All boast great views of the Bund and have been lavishly designed. They're great for a splurge and not always as pricey as they look. Many offer a comparatively inexpensive afternoon tea (¥150 or so), as do the fancy hotels (see p.105), usually between 2 and 5pm.

RESTAURANTS

8½ Otto e Mezzo Bombana Rockbund, 169 Yuanmingyuan Lu, near Beijing Dong Lu ☎60872890, ⓦottoemezzobombana.com/shanghai/; map p.39. The best of the new fine-dining venues in the area. Chef Umberto Bombana has created a menu of Italian cuisine – home-made pastas, raviolis and ragout, all wonderfully done and served in a dining room that's classy without being too grand. Great views of the Pearl Tower from the balcony. ¥500 per person. Daily 4pm–late.

Lao Beijing 老北京 lǎoběijīng 1 Henan Nan Lu ☎63734515; map p.39. This big, chintzy, and well-regarded Beijing duck restaurant is handy for the Bund. Arrive early as the place starts winding down at 8pm. It's not expensive at ¥160 per duck, which feeds two at least. Watch your duck being skilfully eviscerated at the table, wrap it up and slather it with bean sauce, and finish with

duck soup. Just don't expect to be able to go jogging afterwards. Daily 11am–2.30pm & 5–10pm.

Lao Zhengxing 老振兴餐馆 lǎozhèngxīng cānguǎn 556 Fuzhou Lu ☎6322624; map p.39. This grand old Shanghai restaurant is perennially popular for its light, non-greasy Shanghai cuisine, which they've been serving up since 1862. Gold doors lead to a dining hall glittering with gilt, but there's nothing too over the top about the menu, and prices are reasonable, with most dishes costing less than ¥50. House special is the smoky red sauce which graces most of the seafood dishes, including the famous herring and the pork (¥42). Also consider the eight treasures rice, tofu stew and fried river prawns. A good introduction to local cuisine, and not pricey at around ¥130 a head; arrive early and don't expect great service. Daily 11am–11pm.

Lost Heaven the Bund 花马天堂 huāmǎ tiāntáng

CHINA'S REGIONAL CUISINES

The Chinese obsess about food: the Mandarin for "how are you?" – ni chi fan ma – literally translates as "have you eaten yet?" Accordingly, they have created one of the world's great cuisines. It's much more complex than you might suspect from its manifestations overseas, with each region boasting its own delicious specialities. All kinds of Chinese food are available somewhere in the city, including of course the city's own distinctive Shanghai cuisine.

SHANGHAI CUISINE

Shanghai cuisine is sweet, light and oily. Much of the cooking involves adding ginger, sugar and sweet rice wine, but spice is used sparingly. Fish and shrimp are considered basic to any respectable meal; eel and crab may appear too. **Fish and seafood** are often lightly cooked (steamed mandarin fish is especially good), or even served raw; "drunken shrimps", for instance, are simply live shrimps drowning in wine. Crawfish is a popular comfort food; the critters are cooked with chilly, served whole, and eaten with the fingers (plastic gloves are usually provided). Between October and December look out for the local speciality, **hairy crabs** (known as mitten crabs in the West), a grey freshwater crustacean that's harvested in its breeding season. Prise the shell off and you'll find delicious white meat inside, and, if it's a female, maybe the highly prized orange roe.

Meat dishes are well represented too. Sweet and sour spare ribs are given a zesty tang by their heavy sauce. One unmissable local treat is "beggars' chicken", in which the whole bird is wrapped in lotus leaves, sealed with clay and oven-cooked. Every meal will feature so-called "cold" dishes, eaten as appetizers at room temperature; try crispy eel or "drunken chicken" (chicken marinated in rice wine).

The adventurous should try the **thousand-year-old egg** – preserved eggs flavoured with lime and ginger, or the fermented **stinky tofu** – which tastes better than it smells. Finally, don't overlook the humble staples. Shanghai-style fried **noodles** are ubiquitous, and make a great quick lunch. They're similar to chow mein, but the noodles are cut much thicker, and usually fried with pork.

Finally, don't overlook the humble **dumpling**, or xiǎolóngbāo. These are delicious small buns filled with pork and a gelatinous soup – be careful though, as they're steaming hot inside – and served with a sauce made with ginger and vinegar. Also try shēngjiānbāo, a steamed bun with a crispy base and topped with chives and sesame.

17 Yan'an Dong Lu, near Sichuan Nan Lu ☎021/6330 0967, ⓦlostheaven.com.cn; map p.40. Specializing in the cuisine of Yunnan province, this is an expat favourite. The decor is as exotic as the food, though you might consider the lighting on the dark side – the other branch (see map, pp.60–61) has the edge for atmosphere. The chicken with coriander and the lamb ribs are excellent. About ¥200 per person; reservation advised. Daily noon–2pm & 5.30–10.30pm.

M on the Bund 米氏西餐厅 mǐshì xīcāntīng 7th Floor, Five on the Bund, entrance on Guangdong Lu ☎63509988, ⓦm-restaurantgroup.com/mbund/; map p.40. Opened in 1999, *M on the Bund* is famous as the oldest of the Bund's destination restaurants. For years it rather sat on its laurels but new chef Hamish Pollit seems to have brightened things up with his mix of European and North African dishes. Suckling pig and roast lamb (both ¥288) are recommended for dinner. The set lunch won't break the bank at ¥188 per person for two courses. Views over the river are superb – reserve, and ask for a table with a view. Daily 11.30am–2.30pm & 6–11pm.

Mercato 3 on the Bund, 3 Zhongshan Dong Yi Lu ☎63219922, ⓦthreeonthebund.com; map p.40.

Celebrity chef Jean Georges Vongerichten (who has three Michelin stars) serves up Italian home-style cooking in a comfortable rustic-chic environment. The best pizzas in the city – try the salami and ricotta. Reserve, and ask for a seat with a view. Expect to pay around ¥500 per person. There's a late-night menu from 11pm, Thurs–Sun – pizza and two glasses of wine for ¥188. Mon–Wed 5.30–11pm & Thurs–Sun 5.30pm–1am.

Mr and Mrs Bund 6th Floor, 18 Zhongshan Dong Yi Lu ☎63239898, ⓦmmbund.com; map p.40. Local celebrity chef Paul Pairet creates a wide range of imaginative French dishes with a twist – foie gras crumble, a lemon tart served in a lemon, and the like. There's a serve-yourself wine bar, a deck with an amazing view, and the ambience is lively and trendy. It's very hip at the moment, having made it into the San Pellegrino world's best restaurants list, so you'll have to reserve. A meal will set you back at least ¥600 per person, but take note of their late-night deals available after 10.30pm Tues–Sat, when you can get a two-course set menu for ¥200. Lunch Mon–Fri 11.30am–2pm; dinner Tues–Thurs 6pm–2am, Fri & Sat 6pm–4am, Sun & Mon 6–10.30pm.

10

WHERE TO TRY SHANGHAI CUISINE

Jian Guo 328 An intimate neighbourhood venue with a warm atmosphere. Stick with the fish dishes. See p.108.

Lao Zhenxing Simple, unpretentious and always busy; this place keeps them coming with classic Shanghai dishes. See p.102.

Shanghai Ren Jia The Chinese like their restaurants rènào (hot and noisy), and this is a good example. Try those drunken shrimps if you're brave enough. See p.105.

Wang Baohe Popular place for a crab banquet. See p.104.

Xiao Shaoxing Where locals get their drunken chicken. See p.105.

Xinjishi The in-the-know eaterie where the stylish set get their down-to-earth home-style cooking. See p.110.

Food Steets The little restaurants lining Shanghai's food streets and markets are great places to get down with the locals. You won't find many English menus so just point at whatever your neighbour is having, or the critter slithering round the bucket. See p.107.

SICHUAN CUISINE

Sichuan, in China's far west, is renowned for its heavy use of chillis and lip-tingling pepper, though plenty of other flavours, such as orange peel, ginger and spring onions, are used. Classic dishes include hot spiced bean curd (**mápó dòufu**), stir-fried chicken with peanuts and chillis (**gōngbǎo jīdīng**), and fish with pickled vegetables (**suān cài yú**). Try them all out at *Yuxin Sichuan Dish* (see p.111), or, if you'd rather go easy on the spice, at *South Beauty 881* (see p.108).

CANTONESE CUISINE

Cantonese cuisine, from China's south, is the one most foreigners are already familiar with, featuring plenty of lightly seasoned fresh fish and vegetable dishes. A meal of *dim sum* (**diǎnxīn** in Mandarin) comprises tiny flavoured buns, dumplings and pancakes and is often eaten in Shanghai as lunch (in Guangdong Province it's breakfast). There's no shortage of *dim sum* restaurants in Shanghai; try chic *Crystal Jade* (see p.106) or cheap and cheerful *Bi Feng Tang* (see p.106).

NORTHERN CUISINE

The cuisine of northern China is hale and hearty, with steamed buns and noodles as staples. Dishes tend to be heavily seasoned, with liberal use of vinegar and garlic. Beijing duck is the most famous dish, best sampled at *Lao Beijing* (see p.102). The classic winter warmer, hotpot, where diners dip raw ingredients into a heated stock, is the speciality at *Hot Pot King* (see p.107).

10

The Stage, Westin 威斯汀舞台餐 厅 wēisītīng wǔtái cāntīng 1st Floor, Bund Centre, 88 Henan Zhong Lu, near Guangdong Lu ☎ 63350577; map p.39. Upscale but casual, and given a theatrical feel by the open cooking stations, from where chefs prepare a good range of Western and Asian cuisine; a meal will cost about ¥400 per person. It's still the "it" place for a buffet Sunday brunch – ¥538 (plus 15 percent service charge) for as much as you can eat and drink, including champagne and caviar. Come hungry and not too hung over, and pig out while watching the acrobat show. Reservations necessary. Daily 6am–12am; Sunday brunch 11.30am–2.30pm.

Wang Baohe 王宝和酒家 wángbǎohé jiǔjiā 603 Fuzhou Lu ☎ 63223673; map p.39. Billing itself the "king of crabs and ancestor of wine", this local staple has been around for over 200 years and these days rests on its laurels somewhat. It's famous for its crab dishes; eight-course crab set meals start at ¥350 per person. Otherwise try tofu with crab (¥68) and crab dumplings (¥35). During hairy crab season (Oct–Dec) you'll have to reserve well in advance. Daily 11am–2pm & 5–9pm.

CAFÉS

Westin Bakery Bund Centre, 88 Henan Zhong Lu ☎ 63351888; map p.39. Tucked at the back of the over-the-top *Westin* hotel lobby (see p.93), this good-value bakery deserves a mention for being understated (in contrast to the hotel). Tasty cakes, tarts and coffees are served – treat yourself to a lychee vodka truffle (¥7). Daily 9am–7pm.

PEOPLE'S SQUARE

As well as the venues below, check out Yunnan and Huanghe Lu food streets (see box, p.107). If you're doing the sights and looking for a pitstop, it's good to know about *Barbarossa* (see below) and *Kathleen's 5* (see below).

RESTAURANTS

Godly 功德林 gōngdélín 445 Nanjing Xi Lu ☎ 63270218; map p.49. A vegetarian restaurant with temple-themed decor, specializing in fake meat dishes. It's all rather hit and miss: try the meatballs, roast duck, crab and ham, but avoid anything meant to taste like fish or pork, and be wary of ordering just vegetables as they'll turn up too oily. Staff could be livelier. Around ¥60 per head. Daily 11am–2pm & 5–10pm.

Kathleen's 5 赛马餐饮 saìmǎ cānyǐn 5th Floor, 325 Nanjing Xi Lu ☎ 63272221, ⊛ kathleens5.com; map p.49. In a great location – an elegant glass box on top of the old racecourse (that's the one with the clock tower), with views over People's Square. Well-presented Western food; the three-course lunch sets (¥188) are good value – try the beef carpaccio and follow with bass or lamb. The afternoon tea set (¥138) is a treat (see box opposite). Daily 10.30am–midnight.

CAFÉS

Barbarossa 芭芭露莎 bābālùshā 231 Nanjing Xi Lu, inside People's Park ☎ 63180220; map p.49. This mellow, onion-domed Arabian fantasy is beautifully situated by the lotus pond in People's Park, and makes a great pitstop for anyone doing the sights in People's Square. It also functions as a bar and a restaurant but we're calling it a café as that's what it does best. Relax over a drink, smoke a hookah and admire the view of the skyscrapers over the treetops, but don't eat here as the food is overpriced. Note that if you want to come here after seven at night, only the park's north gate will be open. Daily 11am–late.

Jia Jia Tang Bao 佳家 汤包 jiājiā tāngbāo 90 Huanghe Lu ☎ 63276878; map pp.70–71. This cheap and cheerful little place has a huge reputation for that Shanghai signature dish, xiǎolóng bāo (see box, p.102), and other dumpling varieties. Crab dumplings are ¥99 for a steamer of a dozen, the normal varieties around ¥13. There are big queues at meal times and some kinds of dumplings sell out quickly – best get there early. They whip out an English menu when they see a foreigner. Daily 7.30am–7pm.

Yang's Fried Dumplings 小杨生煎馆 xiāoyáng shēngjiānguǎn 97 Huanghe Lu ☎ 5375179; map pp.70–71. This tiny shop has a reputation for the best shēngjiānbāo, or pan fried pork dumplings, in the city, so there's always a queue. Most people buy to take away but there are a few seats. For ¥6 you get four fluffy steaming buns, sprinkled with sesame seeds and with a very hot soup inside. Daily 6.30am–8pm.

THE OLD CITY AND AROUND

The Yu Yuan area has traditionally been an excellent place for snacks – xiǎolóng bāo dumplings and the like – eaten in unpretentious surroundings, but now that the area is firmly on the Chinese-tourist itinerary places get very busy and you'll pay a bit more than in the rest of the city. For quick bites, check out the satay, noodle and corn-on-the-cob stands lining the street bordering the western side of Yuyuan Bazaar. And for something much more upmarket, head south to Xintiandi wannabe The Cool Docks, a set of renovated warehouses filling up with pricey restaurants.

RESTAURANTS

EBI Sushi 和风海老日本料理 héfēnghǎi lǎoriběn liàolǐ Basement, Times Square, 111 Huaihai Zhong Lu ☎ 63918105; map p.54. This unpretentious little

10

AFTERNOON TEA

The fanciest of Shanghai's hotels and restaurants now offer afternoon tea, a good way to sample the city's most luxurious locations without breaking the bank. Between 2 and 6pm, you'll be served tea or coffee, a glass of wine or juice, and a tiered tray of little cakes, sandwiches and pastries. It's particularly worth trying on the Bund, where the venues are glorious (and the only alternative pitstops in the area are the chains):

House of Roosevelt 27 Zhongshan Dong Yi Lu ☏ 23220800, ✆ 27bund.com; map p.40. Though this very fancy restaurant isn't quite up to scratch for the price, the afternoon tea is excellent, and a rare Bund bargain at ¥100 per person. Sit on the rooftop for amazing views. Daily 2–6pm.

Kathleen's 5 5th Floor, 325 Nanjing Xi Lu ☏ 63272221, ✆ kathleens5.com; map p.49. Traditional tea costs ¥138 per person at this elegant and well-located Western restaurant in the former racecourse building (see p.51). Views over People's Park. Daily 2.30–5pm.

New Heights 3 on the Bund, 17 Guangdong Lu ☏ 63210909; map p.40. Good value at ¥128 per person, with plenty of French-style dainties. Book a seat with a view of Pudong. Daily 2–5pm.

Park Hyatt Shanghai World Financial Centre, 100 Century Avenue ☏ 68881234; map p.76. Ring and book a window seat – you'll be on the 87th floor with

fantastic views (see p.116). At ¥210 per person, including a good mix of sweets and savouries, it's actually quite a bargain if you consider the price of visiting the observation deck just above. Daily 2–6pm.

Peninsula Hotel 32 Zhongshan Dong Yi Lu ☏ 23272888; map p.40. Beautifully presented goodies in the city's most luxurious lobby (see p.41), with live violin and cello music all afternoon. Not cheap at ¥250 per person, but that does include a glass of champagne. Daily 2–6pm.

T8 House 8 North Block, Xintiandi, Taicang Lu ☏ 63558999; map p.62. A very tasty and reasonably priced afternoon tea (¥88) in a courtyard house in Xintiandi (see p.59). Tues–Sun 2.30–5pm.

Waldorf Astoria Hotel 2 Zhongshan Dong Yi Lu ☏ 63229988; map p.40. Tasty eats at the *Waldorf* (see p.45) include the signature red velvet cupcake. ¥338 per person. Daily 2–6pm.

Japanese restaurant has nicely understated decor. Either pick one of the red booths or plonk yourself down by the conveyor belt. A sushi set meal is good value at ¥85. Daily 11.30am–2.30pm & 5.30–9pm.

Kebabs on the Grille 克比印度料理 kèbǐ yìndù liàolǐ 8 Cool Docks, 479 Zhongshan Nan Lu ☏ 61526567; map p.54. Most restaurants at this "lifestyle complex", even the good ones, have been short lived, but this looks like a stayer. It's one of the few places in Shanghai to get a good curry, and the view of the plaza and understated decor are a bonus. Try the Kashmiri chicken and garlic *naan* and leave room for the eponymous meaty skewers. The all-you-can-eat Sunday buffet is ¥150. Daily 11am–10.30pm.

Lu Bo Lang 绿波廊 lùbōláng 115–131 Yuyuan Lu, just south of the Huxing Ting Tea House ☏ 63280602; map p.54. Tourist-friendly venue, tricked out with chinoiserie and with decent, if pricey, *dim sum* and Shanghai dishes such as crab and cabbage; a meal will cost about ¥120 a head. Daily 11am–2pm & 5–8.30pm.

Nan Xiang 南翔馒头店 nánxiáng mántóudiàn 85 Yuyuan Lu ☏ 63554206; map p.54. A famous dumpling place that's on the "must-do" list for Chinese tourists, meaning that sometimes it's just too busy to bother with. The ground floor is for proles to munch your standard pork and crab; the higher you go, the fancier the decor

and the dumplings become, though the staff don't get any less surly. Most customers are here for takeaway – eat in and there's a minimum spend of ¥60 per person which will get you a decent selection of dumplings. Daily 7.30am–9pm.

Quanjude 全聚德烤鸭店 quánjùdé kǎoyādiàn 4th Floor, 786 Huaihai Zhong Lu ☏ 54045799, ✆ quanjude.com.cn; map p.54. Part of the Beijing duck restaurant chain, with a whole duck (which will feed three) going for ¥160. Service is slow, so be prepared for a wait. Watch the bird carved at your table, then smear it with sauce and wrap it in a pancake, and finish with duck soup. You can even have a side order of duck tongues. It's rich and fatty, so not for dieters. Daily 11am–11pm.

Shanghai Ren Jia 上海人家 shànghǎi rénjiā 141 Yunnan Nan Lu ☏ 63513060; map p.54. Huge, bustling chain restaurant with a cheap and cheery atmosphere and interesting twists on standard Shanghainese fare. It's best to come in a large group so you can order and share multiple dishes. Roasted pig's trotter (¥58) is the house speciality, and they also serve "drunken shrimp"; the critters come to the table live and soaked in booze – you pull off their heads and eat them while they twitch. Daily 11am–2pm & 5–9pm.

Xiao Shaoxing 小绍兴饭店 xiǎoshàoxīng fàndiàn 118 Yunnan Nan Lu (east side), immediately north of

Jinling Zhong Lu ☎ 68662270; map p.54. Old-fashioned Chinese-style dining – bright and noisy and with big tables; the waitresses expect you to call for their attention – so hardly suitable for a date, but it's fun for a group. It's famous in Shanghai for its "drunken chicken" (the meat is steeped in rice wine), which costs ¥80; other dishes are much cheaper. Adventurous diners might wish to sample the blood soup or chicken feet. Daily 11am–2pm & 5–8.30pm.

CAFÉS
Delifrance 德意法兰西 déyì fǎlánxī Basement, Times Square, 381 Huaihai Zhong Lu; map p.54. Cheap and tasty coffee and pastries in a faux Parisian café. A good place for breakfast. Daily 8am–10pm.

10 THE OLD FRENCH CONCESSION

This is the area where most expatriates eat and correspondingly where prices begin to approach international levels. Menus are in English, and English will be spoken, too. In Xintiandi, an olde-worlde complex of upscale bars, restaurants and cafés (see p.59), you're spoilt for choice but you won't see much change from ¥200. Breakfast options are somewhat limited; try to find the branches of *Wagas* or *Manabe* (see p.101).

RESTAURANTS
1221 1221餐馆 yīèrèryī cānguǎn 1221 Yan'an Xi Lu, by Pan Yu Lu ☎ 62136585; map pp.60–61. It's a little out of the way, a 10min walk east of Yan'an Xi Lu subway stop, but this is a pretty decent, foreigner-friendly Shanghainese restaurant. Decor is modern and minimalist so don't expect an evocation of Old Shanghai in anything but the food. The drunken chicken and *xiang su ya* (fragrant crispy duck) are good, as are the onion cakes. It's a good choice for vegetarians too. About ¥1200 per person. Reserve. Daily 11.30am–11pm.

★ **Bi Feng Tang** 避风塘 bìfēngtáng 175 Changle Lu ☎ 64670628; map pp.60–61; 58 Haining Lu, near Wusong Lu ☎ 63953568; map pp.60–61. This chirpy Cantonese chain selling tasty *dim sum* is a popular place to end a night out in the Old French Concession. Mon–Fri 10am–5am, Sat & Sun 8am–5am.

★ **Charmant** 小城故事 xiǎochéng gùshì 1414 Huaihai Zhong Lu ☎ 64318107; map pp.60–61. A good place to know about – convenient and cheap, *Charmant* functions as much as a café as a restaurant, and is open until the early hours, making it a handy last spot after a night on the tiles. Slip into a window booth and linger over a peanut smoothie, which is nicer than it sounds, or a hot chocolate (¥25). For meals (around ¥80 per head), the Taiwanese-style pork or tofu and the cold chicken noodles are recommended. Daily 11.30am–4am.

Cheng Cheng's Art Salon 屋里香私房菜 wūlǐxiāng sīfángcài 164 Nanchang Lu, near Sinan Lu ☎ 53065462; map pp.60–61. If you're bored of trendy minimalism, try this place, occupying a renovated colonial building quirkily decorated with all manner of paintings and bric-a-brac. It serves Shanghai home-style cooking, not too oily, and is pretty reasonably priced: try the chicken with shallots (¥30) or asparagus with crab (¥88). Daily 11.30am–2pm & 5–10pm.

★ **Chun** 春 chūn 124 Jinxian Lu, near Maoming Lu ☎ 62560301; map pp.60–61. This is like having dinner in someone's front room: there's no sign outside, only four tables and no menu – you just turn up and eat whatever the robust lady boss puts in front of you. Needless to say, the Shanghai dishes on offer are excellent and, don't worry, it's all very cheap – a meal for two will cost less than ¥100. You'll certainly have to reserve, and there's no English spoken, so get a Chinese speaker to do it for you. Daily 6–9pm.

★ **Crystal Jade** 翡翠酒家 fěicuì jiǔjiā Unit 12A–B, 2nd Floor, No. 7 Building, South Block, Xintiandi ☎ 63858752; map pp.60–61; B110 Hong Kong Plaza, 300 Huaihai Zhong Lu ☎ 6335 4188; map pp.60–61. Good Cantonese food, sophisticated looks and down-to-earth prices (around ¥80 per head) make this the place to eat in Xintiandi, and one of the best in town for *dim sum* and xiǎolóng bāo. Even being tucked away at the back of the upper floor of a shopping centre doesn't dent its popularity – you'd better reserve. Try the barbecued pork and leave room for mango pudding. Solitary diners are made to feel comfortable at the long central table. There's a second less swanky – but also less busy – branch in the Hong Kong Plaza. If it's a weekend night and you haven't booked, go there. Both branches daily 11am–3pm & 5–11.30pm.

Cuivre 1502 Huaihai Zhong Lu ☎ 64374219, ⓦ cuivre .cn; map pp.60–61. This glamorous French restaurant would be a great place for a date, as it's hip – menus are on iPads and the bar stools are made of bicycles – but not pretentious. The food is reliably good, portions are generous and there's a good wine list. Try the fois gras sushi as a starter then follow with the lobster risotto. Around ¥300 per person. Reservations essential. Dinner daily 6–10.30pm; lunch Sat & Sun noon–2pm.

Din Tai Fung 鼎泰丰 dǐngtàifēng 11A, 2nd Floor, Building 6, Xintiandi South Block, 123 Xingye Lu ☎ 63858378, ⓦ dintaifung.com.tw; map pp.60–61. The winning formula at this Taiwanese chain is to offer good Shanghai street food in upscale surroundings, with chefs cooking away behind a glass wall. Its pork dumplings (xiǎolóng bāo) are excellent, but don't neglect the other varieties, particularly shrimp and crab roe. Eating here is a lot more expensive than eating in the street, of course, at around ¥100 per person. Daily 11am–3pm & 5–11pm.

FOOD STREETS

With the destruction of "snack lane" Wujiang Lu, street food, so prevalent elsewhere in China, has pretty much disappeared from the city centre. But there are still some notable food streets lined with cheap restaurants, which come alive at night, turning into forests of neon. The most popular with visitors is the area **around Yuyuan Bazaar** (see p.55), which has plenty of venerable dumpling shops, but for a more local experience, head to **Huanghe Lu** (黄河路; huánghé lù), due north of People's Park – in particular the section north of Beijing Xi Lu – where you'll find a large concentration of restaurants and vendors, many of them open 24 hours. *Yang's Fried Dumplings* (see p.104) and *Jia Jia Tang Bao* (see p.104) have great reputations for, respectively, dumplings and xiǎolóng bāo, though there's always a queue. Sit-down places offer Shanghai staples such as hóngshāo ròu and lion's head meatballs.

Yunnan Lu (云南路; yúnnán lù; see map p.54), a block to the east of People's Park, is the most established of the food streets, though these days it's more of a restaurant row, with ingredients, including snakes and toads, on display on the pavement.

Finally, for an unusual gastronomic experience, head to the 24-hour wholesale seafood market at **920 Tongchuan Lu** (铜川路水产市场; tóngchuān lù shuǐchǎn shìchǎng) in the north of the city. There's a huge selection of live seafood on offer, including turtles and sea snakes, all sold by the *jin* (half kilo). Abalone cost around ¥10 each, crabs around ¥35, lobster ¥150 – pricey but still cheaper than you'd pay elsewhere; humbler options such as turbot or salmon will set you back ¥30 or so. You may have to barter as prices aren't always marked. Having made your choice, take it to any of the little restaurants at the side, where it's cooked for you by weight (¥20 per kilo). If they're not busy, restaurant staff will help you buy your fish at the market (and get a good price). It's a warts-and-all kind of place, noisy and smelly, but memorable, and you won't get fresher fish. It's also the cheapest place in the city for a crab feast. The market is a little way out; head to Zhenru subway stop on line #11 and take a taxi the rest of the way (¥15).

elEfante 20 Donghu Lu ☎ 54048085, 🌐 el-efante.com; map pp.60–61. Chef Willy Trullas cooks up Mediterranean fare in this stylish and upmarket venue, the latest "in" place for expats. Crab salad (¥98) and pork belly (¥78) are a couple of recommended dishes, but you can't really go wrong from the extensive tapas and seafood menu. When it's sunny out, ask for a table on the patio. ¥400 per person. Tues–Sun 11am–3pm & 6–10.30pm.

Fu 1039 福一零三九 fú yīlíngsānjiǔ Lane 1039, Yu Yuan Lu ☎ 52371878, Ⓜ Jiangsu Lu; map pp.60–61. Located in a well-restored 1930s mansion, this is one of those places that looks like it's going to be fearsomely expensive but isn't (about ¥200 per head). It clearly doesn't feel the need to brag – you can't see it from the street and there's not even a sign; to find it, head up the lane at 1039 Yuyuan Lu (close to the Jiangsu Lu station) for about 100m then turn left. The cuisine is sweet and mild Shanghainese, and includes dishes such as steamed carp drizzled with Shaoxing wine and sautéed chicken with mango. Not much English is spoken but there's a picture menu. Daily 11am–2pm & 5–11pm.

Fulin Xuan 福临轩饭店 fú lín xuān fàn diàn 2nd Floor, 300 Huaihai Zhong Lu, near Huangpi Nan Lu ☎ 63756577; map pp.60–61. Typically massive Cantonese place with an English menu and a good reputation among locals. Good for *dim sum* of course, and the beef with black pepper and Hong Kong-style clay-pot rice are recommended.

Not pricey at around ¥80 a head. Daily 11am–11pm.

Grape 葡萄园 pútáo yuán 55A Xinle Lu, near Xiangyang Bei Lu ☎ 54040486; map pp.60–61. Unchallenging decor and some English-speaking staff make this Shanghainese place popular with expats, but it's good enough to draw the local crowd too. Try the lamb with leek or duck pancakes and make room for a few of their savoury cold dishes, or take the opportunity to give bullfrog and eel a go. Reasonable at ¥100 a head, and the place is well located for some postprandial window-shopping. Daily 11am–midnight.

★ **Guyi Hunan** 古意湘味浓 gǔyì xiāngwèinóng 89 Fumin Lu, near Julu Lu ☎ 62495628; map pp.60–61. This popular institution is the best in the city to sample Hunan cuisine – known for being hot and spicy and for its liberal use of garlic, shallots and smoked meat. Reserve in advance and bring a few people to sample a good range of dishes. Go for the chilli-sprinkled spare ribs, fish with beans and scallions, or tangerine-peel beef, which tastes better than you might expect. The chef's speciality, open face fish, is as tasty as it is ugly. About ¥120 per head. Daily 11am–2pm & 5.30–10.30pm.

Hot Pot King 来福楼 láifú lóu 2nd Floor, 146 Huaihai Zhong Lu, by Fuxing Xi Lu ☎ 64736380; map pp.60–61. An accessible, friendly place to sample local favourite hotpot, with English menus, understanding staff and tasteful decor. Order lamb, glass noodles, mushrooms and tofu, and chuck

10

them into the simmering pot in the middle of the table. Perfect for winter evenings, or to fill up after the bars (it's open very late). ¥90 per person. Daily 11am–4am.

Jian Guo 328 建国 328小 馆 jiànguó sān èr bā xiǎoguǎn 328 Jianguo Xi Lu, near Xiangyang Nan Lu ☎64713819; map pp.60–61. This tiny neighbourhood restaurant is a smart place to eat Shanghainese; it's relaxed, inexpensive and quiet, there's no smoking, and the Taiwanese owner is attentive. Plus they don't use MSG and the food isn't too oily. The menu is long and features all the local classics – among the choice dishes are yellow croakers with scallions (¥58) and deep-fried duck leg (¥38). Eating here shouldn't cost more than ¥100 per person, but you'll probably have to reserve and there's not much English spoken. Daily 11am–9.30pm.

KABB 凯博西餐厅 kǎibó xīcāntīng 181 Taicang Lu, 5 Xintiandi Bei Lu ☎33070798; map pp.60–61. This casual American-style bar and grill is one of Xintiandi's more relaxed places, though it's still advisable to reserve, especially if you want the coveted outside seating. Portions of wraps, nachos, steaks, burgers and the like are huge, and it's especially good value at breakfast and lunchtime. About ¥100 per person. Daily 7am–1am.

★ **Lost Heaven** 花马天堂云南餐厅 huāmǎtiāntáng yúnnán cāntīng 38 Gaoyou Lu, near Fuxing Xi Lu ☎64335126, ⓦlostheaven.com.cn; map pp.60–61. This fashionable venue, sister of the Bund branch, serves food from China's southwest, a cuisine that has Southeast Asian notes to it – try the stir-fried beef, goat's cheese and scallion chicken. With candlelit tables, dark-wood floors and stone-mask decorations, the ambience is wonderfully atmospheric, if a little dark. ¥250 per head. Daily 11.30am–1.30pm & 5.30–10.30pm.

Molokai 摩罗 街 móluó jiē Xintiandi South Plaza, Building 6, 123 Xingye Lu ☎53210881; map pp.60–61. Clean and smart Hong Kong-style diner in Xintiandi that looks pricier than it is. The menu is erratically international, but for the best that the place has to offer, stick with Cantonese dishes such as shrimp wontons (¥28) and scrambled egg with shrimp (¥52). Finish with a chocolate brownie (¥38). Daily 11am–11pm.

Pinchuan 品川 pǐnchuān 47 Taojing Lu ☎64379361; map pp.60–61. Sichuan cuisine, decent service, and comfortable, upscale surroundings but reasonable prices (¥120 or so a head) make this an expat favourite. The spice quotient is tame for purists but will suit those who want a gentle introduction to the fiery cuisine. Try the mápó doùfu and "saliva chicken" (kǒu shǔi jī). Daily 11am–2pm & 5–10pm.

Shen Yue Xuan 申粤轩 shēnyuè xuān 849 Huashan Lu ☎62511166; map pp.60–61. The best Cantonese place in Shanghai, situated in an old mansion and serving scrumptious *dim sum* at lunchtime. In warmer weather you can dine alfresco in the garden, a rarity for a Cantonese restaurant. About ¥80 a head. Daily 11am–11pm.

Shinmachi 新町 xīn tīng 159 Madang Lu, Xintiandi ☎33661281; map pp.60–61. Dark wood fittings and 50s Tokyo memorabilia give this charming Japanese restaurant a quaintly vintage look. There's a wide range of prices – a bowl of ramen will cost you ¥50, wagyu beef ten times that. Bento box set lunches are cheap at ¥88. There's a *teppan-yaki* kitchen on the ground floor, and you'll find the sushi bar above. Being reasonably priced and centrally located, it's popular so reserve. Daily 11.30am–2.30pm & 5.30–11.30pm.

Shintori Null 2 新都里无二店 xīndūlǐ wúérdiàn 803 Julu Lu ☎54045252; map pp.60–61. This nouvelle Japanese trendsetter is easy to miss first time: push open an unmarked door, then head down the bamboo-lined path. First sight of the venue, with its clamorous open kitchens and industrial chic decor, is startling, but so are the prices; take someone you want to impress and be prepared to spend around ¥500 per person. The set lunch (only on the weekend) is reasonable at ¥100. Entertaining presentation will give you something to talk about, though you'd better order a lot or you'll be complaining about the small portions. Finish with green tea tiramisu (¥60). Mon–Fri 5.30–10.30pm, Sat & Sun 11.30am–10.30pm.

Shu Di La Zi Yu Guan 蜀地辣子鱼馆 shǔdì làziyú guǎn 187 Anfu Lu, on the corner with Wulumuqi Zhong Lu ☎54037684; map pp.60–61. Never mind the tacky decor – concentrate on the excellent, inexpensive Sichuan and Hunanese cuisine. A big pot of Sichuan spicy fish is a must, but also recommended are bamboo fragrant chicken (zhu xiang ji) and the old fave mápó doùfu – spicy tofu. A bargain at around ¥70 a head. Daily 11am–2pm & 5–9pm.

Simply Thai 天泰餐厅 tiāntài cāntīng 5-C Dongping Lu ☎64459551; map pp.60–61. A pretty decent Thai joint, with an eclectic range of reasonably priced dishes (less than ¥100) and a smart but informal setting with a leafy courtyard. Try the stir-fried asparagus and fish cakes. There's also a branch in Xintiandi but it's not nearly as good. Daily 11am–11pm.

South Beauty 881 俏江南 qiào jiāngnán 881 Yan'an Zhong Lu, opposite the Exhibition Centre ☎62475878; map pp.60–61. Foreigner-friendly Sichuan food in what looks like an English country house. Speciality of the house is beef in boiling oil, cooked at your table. Linger afterwards for drinks in the fantastic bar and imagine yourself starring in a Merchant Ivory production. There's even a cigar room. ¥200 per person, but watch out for hidden extras like the charge for a glass of water. Other branches around town don't quite replicate the atmosphere here. Daily 11am–3pm & 5–11pm.

10

T8 House 8, North Block, Xintiandi, Taicang Lu ☎63558999, ⓦt8shanghai.com; map pp.60–61. Fine Continental-style dining, courtesy of a Swedish chef in an elegant reconstruction of a courtyard house. Reserve, and ask for one of the booths at the back if you want quiet or a seat by the open kitchen if you want spectacle. The menu of fusion dishes changes with the season, but there is always a tasting menu for around ¥800. Fabulous desserts include a chocolate addiction platter. ¥500 a head. Afternoon tea is ¥88 (see box, p.105). Daily 11.30am–2.30pm & 6.30–11.30pm, plus afternoon tea Tues–Sun 2.30–5pm.

★ **Xinjishi (Jesse Restaurant)** 新吉士餐厅 xīnjíshì cāntīng 41 Tianping Lu ☎62829260; map pp.60–61. The decor is a bit tatty but there's nothing at all wrong with the tasty and reasonably priced home-style cooking (most dishes are around ¥70). Dishes are from all over the country, but go for the soy-braised pork, pickled eggplant, crab-flavoured tofu and other local faves. It's always packed, so reserve. It's spawned a chain, but none of the new branches are nearly as good. Daily 11am–4pm & 5.30pm–midnight.

Xibo 锡伯新疆餐厅 xībó xīnjiāng cāntīng 3rd Floor, 83 Changshu Lu, near Julu Lu ☎54038330, ⓦxiboshanghai.com; map pp.60–61. Xinjiang cuisine, from China's far northwest, has always been popular in Shanghai but usually the speciality restaurants are loud and gaudy. This cosy venue is a winner for its understated, classy decor and for its well-presented dishes from Xinjiang's Xibo minority people. The flavours are spicy and Central Asian. Big plate chicken– a huge spicy stew to share – is a favourite, and make sure you order some lamb skewers on the side. Roasted aubergine with peppers is the best of the vegetable dishes. Pleasingly affordable at around ¥150 a head. Daily 11am–midnight.

Ye Shanghai 夜上海 yè shànghǎi House 6, North Block, 338 Huangpi Nan Lu, Xintiandi ☎63111323; map pp.60–61. Shanghai cuisine in an understated take on colonial chic. Tucked away down an alley, it's actually one of the best Xintiandi places, with a very good three-course lunch deal (¥88). Otherwise, go for drunken chicken, prawns with chilli sauce or one of the many crab dishes as a good introduction to local flavours. Around ¥200 per person. Daily 11.30am–2.30pm & 6.30–10pm.

CAFÉS

Boonna 布那咖啡店 bùnà kāfēidiàn 1690 Huaihai Zhong Lu, near Wuxing Lu ☎64330835; map pp.60–61. Unfussy, laidback little café, set back from the busy road, with lots of shaded outdoor seating. Surfing the free wi-fi on a MacBook is not mandatory but would certainly help you fit in with this international hipster crowd. Coffee for ¥15 and lunch sets for ¥35. A handy French Concession pitstop. Daily 8am–midnight.

Café del Volcan 80 Yongkang Lu ☎156 1866 9291, ⓦcafevolcan.com; map pp.60–61. This tiny Australian-owned boutique makes the best coffee in Shanghai. Though it isn't cheap at ¥36 for a latte, there's always a queue. All beans are roasted on the premises, and baristas are keen to chat about what makes their brew special. No wi-fi. Mon–Fri 8am–8pm, Sat & Sun 10am–6pm.

★ **Citizen Bar and Café** 天台餐厅 tiāntái cāntīng 222 Jinxian Lu ☎62581620, ⓦcitizenshanghai.com; map pp.60–61. A great Continental-style café tucked away in an elegantly gentrified neighbourhood. It's very popular with French expats – perhaps because of the good coffee, free wi-fi and the limitless potential for people-watching from the balcony. Food is a bit pricey but there's a wide choice of bar snacks and it's a very civilized venue for a pre-dinner cocktail or a slice of apple pie. Daily 11am–1am.

Farine Ferguson Lane, 378 Wukang Lu ☎64335798, ⓦfarine-bakery.com; map pp.60–61. Artisanal bread and pastries, all baked on the premises. Excellent coffee too (though pricey at ¥38), and the outside seating is good for watching the smart set swagger by. Tues–Sun 7am–8pm.

★ **Kommune** 公社酒吧 gōngshè jiǔbā Building 7, Lane 210, Taikang Lu ☎64662416; map pp.60–61. Hip café located at the heart of Tianzifang – head north up the alley, take the first left and it's just there. Very popular with the designer set, especially for weekend brunch. The pleasant courtyard makes it one of the best places for outside dining, especially on Wednesday nights when there's an Australian-style barbecue (¥100). Deli sandwiches from ¥38. Daily 8am–10pm.

Le Café des Stagiaires 54–56 Yongkang Lu, near Xiangyang Lu ☎34250210, ⓦcafedesstagiaires.com; map pp.60–61. This artsy café and bar on buzzing Yongkang Lu has plenty of panache. It's attractively decorated with European memorabilia, and the loos are papered with CVs – the name is French for "intern". As well as coffee, there's a good wine list and simple French food and pizza on offer. Daily 9am–11pm.

Old China Hand Reading Room 汉源书屋 hànyuán shūwū 27 Shaoxing Lu, by Shaanxi Nan Lu ☎64732526, ⓦhan-yuan.com; map pp.60–61. Bookish but not fusty, this is the place to come for leisurely reflection. There's a huge collection of tomes to peruse or buy, many printed by the café press, which specializes in coffee-table books about French Concession architecture. Period furniture, big picture windows and – what's that eerie quality? Oh, silence. Afternoon coffee with a scoop of ice cream and biscuits is ¥45. No meals. Daily 10am–midnight.

Pier 39 39号码头 sānshíjiǔhào mǎtóu 172 Jinxian Lu ☎62581939; map pp.60–61. Bright and breezy little California-style café, popular with expats for its big salads and clam chowder, which comes inside a sourdough loaf

(¥52). Free delivery. Daily 11am–10pm.

Pantry 205 Wulumuqi Nan Lu ☎ 138 1871 9543; map pp.60–61. This co-op sells the best baked goods, preserves and biscuits in town. They do small set meals for breakfast, lunch and afternoon tea. Daily 8am–6pm.

Sunflour 322 Anfu Lu ☎ 64737757, ⊛ sunflour.com .cn; map pp.60–61. Popular if pricey bakery and café selling breads, pastries and sandwiches to take away or eat sitting in. Decent breakfasts too, including perhaps the city's best full English. Daily 7am–10.30pm.

Urban Tribe 城市山民 chéngshì shānmín 133 Fuxing Xi Lu ☎ 64335366; map pp.60–61. It's a boutique selling ethnic knick-knacks really, but there's a nice bamboo garden at the back with coffee served in cute handmade cups (¥20). Daily 9.30am–10pm.

Vienna Café 维也纳咖啡馆 wéiyěnà kāfēiguǎn 25 Shaoxing Lu, near Ruijin Er Lu ☎ 6445213; map pp.60–61. Popular and rather charming Austrian-style café, almost managing that fin-de-siècle vibe. You can't fault their strudel or *Kaiserschmarrn* – pancake served with apple sauce. There's a film night every Thursday evening. Daily 8am–8pm.

Whisk 威斯忌 wēisījì 1250 Huaihai Zhong Lu, near Changshu Lu subway stop ☎ 54047770; map pp.60–61. Minimalist decor and a chocolate-themed menu. They do meals, but they're so-so – come for the speciality hot chocolate or one of the many varieties of chocolate cake naughtiness. Shame there's a minimum spend (¥40), a maximum time (2hr), and spotty service. Daily 8.30am–11.30pm.

Xianzonglin 仙踪林 xiānzōnglín 671 Huaihai Zhong Lu; map pp.60–61. A Taiwanese chain café that specializes in bubble tea – that's the sweet stuff with gooey balls in it. The huge drinks list includes plenty of oddities such as blueberry tea. Sip while you sit on a swing – teenagers will love it. Daily 10am–10pm.

JING'AN

Jing'an is a good area for international cuisine, and though you won't find any romantic converted villas there are some surprisingly intimate venues. For something more local, try Huanghe Lu food street (see box, p.107).

RESTAURANTS

Bali Laguna 巴厘岛 bālí dǎo 189 Huashan Lu, inside Jing'an Park, near Yan'an Zhong Lu ☎ 62486970; map pp.70–71. A popular Indonesian restaurant; the food, such as seafood curry served inside a pineapple (¥88), is just okay, but the park location makes for a lovely ambience on a sunny day, and there's lots of outdoor seating. Note that it is only open for lunch. Daily 11.30am–2.30pm.

Coconut Paradise 椰香天堂泰国料理 yēxiāng tiāntáng tàiguó liàolǐ 38 Fumin Lu, near Yan'an Zhong Lu ☎ 62481998; map pp.70–71. This renovated French-style villa hosts arguably the city's best Thai restaurant; thanks to the many candles and the Buddhist theme of the decor, it's certainly the most atmospheric. Eat in the garden if the weather permits. Great for a date, and less pricey than it looks at ¥150 a head. Daily 11am–2pm & 5–11pm.

Downhome Kitchen 老灶店 lǎozàodiàn Building 15, 48 Yuyao Lu, the New Factories ☎ 52135277; map pp.70–71. Located in a complex of trendy bars, this place is something of an anomaly, designed, rather self-consciously, to evoke "olde Shanghai" – you even sit on stools. There's a good, reasonably priced range of Shanghainese dishes such as fried eggplant with chilli pepper and braised pork belly, although service could be quicker. A good starting point for a night out and not pricey; a meal will cost around ¥70 per head. Daily 11am–2pm & 5–9.30pm.

★ **Little Sheep** 小肥羊火锅 xiǎoféiyáng huǒguō 777 Jiangning Lu ☎ 52891717, ⊛ littlesheep.com; map pp.70–71. Cheap and cheerful Mongolian hotpot chain that's highly regarded, though it's pretty ordinary looking. There's a picture menu, so just pick a bunch of ingredients, including plenty of thinly sliced lamb, throw them into the pot, and work on steaming up the windows. ¥60 per person. Daily 10.30am–4am.

Lynn 琳怡中餐厅 línyí zhōngcāntīng 99 Xikang Lu, near Nanjing Xi Lu ☎ 62470101; map pp.70–71. This demure, Art Deco-styled Shanghainese and Cantonese restaurant is popular with the trendy Chinese crowd, especially at weekends, when there's an ¥88 all-you-can-eat *dim sum* deal. It's noisy, so don't take a date, but it's hard to fault the food. Daily 11.30am–2.30pm & 6–10.30pm.

New York Style Pizza Basement, Email Fashion Plaza, 1699 Nanjing Xi Lu ☎ 62472265; map pp.70–71. An undemanding diner that does decent pizza; ¥10 a slice, ¥70 for the whole goddamn thing. Good for post-booze munchies. Daily noon–10.30pm.

★ **Yuxin Sichuan Dish** 渝信川菜 yúxìn chuāncài 3rd Floor, 333 Chengdu Bei Lu ☎ 52980438; map pp.70–71. The best Sichuan food in the city, in a huge, no-nonsense dining hall. It's very popular with families and the white-collar crowd, so reservations are recommended. Go for the *kou shui ji* (spicy chicken) and *sha guo yu* (fish pot), with which you can work on developing a face as red as the peppers. About ¥90 per person. Little English is spoken but there's a picture menu. Daily 11am–2pm & 5–9.30pm.

CAFÉS

Aura 埃哇餐厅 āiwā cāntīng 171 Jiaozhou Lu ☎ 62532779, ⊛ auracoolzey.com; map pp.70–71. This cosy little hideaway, crisply decorated and offering free wi-fi, is aimed at the trendsetters staying at the *URBN* hotel next door. Coffee or a milkshake cost a pricey ¥25, pizzas start at ¥76. Daily 10am–11pm.

Bandu 半度音乐 bàndù yīnyuè 50 Moganshan Lu ☎62768267, ⊛bandumusic.com; map pp.70–71.

The best of the Moganshan Art District cafés, this intimate hideaway hosts performances of Chinese folk music every Saturday at 8pm (book tickets in advance as it can sell out). The food – basic noodle dishes – is undistinguished though. Daily 11am–7pm, Fri & Sat 11am–11pm.

PUDONG

10

Pudong is rather soulless, and the most notable restaurants are those attached to the swanky hotels. For cheap eats, try the Superbrand Mall or the basement food court of the Jinmao Tower (see p.77), or head to the World Financial Centre, where there's a branch of *Element Fresh* (see p.101), which provides one of the few opportunities for casual Western dining in the area.

Jade on 36 翡翠36餐厅 feīcuì sānshíliù cāntīng 36th Floor, Tower 2, Pudong Shangri-La, 33 Fucheng Lu ☎68828888, ⊛jadeon36.com; map p.76. Celebrity chef Franck-Elie Laloum prepares classic French food in a grand venue with an amazing view of the Bund – a place to splurge or impress visitors. Foie gras, prawn and beef rib is recommended, but it's very pricey – at least ¥650 a head. Lavish, no-holds-barred Sunday brunch is ¥858. The attached bar is very swish too. Mon–Sat 6–10.30pm, Sunday brunch 11.30am–3pm.

Qian Xiang Ge 黔香阁 qiánxiānggé 171 Pucheng Lu, near Shangcheng Lu ☎58871717; map p.76. Big, busy and unpretentious dining hall serving spicy/sour

Guizhou cuisine, with most patrons going for the excellent sour fish soup (*suantang yu*) or spicy chicken (*dao han ji*). Everything comes with pickled vegetables. ¥120 per head. Daily 11am–2pm & 5–10pm.

★ **Yi Café** – 咖啡 yī kāfēi Level 2, Tower 2, Pudong Shangri-La, 33 Fucheng Lu ☎68828888; map p.76. This slickly designed place has ten show kitchens dishing up an enormous range of international cuisines. It's all you can eat – weekday lunch is ¥238, and the very popular weekend brunch is ¥298. Dinner is always ¥308 (plus 15 percent service charge). At other times, expect to pay around ¥400 per head. Daily 6am–10.30am & 11am–11pm.

HONGKOU

Old Film Café 老电影咖啡吧 lǎo diàn yǐng kā fēi bā 123 Duolun Lu ☎56964763; map p.82. If you're in the area, this charming old house, full of period detail and wallpapered with old film ads, is the place for refreshment.

Film buffs will be excited by the possibility of watching the fine collection of old Chinese and Russian films – just ask the owner and he'll put one on for you. Daily 10am–1am.

BAR ROUGE

Drinking and nightlife

Shanghai's cosmopolitan denizens are famous for their thirst for novelty, love of style and dedication to the good times; the city's always been good at putting on a do. Today you'll find plenty of parallels with the glory days of "taxi girls" (see box, p.65), flower houses and anything-but-innocent "tea dances". So far as China goes, this is party central. There's something for all tastes, from spit-and-sawdust dives to exclusive cocktail bars, cheesy mega discos to slick DJ clubs. That said, the scene is nothing if not capricious and places go in and out of fashion and open and close with the seasons.

ESSENTIALS

Information For bang up-to-date information on the nightlife scene, check out ⓦ smartshanghai.com or an expat listings magazine (see p.24).

Where to drink There are a number of bar districts in Shanghai, and it's well worth taking in more than one over the course of the evening. The best nights in the city tend to involve a bit of bar-hopping – just remember how cheap taxis are. The biggest range of watering holes can be found in the Old French Concession. Xintiandi is upmarket, perhaps just a little too respectable, but a good place for a civilized drink if you can afford it. Yongkang Lu is a pleasingly laidback new bar strip, but note that it's in a residential area, and locals get furious at noise after 10pm (they've been known to throw water from their windows at revellers in the street). To the west, Hengshan Lu is a more diffuse zone, stretching for several kilometres, with bars catering to most tastes but veering towards the expat-friendly just-like-home pastiche. The Bund is the fastest rising new area; here, an air of exclusivity is reflected in the prices. If you're horny and dumb enough to follow one of the ubiquitous touts promising to take you to a "lady bar", then you deserve the subsequent shakedown. Anyway, it's not as if there's a shortage of "independent female contractors" in the regular dive bars.

Opening hours Bar hours are flexible; a bar tends to close when its last barfly has lurched off – though all places open till at least midnight, and on the weekends much later. Clubs open at around 9pm, get going after midnight, and close at 4am or later.

Prices Though Chinese beer can be cheaper than bottled water in shops, bar prices can come as something of a shock; even in the shabbiest dive, a small bottle of Tsingtao will cost upwards of ¥25. In the swankiest venues it will be more than ¥50, and for a cocktail you won't get much change from a ¥100 note. But just about everywhere has a happy hour (two drinks for the price of one), and these are generally long – sometimes 5 to 8pm. Wednesday is often ladies' night, with many places offering free drinks for women before midnight. Look out too for open bar nights – all you can drink for around ¥100 – advertised in expat magazines. Only the swankiest venues have cover charges, and they usually include one free drink. However, one annoying practice common in clubs is having to pay to sit at a table – a waitress will soon shoo you off if you blanch at the (often ridiculous) price.

BARS

Some of the venues listed under cafés work very well after dark as bars, notably *Citizen Bar and Café* (p.110), *Café des Stagiaires* (see p.110), and *Barbarossa* (see p.104). Most fancy restaurants have civilized bars attached, great places for a quiet cocktail: notably *T8* (see p.105), *Jade on 36* (see p.112), *Lost Heaven on the Bund* (see p.102), *8½ Otto E Mezzo Bombana* (see p.102) and *South Beauty 881* (see p.108).

THE BUND AND NANJING DONG LU

Bar Rouge 7th Floor, No. 18 The Bund ☎63391199, ⓦ bar-rouge-shanghai.com; map p.40. Staff are snobbish, the clientele is pretentious, but the terrace has unrivalled views over the Bund. Cover is ¥100 on weekends and you won't get much change from a red bill for a drink, but go for one, check out the view, and then hit somewhere less posey. Happy hour daily 6–9pm; themed parties on Thursdays. Daily 6pm–3am.

★ **Captain Bar** 船长酒吧 chuánzhǎng jiǔbā 6th Floor, 37 Fuzhou Lu, by Sichuan Zhong Lu ☎63235053; map p.40. This relaxed venue is one of the few in the area where you won't feel the need to dress up. Never mind the unremarkable interior, it's all about the terrace, with its fabulous view of Pudong. It sits atop a backpacker hostel (see p.97), though most guests are put off by the prices – with draught beer at ¥40 – although it's still the cheapest in the area. Happy hour till 8pm. Daily 5pm–late.

BRIGHT LIGHTS, BIG CITY

Shanghai at night, between dusk and about 10pm, is lit up like a pinball game. The city sucks up so much of China's energy that the national grid can't take it, and power cuts are endured in the sticks. The best places to appreciate the awesome spectacle are:

100 Century Avenue Bar See p.116. The cocktails are expensive, but the view makes it worth it.

Captain Bar See above. The only Bund bar that won't empty your wallet.

Huangpu River night cruise See p.45. Touristy, but fun.

Marriott Hotel lobby See p.93. An awesome view of People's Square, but be discreet: if too many people begin turning up, they'll probably start charging.

Nanjing Dong Lu See p.46. You might not want to buy anything here, but the lights are spectacular.

Vue See p.115. This hot new bar has great views of Pudong from its terrace.

Yuyuan See p.55. This olde-worlde Chinatown mall takes on a whole new aspect when the neon comes on.

★ **Glamour Bar** 魅力酒吧 mèilì jiǔbā 6th Floor, M on the Bund, 20 Guangdong Lu, by Zhongshan Dong Yi Lu ☏63293751, ⊛m-theglamourbar.com; map p.40. Pink, frivolous and fabulous, this is one of Shanghai's best bars (one of the world's best, according to Condé Nast). There's also a good view of the Bund and a schedule of cultural events such as book launches and readings. Cocktails from ¥85; go for the *mojito* or the champagne selection. Daily 5pm–late.

Long Bar Waldorf Astoria, Lobby Level 2, Zhongshan Dong Yi Lu, near Guangdong Lu ☏6322 9988; map p.40. Sophisticated, retro lounge with an Art Deco look and, as you might have guessed, a very, very long bar – over thirty metres, modelled on the original that once graced this address (see p.45). The drinks menu is lengthy too, with plenty of mellow whiskies. Live jazz on weekends. Mon–Sat 4pm–1am, Sun 2pm–1am.

Peace Hotel Jazz Bar 和平饭店爵士酒吧 hépínfàndiàn juéshíjiǔbā Peace Hotel, 20 Nanjing Dong Lu, the Bund ☏63216888; map p.39. Famous in the 1920s for its eight-piece dance band, this bar has recently been refitted in a retro, Art Deco style. The resident jazz band, whose average age is 77, play from 7.30pm. There are rather too many columns in front of the stage, and the clientele is touristy rather than hip; still, as a historical curio, it's worth dropping in for a couple of (pricey) drinks. Minimum spend is ¥100 per person. Daily noon–2am.

Vue 32nd & 33rd Floor, Hyatt on the Bund, 199 Huangpu Lu, north of Suzhou Creek ☏63931234, ext 6348; map p.82. This sleek designer bar has fantastic views of the Bund, and there's a jacuzzi on the outdoor terrace so take your swimwear (or rent it from the bar). Cocktails for around ¥80. Tuesday is ladies' night; ¥100 cover at weekends. Sun–Thurs 6pm–1am, Fri & Sat 6pm–2am.

THE OLD FRENCH CONCESSION

The Apartment 47 Yongfu Lu ☏64379478; map pp.60–61. A New York-style loft bar that's become an expat favourite. There's a big bare-brick bar area, a quieter dining room, and an airy patio upstairs. It feels very clubby at weekends – expect to do some shouting and dancing. Sun–Thurs 11am–2am, Fri & Sat 11am–3am.

The Bell Bar Lane 248 Taikang Lu ☏138 1777 8890, ⊛bellbar.cn; map pp.60–61. This casual little backpacker bar is the best place to drink in the Tianzifang warren. Amiable bartenders create a homely atmosphere – try the strawberry martini, browse the book exchange and swap travel stories with the staff. Head north up Lane 248, and take the third turning on the right. Happy hour 5–8pm. Daily 11am–2am.

Constellation 酒池星座 jiǔchí xīngzuò 96 Xinle Lu ☏54040970; map pp.60–61. This discreet little cocktail bar has a good reputation thanks to attentive, bow-tied staff who know what they're shaking up. Show up early if you want to be guaranteed a seat and be aware that it can get very crowded. Daily 7pm–2am.

Cotton Club 棉花俱乐部 miánhuā jùlèbù 1416 Huaihai Zhong Lu, near Fuxing Xi Lu ☏64377110, ⊛thecottonclub.cn; map pp.60–61. A long-running, relaxed jazz club with none of that bristling Shanghai attitude. Music gets going at 9.30pm, a bit later at weekends. Jam sessions on Tuesdays. Tues–Sun 7.30pm–1.30am.

★ **Dada** 115 Xingfu Lu, between Fahuazhen Lu and Pingwu Lu ☏150 0018 2212; map pp.60–61. It might be a bit of a way out, but this clubby lounge bar is worth searching out for its laid-back ambience and hip young crowd. Music, mostly house and electro, is by talented independent promoters Antidote. Drinks are cheap and there's always a deal on. Look out for their special events – flyers are scattered around town. Daily 8pm–late.

El Coctel 2nd Floor, 47 Yongfu Lu, near Fuxing Xi Lu ☏64336511; map pp.60–61. This dark, elegant but laidback venue has quirky soft furnishings and a menu of classic cocktails (most of which will set you back ¥70 or so), swirled together by expert mixologists – try the Cosmo. It's a place to recline and people-watch, rather than bop, and the table service is attentive. Shame they allow smoking – but do snaffle one of their matchboxes. You'll probably need to reserve on the weekend, otherwise you'll have to wait on the staircase for a table. Daily 5pm–3am.

Izumi 21 Yongjia Lu ☏64710260; map pp.60–61. A small, dark and discreet Japanese Izakaya-style bar with a friendly owner; drinks include a good list of rice wine-based cocktails. With jazz on the playlist, it's an excellent place for a civilized sake. Daily 7pm–2am.

JZ Club 爵士 juéshì 46 Fuxing Xi Lu, near Yongfu Lu ☏64310269, ⊛jzclub.cn; map pp.60–61. A popular venue, dark and velvety but not smoky, with live jazz every night from 10pm. High tables and a gallery ensure that the performers are the stars. Drinks are pricey (starting at ¥55) but there's usually no cover. Daily 7pm–2am.

La Buvette 58 Yongkang Lu, near Xiangyang Nan Lu; map pp.60–61. Colourfully decorated, with a Latin theme. It's tiny, and most drinkers spill onto the street to mingle with patrons from the neighbouring bars. Cocktails start at a reasonable ¥38. Tues–Fri 4pm–late, Sat & Sun 2pm–late.

Paulaner Bräuhaus 宝莱纳 bǎoláinà House 19–20, North Block, Xintiandi, Taicang Lu ☏63203935; map pp.60–61; 150 Fengyang Lu ☏64745700; map pp.60–61; Riverside Promenade, Binjiang Dadao ☏68883935; map p.76. These giant beer halls feature greeters in *Lederhosen*, and Filipino bands. They run their own microbrewery and offer German food, although the beer's not cheap, with the smallest lager costing ¥68 (a litre is ¥105). Daily 11am–2am.

11

People 7 人间银七 rénjiānyínqī 805 Julu Lu, close to Fumin Lu ☎ 54040707; map pp.60–61. This hip bar trades on its exclusivity. Not only is there no sign, there's even a special code to get in: put your hands into the third and seventh of the nine lighted holes outside. A door slides back revealing a two-storey lounge bar with walls of exposed concrete, spotlights, comfy white sofas and a long eerily lit bar. The quirky elements – glasses with curved bottoms so they keep rolling round, baffling toilet doors with fake handles – will either delight or annoy. Daily 6pm–midnight.

Senator 98 Wuyuan Lu, near Wulumuqi Zhong Lu ☎ 54231330; map pp.60–61. A stylish and sophisticated speakeasy from the people behind *Citizen* (see p.110). It's intimate and cosy and the staff really know their cocktails; tell them your mood and tastes and they'll suggest a drink to fit. They have a vast range of bourbons and most of the recipes are prohibition era. Daily 5pm–1am.

Yuan 元坊 yuán fāng 17–2 Xiangyang Bei Lu ☎ 64330538; map pp.60–61. This funky and stylish bar is Chinese owned and staffed, and serves imaginative cocktails (starting at ¥68) with a Chinese twist – ingredients include rice wine, ginseng and osmanthus. The ambience is fun and theatrical, and the kitschy chinoiserie decor has been chosen with a knowing wink. Mon–Sat 5pm–1am.

Zapatas 5 Hengshan Lu, near Dongping Lu ☎ 64334104, ⓦ zapatas-shanghai.com; map pp.60–61. No Mexican anarchist would be seen dead in the company of the lascivious frat-house crowd here who, come the revolution, will be first against the wall. Never mind, it's a heaving party on Monday and Wednesday nights, when ladies are offered free margaritas before midnight. Tequila gets poured into the mouths of anyone dancing on the bar. Enter through the garden of *Sasha's*, the nearby restaurant. Daily 5pm–late.

JING'AN

Kaiba 开巴 kāibā 479 Wuding Lu, near Shanxi Bei Lu ☎ 62889676, ⓦ kaiba-beerbar.com; map pp.70–71. A favourite with the after-work crowd, this big Belgian bar has a great beer selection, with over fifty imported bottled European beers and plenty more on draft. It's not cheap – a Duvell will set you back ¥70 – but happy hour runs from 4–9pm on weekdays, 2–7pm on weekends. Daily 11am–2am.

Malone's 马龙 mǎlóng 255 Tongren Lu, near Nanjing Xi Lu ☎ 62472400, ⓦ malones.com.cn; map pp.70–71. Sports bar popular with the expat business crowd and popular for its burgers. House band plays reliable crowd-pleasers every night. Daily 10am–2am.

Windows Too 蕴德诗酒吧 yùndéshī jiǔbā J104, Jingan Temple Plaza, 1699 Nanjing Xi Lu, by Huashan Lu ☎ 62889007, ⓦ windowsbar.com; map pp.70–71. Packs them in nightly thanks to a revolutionary idea – cheap beer at ¥15 a bottle, noisy hip-hop, no class and no pretensions. It's popular with those at the bottom of the Shanghai foreigner food chain – students, teachers and backpackers – and those who'll deign to talk to them. ¥50 cover on the weekend. Daily 10am–late.

PUDONG

100 Century Avenue 世纪100 Shìjì yībǎi Park Hyatt, 91st Floor, World Financial Centre, 100 Century Avenue ☎ 38551428, ⓦ 100centuryavenue.com; map p.76. This is the world's highest bar. Fantastic views, obviously, and live music every night from a Filipino band. But it's pricey – a beer is ¥80, and there's a cover of ¥100. Daily 11.30am–2.30pm & 5.30–10.30pm.

Cloud Nine 九重天酒吧 jiǔchóngtiān jiǔbā 87th Floor, Grand Hyatt Hotel, Jinmao Tower, 88 Shiji Dadao ☎ 50491234; map p.76. Inside it's all rather dark and metallic, but never mind, the view is astonishing. Unfortunately staff steer those not staying at the *Hyatt* away from the coveted window-side tables facing the Bund. Minimum spend is ¥120 per person, and cocktails start at ¥80. Mon–Fri 5pm–1am, Sat & Sun 2pm–1am.

Flair 58th Floor, Ritz-Carlton Pudong, 8 Century Avenue ☎ 20201778; map p.76. The terrace at this suave lounge bar has a jaw-dropping view – right into the Pearl Tower. You won't get change from a red bill for a drink, and beware, there's a ¥350 minimum spend per person. Tapas and seafood available. Spectacular, yes. Value for money, no. Daily 5pm–2am.

Paulaner Bräuhaus 宝莱纳 bǎoláinà Binjiang Dadao, near Shangri-La Hotel ☎ 68883935; map p.76. Another branch of the German-style pub chain (see p.115) with pricey Paulaner beer from its own microbrewery. Good views of the Bund make it worth considering. Daily 11am–2am.

CLUBS

The dancing scene in Shanghai will be familiar to anyone who's been clubbing in any Western capital – you won't hear any local sounds or much that's not mainstream – but at least the door prices are cheaper. Most places have international DJs and plenty of famous faces have popped in for a spin of the decks. One Chinese innovation is the addition of karaoke booths at the back. Note that there are also dancefloors in meat markets *Windows Too* (see above) and *Zapatas* (see above), in poser palace *Bar Rouge* (see p.114) and hipster hideout *Dada* (see p.115).

Cirque le Soir 4th Floor, South Bund 22, 22 Zhongshan Dong Er Lu ☎ 0400 9910088, ⓦ cirquelesoir.com; map

p.54. Intriguing gothic nightclub with a show of twisted cabaret acts. Masked dwarves, magicians, burlesque dancers

GAY AND LESBIAN SHANGHAI

These days, China is fairly relaxed about homosexuality; at least it's no longer on the official list of psychiatric diseases. Shanghai is the Chinese city most accepting of alternative lifestyles, though anyone used to the scene in a Western city will find things tamer here and most clubs are aimed at men.

Eddy's Tianping Lu, just off Huaihai Lu ☎62820521, ⓦeddys-bar.com; map pp.60–61. Long-standing lounge; dark and severe in decor but with a friendly, older crowd. Daily 7pm–2am.

Shanghai Studio Building 4, Lane 1950, Huaihai Zhong Lu ☎62831043, ⓦshanghai-studio.com; map pp.60–61. Part lounge bar, part gallery, part underground maze, *Shanghai Studio* is aimed at the media set and has a ¥100 open bar on Thursdays.

390 Bar 390 Panyu Lu, near Fanhuazhen Lu ☎18621249854, ⓦ390shanghai.com; map pp.86–87. Big- new live-music venue, with a lounge bar at the front and a dance club behind. Relaxed and friendly, but the concept is a little off the wall, so check to see whether it's still open. Daily 5pm–2am.

11

and the like perform around the tables, then put on a grand finale at midnight. You have to reserve a table, and it's classy, so dress up. There's a minimum spend and you can expect to throw down about ¥800 per person. Wed–Sat 9pm–4am.

The Geisha 艺 yì 390 Shanxi Nan Lu, near Fuxing Zhong Lu ☎64030244, ⓦthegeisha-shanghai.com; map pp.60–61. Small but well formed, with a Japanese theme to the decor and the cocktails. A nicely mixed crowd bops to club classics. It gets rammed on the weekend; there's an open-air lounge specializing in sake upstairs, for when the dancefloor gets too busy. Wednesday night is ladies' night – free martinis till midnight. Happy hour Monday to Friday 5–8pm. Tues–Sat 6pm–late.

Muse 同乐坊 tónglè fāng 68 Yuyao Lu, New Factories, near Xikang Lu ⓦmuseshanghai.com; map pp.70–71. Glitzy megaclub, with house music downstairs and hip-hop up. At least ¥70 cover, beers are ¥40. A little more sophisticated than usual. Open till 2am on weekdays, 4am on Fri and Sat.

Number 88 88酒吧 bāshíbā jiǔbà A Mansion, 2nd Floor, 291 Fumin Lu, near Donghu Lu ☎61360288, ⓦno88bar.com; map pp.70–71. Fun to check out, if you're in the right frame of mind – it's fiercely tacky but exuberant. Young, moneyed Chinese bop to club classics or play dice at the back, in a kitschy *Tomb Raider* wonderland. The music is as all over the place as is the decor. Cover is ¥50. Daily 8.30pm–6am.

Shelter 庇护所 bìhù suǒ 5 Yongfu Lu, near Fuxing Xi Lu ☎64370400; map pp.60–61. This dramatic, claustrophobic venue inside a converted bomb shelter is the centre of Shanghai's underground music scene. International DJs play hip-hop, electro and dubstep to an enthusiastic crowd that, refreshingly, hasn't dressed up (no point anyway, it's too dark). Cover is ¥30 or so, beers from ¥20, cocktails from ¥30. It doesn't really get going till after midnight. Wed–Sat 10pm–late.

ACROBATS AT THE SHANGHAI CENTRE THEATRE

Entertainment and art

Shanghai has a great range of arts venues, and plenty of interested people to fill them. There's lots of money around for prestigious projects such as the grand Power Station of Art in Puxi (see p.57) and the lovely new concert hall, the Oriental Arts Centre (see p.79), and Shanghai's major art, literary and film festivals are building considerable reputations (see p.26). Most visitors take in an acrobatics show and perhaps an opera, but there's growing music, dance and drama scenes too, and no one should miss the contemporary art that flourishes in the city. When it comes to cutting-edge new work, however, Shanghai doesn't quite measure up on the international stage. Performances and exhibitions tend to be safe and conventional; the government's heavy-handed censorship makes any even mildly contentious form of cultural production impossible.

ESSENTIALS

INFORMATION

To find out what's on, check an expat magazine such as *Time Out* or *City Weekend*, or the website ⓦ smartsshanghai .com. *China Daily* has listings of big cultural spectaculars such as visiting ballet troupes.

BOOKING TICKETS

Credit card bookings haven't yet caught on in China, but you can still get tickets in advance without the hassle of going to the venue. For both of the following, tickets will be delivered to your home or hotel, and you pay cash on arrival, plus a small delivery charge.

Shanghai Cultural Information and Booking Centre ☎ 62172426, ⓦ culture.sh.cn/English. Tickets booked here are delivered at no extra charge provided you book more than three days before the performance.

SmartShanghai ⓦ smartsshanghai.com/smartticket/. Useful and easily navigated English-language website.

DRAMA AND DANCE

Most Shanghai theatre is light-hearted fare about the trials of urban dating life, in Chinese of course, though some troupes occasionally put on shows in English. Dance is popular, but it's almost always the conservative end of the spectrum. If you're into modern dance, look out for the work of choreographer Jinxing, China's most high profile transsexual and one of the scene's few innovators. The big draws at the moment are imported musicals and ballets – worth investigating as they are cheaper than they would be at home.

Majestic Theatre 美琪大剧院 měiqí dàjùyuàn 66 Jiangning Lu, near Nanjing Xi Lu ☎ 62174409; map pp.70–71. One of Asia's best theatres when it was built in 1941. Today, musicals are the main fare, but the programme is interspersed with some English-language drama, dance competitions and Chinese opera.

Shanghai Art Theatre 艺海剧院 yìhǎi jùyuàn 466 Jiangning Lu, near Kangding Lu ☎ 64278199; map pp.70–71. This airy modern complex tends to show classical Chinese opera and rather rusty old Chinese dramas.

Shanghai Culture Square 文化广场 wénhuà guǎngchǎng 225 Shaanxi Nan Lu, near Fuxing Zhong Lu ☎ 54619961, ⓦ shculturesquare.com; map pp.60–61. This prestigious new venue seats more than two thousand, and is usually home to musicals, both imported and domestic.

Shanghai Dramatic Arts Centre 上海话剧艺术中心 shànghǎi huàjù yìshù zhōngxīn 288 Anfu Lu ☎ 51695229, ⓦ china-drama.com; map pp.60–61. Slick productions in a modern auditorium; performances are usually of classics or crowd pleasers. Western plays performed in Chinese are accompanied by English supertitles on an electronic screen.

Shanghai Grand Theatre 上海大剧院 shànghǎi dàjùyuàn 300 Renmin Dadao ☎ 63273094, ⓦ shgtheatre.com; map p.49. Popular contemporary dramas, operas and classical ballet are all staged at this lovely venue, which also plays host to most visiting musicals. Regular performances by the in-house Shanghai Symphony Orchestra (see p.120).

12

CHINESE OPERA

Chinese opera is a unique combination of song, dance, acrobatics and mime. It's highly stylized, with every aspect of the performance, from costumes and make-up to movements, imbued with a specific symbolic meaning. Colour is very significant, red for example signifying loyalty and blue cruelty. Plots feature straightforward goodies and baddies, often concerning young lovers who are forbidden to marry, supernatural interventions and so on. The main barrier to appreciation for the uninitiated is the percussive din of the accompanying orchestra. These days – with the fan base growing increasingly elderly and in the hopes of appealing to a younger audience – shows have been shortened from four hours to an hour or two, and include plenty of slapstick and martial arts. There are hundreds of regional variations, such as Yue opera from nearby Zhejiang Province, Kun opera from Jiangsu and the local form, Hu.

Wanping Theatre 857 Zhongshan Er Lu ☎ 64392277; map pp.70–71. Nightly, tourist-friendly show based on the adventures of the monkey king, broadly adapted from the Chinese classic novel *Journey to the West*. Performances are at 7.30pm; tickets start at ¥80.

Yifu Theatre 天蟾逸夫舞台 tiānchán yìfū wǔtái 701 Fuzhou Lu ☎ 63225075; map p.49. One of the few places in Shanghai where you can hear provincial opera forms. There's a different show every night of the week and a brisk English summary at the start explains the plot. Tickets – ¥30 to ¥300 – can be bought on the day and shows start at 7.15pm (some afternoon performances).

ACROBATICS

Acrobatics have a long tradition in China and acrobatic shows are a guaranteed crowd pleaser. The style may be vaudeville but the stunts are spectacular – a dozen people stacked on one bicycle and the like. Performances have a little bit of everything: plate spinners, hoop divers, a comedy turn, jugglers and all sorts of feats of gymnastics. Many of the performers will have been trained for their roles since childhood in specialist schools.

Shanghai Centre Theatre 上海商城剧院 shànghǎi shāngchéng jùyuàn 1376 Nanjing Xi Lu, by Xikang Lu ⓣ62798948; map pp.70–71. Plenty of stunts. Performances are every day, starting at 7.30pm and finishing by 9pm, and tickets cost ¥100–280.

Shanghai Circus World 上海马戏城 shànghǎi mǎxìchéng 2266 Gonghe Xi Lu ⓣ66527750, ⓦera-shanghai.com; ⓜShanghai Circus World (line #1). The gold-coloured central dome hosts "*ERA, the Intersection of Time*". Never mind the daft name, the shows here are good old-fashioned spectaculars, the city's best, with audiovisual trickery enhancing the awe-inspiring acrobatic cavortings. Performances run daily at 7.30pm. Tickets range from ¥140 to ¥580, but the pricier seats don't seem to have that much of an advantage over the cheaper ones.

LIVE MUSIC

Shanghai's music scene doesn't yet rival Beijing's, but it's only a matter of time as more venues open, new talent is trained in the impressive music schools, more international artists make appearances, and more disaffected kids buy electric guitars. Jazz devotees should head up to Fuxing Xi Lu for the *JZ Club* (see p.115) or nearby *Cotton Club* (see p.115). There's plenty of hip-hop around, but it's all about fashion and posing and the scene has yet to produce any music of note. The indie music scene is not nearly as good as Beijing's, but it's there, and it's worth dipping a toe into the venues listed here. Try and catch indie popsters Cold Fairyland and Candy Shop, or folk-punk rockers Top Floor Circus.

CLASSICAL MUSIC

In addition to the venues listed below, classical concerts are also held at the Shanghai Grand Theatre (see p.51) – check the website.

Jinmao Concert Hall 金茂音乐厅 jīnmào yīnyuètīng Annexe of Jinmao Tower, 88 Shiji Dadao ⓣ50472612, ⓦjinmao88.com/en/jinmao_edifice_odeum.htm; map p.76. Small venue for classical music recitals, with reasonably priced tickets from ¥60.

Oriental Arts Centre 上海东方艺术中心 shànghǎi dōngfāng yìshù zhōngxīn 425 Dingxiang Lu, near Shiji Dadao ⓣ68541234, ⓦshoac.com.cn; map p.78. A fantastic 40,000-square-metre behemoth with superb acoustics (see p.79). At night the ceiling sparkles and changes colour according to the tunes being played.

Shanghai Concert Hall 上海音乐厅 shànghǎi yīnyuètīng 523 Yan'an Zhong Lu near Xizang Zhong Lu ⓣ63862836, ⓦshanghaiconcerthall.org; map p.54. This lovely old building was moved at tremendous cost sixty metres east in 2003, in order to get it away from the din of Yan'an Lu. Today it's the city's premier venue for classical music. Tickets from ¥80.

Shanghai Symphony Orchestra Hall 上海交响乐团演奏厅 shànghǎi jiāoxiǎngyuètuán yǎnzòutīng 105 Hunan Lu ⓣ64372735, ⓦsh-symphony.com; map pp.60–61. Home to the Shanghai Symphony Orchestra, who are very good, if rather conservative in their repertoire.

ROCK AND POP MUSIC

MAO Livehouse 308 Chongqing Lu, near Jianguo Zhong Lu ⓣ64450086, ⓦmao-music.com; map pp.60–61. A decent-sized, centrally located venue for local and international rock and indie bands. The sound system passes muster and drinks are cheap, at around ¥20 a beer. Variable cover charge, usually around ¥50.

Mercedes Benz Arena 梅赛德斯-奔驰文化中心 méisàidésī-bēnchí wénhuà zhōngxīn 1200 Expo Avenue, near Gaoke Xi Lu, Pudong ⓣ400 181 6688, ⓦmercedes-benzarena.com/index.php/enhome; ⓜYaohua Lu. A legacy of the 2010 Expo, this giant UFO-like building seats 18,000. It hosts big international names such as Justin Beiber and Elton John.

Shanghai Stadium 上海体育场 shànghǎi tǐyùchǎng 666 Tianyaoqiao Lu ⓣ64266666, ext 2567; ⓜShanghai Stadium; map pp.86–87. Venue for mega gigs by visiting bands such as the Rolling Stones and Korean superstar Rain, as well as home-grown idols. Tickets are cheaper than they would be in the West, usually around ¥120.

★ **Yuyintang** 育音堂 yùyīntáng 851 Kaixuan Lu, by Yan'an Xi Lu subway stop ⓣ52378662, ⓦyytlive.com; map pp.86–87. This grungy venue is ground zero for the converse shoes and black-nail-varnish set, hosting rock/punk and electro gigs every weekend with a varying cover of around ¥30. It's all pretty rough and ready, with concrete floors and graffitied walls, but the sound system is surprisingly good, and bottles of beer are only ¥15.

FILM

When it comes to pulling in the box-office receipts, China is second only to the US, yet the country's notoriously prickly censors pass only thirty-four foreign films a year for domestic Chinese consumption. There are plenty of cinemas to see them in, but generally all films are dubbed into Mandarin; exceptions are noted below. During the Shanghai Film Festival (see p.27) there is more varied fare on offer. Expat-oriented screenings of hip, arthouse or exploitation films are held every Tuesday night at 9pm at *Dada* bar (see p.115), and of more mainstream Western films at the *Vienna Café* (see p.111) every Thursday at 7.30pm.

Broadband International Cineplex 万裕国际影城 wànyù guójì yǐngchéng 6th Floor, Times Square, 99 Huaihai Lu ☎63910363, ☜swy99.com; map p.54. Multiplex showing Chinese releases – although unusually it has English-speaking staff. Tickets ¥60 and up.

Cathay Theatre 国泰电影院 guótài diànyǐngyuàn 870 Huaihai Zhong Lu ☎54040415, ☜guotaifilm.com; map pp.60–61. Grand, rather creaky old venue with cheaper tickets than the multiplexes (from ¥15) for much smaller seats.

IMAX Science and Technology Museum ☎68622000, ☜sstm.org.cn; map p.78. Daily science spectaculars – stories about tigers, dinosaurs, and so on, on a huge curved screen or in a 3D theatre.

Paradise Warner Cinema City 永华电影城 yǒnghuá diànyǐngchéng 6th Floor, Grand Gateway, 1 Hongqiao Lu, Xujiahui ☎64076622, ☜paradise warner.com; map pp.86–87. Shows foreign films in their original language, alongside Chinese releases (in Mandarin only). Tickets from ¥60.

Peace Cinema 和平影都 hépíng yǐngdū 290 Xizang Zhong Lu ☎63225252, ☜shdgm.com; map p.49. Huge, centrally located cinema just off People's Square boasting the city's only IMAX screen that shows features. Tickets start at ¥50, IMAX tickets are ¥80.

Shanghai Film Art Centre 上海影院中心 shànghǎi

SHANGHAI CINEMA

China's first-ever moving picture was shown in Shanghai in 1914, at a teahouse variety show, and the nation's first cinema was built here twelve years later. By the 1930s film had caught on both with the foreign population and with the locals and a number of studios had opened. Influenced by the May Fourth Movement, which challenged imperialism and social conservatism, film-makers eschewed the formalism and abstractions of Chinese drama, and sought to make naturalistic films. One classic from the era, *Sister Flower* (1933), tells the story of twin sisters separated at birth, one of whom ends up in Shanghai while the other remains a poor villager. *Spring Silk Worm*, from the same year, portrays grim decline in Zhejiang Province, and points the finger at Japanese colonialism. The most celebrated film of the time was *The Goddess* (1934), about the struggle of a prostitute to have her son educated; it features a standout performance from the tragic beauty Ruan Lingyu, China's Garbo, who killed herself a year later.

When the Japanese invaded in 1937 Shanghai's studios were closed, and film-making talent fled. Despite the turmoil, the Shanghai film-makers made one last great work, the epic *Spring River Flows East*, telling the story of a family torn apart by the conflict.

When the Communists took over things didn't get any easier. Officially derided as bourgeois, the studios managed to release only one privately funded film, *The Life of Wu Xun* (1949), the story of a nineteenth-century philanthropist. Mao damned it as revisionist and closed the studios down. From then on Chinese film-makers were only allowed to shoot dry government propaganda. Though the studios have yet to return, a new film school has opened and the city has once more begun to be depicted in contemporary Chinese cinema, most notably in Lou Ye's tragic love story *Suzhou Creek* (2002).

Shanghai's decadent prewar days have a perennial appeal to film-makers, it would seem, providing the setting for the stilted Merchant Ivory boreathon *The White Countess* (2004), and the adaptation of Somerset Maugham's *The Painted Veil* (which includes a CGI Bund); but it is Zhang Yimou's *Shanghai Triad* (1995) which really set the standard for that whole "gangsters and *qipao*" concession-era genre. The brutal end to those days is shown in Steven Spielberg's excellent adaptation of J.G. Ballard's classic novel, *Empire of the Sun* (1987). These days, Shanghai has an intriguing new role as a city of the future – science fiction films *Code 46* (2008) and *Looper* (2012) were shot here.

The old Chinese classics, and others of the time, can be seen at the *Old Film Café* (see p.112), or you can buy them on DVD from the Foreign Language Bookstore (see p.131) or from the shop in the Shanghai Grand Theatre (see p.131).

yīngyuàn zhōngxīn 160 Xinhua Lu, near Panyu Lu ☎62804088, ⊚filmcenter.com.cn; ⊚Jiaotong University. The only vaguely art-house cinema in town which has at least some non-mainstream content. Tickets from ¥45, half-price on Monday and Tuesday. The main venue for the Shanghai Film Festival.

UME International Cineplex 国际影城 guójì yīngchéng 5th Floor, South Block, Xintiandi ☎63733333, ⊚http://bs.ume.com.cn/tplt/201312251 52739.shtml; map p.62. Foreign films, subtitled rather than dubbed. When you call, an English schedule will follow the Chinese. Tickets star at ¥50.

ART

Of all the arts, the most thriving scene, and certainly the most accessible to the visitor, is contemporary art. Chinese art is hot, and is being snapped up by international dealers, though it remains to be seen how worthwhile this hyped-up work will turn out to be; much is a sophisticated form of chinoiserie, selling an image of China for foreign consumption. Still, there's plenty of good stuff out there, and for once the government is not meddling too much.

As well as new government-run art museums such as the staid Duolun (see p.82) and Power Station of Art (see p.57), more exciting private ventures, among them MoCA (see p.52), Rockbund (see p.42) and the Shanghai Gallery of Art (see p.122), are stimulating the scene; and every other year, the Shanghai Biennale (see p.27) seems to get bigger. But the first stop for the artily inclined has to be 50 Moganshan Lu, a derelict suburban textile factory that was first taken over by artists in the 1990s when rents were cheap – it has since become one of the city's premier tourist attractions (see p.72). In addition, the galleries below are well worth checking out.

Around Space 703 Chuang Ye Building, 33 Sichuan Lu ☎33050100, ⊚aroundspace.org; map p.40. This small space tucked behind the Bund shows contemporary painting by cool Chinese artists. Tues–Sun 10.30am–6.30pm.

Art Labor画廊 huàláng Building 4, 570 Yongjia Lu, near Yueyang Lu ☎34605331, ⊚artlaborgallery.com; map pp.60–61. Packing a big punch for a small gallery, this is one of the best places to see emerging local artists, usually exhibited alongside artists from abroad. Tues–Sat 11am–7pm & Sun 12–6pm.

Galerie Beaugeste 比极画廊 bǐjí huàláng 519, Building 5, Lane 210, Taikang Lu ☎64669012, ⊚beaugeste-gallery.com; map pp.60–61. Slick photography gallery among the boutiques in Tianzifang (see p.64). It's small, but the shows are always interesting. Weekends 10am–6pm, Mon–Fri call ahead.

Shanghai Gallery of Art 外滩三号沪申画廊 wàitānsānhào hùshēn huàláng 3rd Floor, Three on the Bund, Zhongshan Dong Yi Lu ☎63215757, ⊚threeonthebund.com; map p.40. An impressive space in a beautiful and upscale building, just above the Armani flagship store, that hosts safe shows of established big hitters. Daily 11am–9pm.

Shanghai Sculpture Space (Red Town) 上海城市雕塑艺术中心 shànghǎi chéngshì diāosù yìshù zhōngxīn 570 Huaihai Xi Lu ☎62807844, ⊚sss570 .com; map pp.60–61. Occupying an old steel factory, this charming sculpture gallery has more than two thousand square metres of floor space, home to a permanent display of quirky but uneven work, which continues into the grounds. Tues–Sun 10am–4pm.

CHINESE CONTEMPORARY ART AND ARTISTS

As China opened up, artists discovered and imitated Western forms, from surrealism to Dada to Pop, but the best absorbed international trends and made from them something that is distinctly Chinese. Now it's hard to speak of any dominating "isms" but documentary realism remains a strong strain in Chinese art, with artists given leeway to bring up, albeit obliquely, issues whose discussion is curtailed in other forums; for example, pollution, corruption and the destruction of the urban environment are common themes. Artists who exemplify this subtly political approach include Yang Fudong, notable for his wistful images of city life and migrant workers, and Cui Xiuwen, whose work includes film of women in a toilet at a karaoke bar. Just as strong is a theme of nostalgia, retreat or introspection – plenty of artists don't want to be commentators. Artists like Liu Wei, with his decaying cities, or Gu Dexin, who makes fruit and flesh confections, embody this trend.

Other artists to look out for at the moment include Zhang Huan, who uses his body as a canvas, and Cai Guo-Qiang, who makes art with gunpowder. One of the most recognizable figures is Yue Minjun, whose absurdist paintings of laughing figures have been much copied. You won't see anything of China's most famous contemporary art impresario, Ai Weiwei, as his work is judged as just too contentious.

TIANZIFANG

Shopping

Shanghai is excellent for shopping, with something for all tastes, whether you like getting stuck into teeming markets or swaggering about with the glitterati. And with the yuan artificially pegged at a low rate (at least for the moment), for foreign visitors it's all great value too.

13

The Shanghainese love **luxury goods**, and it's not uncommon to find young women spending several months' salary on a handbag – it's advertising status in a society that only recently lost traditional forms of hierarchical display. But all those glitzy brand names that give the streets their sheen are not good value at all; high-end goods and international brands are generally 20 percent more expensive than they would be in the West. Ignore them, and instead plunge into the fascinating world of **boutiques and markets**, where you'll find goods that are quirky, original, bespoke and a bargain. Shanghai's **best buys** are international brand designer clothes from factory outlet stores; tailored clothes and made-to-order shoes; originals by local designers; fake name-brand labels; and quirky homeware such as handmade porcelain and jewellery. It's a rare visitor who doesn't end up having to buy another bag to keep all his new goodies in.

ESSENTIALS

Opening hours Shops and markets are open every day and generally from 10am to 8pm; malls open till 10pm (though many of the shops inside close at 9pm).

Paying Only in the most high-end shops will you be able to use a credit or debit card. You can exchange goods with a receipt except in small shops.

Regulations and customs Keep in mind that most Western countries take a dim view of designer knock-offs.

If you're packing more than a couple of look-a-like Vuittons, they could be confiscated. Technically, you cannot take items out of China that are over 200 years old, but you'd be hard-pressed to find anything that old in Shanghai anyway. If you manage to find something over 100 years old, it'll require authentication from the Antiques and Relics Bureau; the store should help you and the process shouldn't cost you anything.

MALLS

Malls have transformed the retail environment of modern China, and nowhere have they been embraced as enthusiastically as in Shanghai. Aspects of mall culture that Europeans disdain – artificiality, the absence of the authentic bustle of the street, a veneer of exclusivity – are in China seen as advantages. Perceived as upscale, they have the most expensive brands on the ground floor, then it all gets more affordable above, and there's always a food court or a clutch of restaurants too.

Grand Gateway 港汇广场 gǎnghuì guǎngchǎng 1 Hongqiao Lu ☎ 64070111; map pp.86–87. A megalosaurus of a mall with direct access to the metro. It's a little cheaper and a lot busier than the others. Daily 10am–10pm.

> ## WHERE TO SHOP
>
> For souvenirs the first place to head for is **Yuyuan Bazaar** (see p.55), **Qibao** (see p.134) or **Tianzifang** (see p.64) where you can get all the perennial favourites: chopsticks, kites, fans, signature chops, tea and teapots, but there are plenty of other less obvious options (see p.129). Nanjing Dong Lu (see p.46) used to be known as the golden mile but these days it's pretty prosaic, with stores full of cheap clothes – although at least it's pedestrianized. Most foreign visitors will be more impressed with the retail opportunities offered around the corner on **the Bund**, where luxury brand names have opened showpiece stores – though all but the absurdly wealthy will have to make do with window-shopping. Pricey luxury goods are also available in the malls of **Nanjing Xi Lu** (see p.69) or yuppie playground **Xintiandi** (see p.59).
>
> The most chic area to shop is the **Old French Concession**; central Huaihai Zhong Lu itself is full of familiar brands, but the streets off it, such as Nanchang Lu, Shaanxi Nan Lu and Maoming Lu, are full of fascinating little boutiques, making this the place to forage for fashionable gear. For local crafts, and anything that's a bit more creative, head to the Tianzifang area (see p.64).
>
> For stores geared to local tastes, check out **Xujiahui** (see p.86); as soon as you exit Xujiahui subway you're bang in the middle of a dense concentration of retail outlets – the Grand Gateway Plaza, Pacific Department Store, Metro City and the Oriental Department Store – aimed at the burgeoning middle classes. This is a good place to come for electronic equipment and affordable fashion.
>
> **Serious shoppers** should first get themselves to the Foreign Language Bookstore or Garden Books (see p.131), both of which sell a little white book with no English title, published by Shanghai Creative Bazaar. It's full of photos from fifty of the city's most interesting shops, with interviews with their owners, a blurb on each and all addresses listed in Chinese.

13

Plaza 66 恒隆广场 hénglóng guǎngchǎng 1266 Nanjing Xi Lu ☎62790910; map pp.70–71. The fanciest mall's high-end stores are characterized by sleek, glassy-eyed staff who outnumber the customers. You could spend hours here without seeing anyone buy anything. The ground-floor *Atrium* café is good for a coffee and the toilets are sparklingly clean. Daily 10am–10pm.

Raffles Mall 莱福士广场 láifúshì guǎngchǎng 268 Xizang Zhong Lu, the corner of Fuzhou Lu ☎63403333; map p.49. A good mall should be a cocktail of the fabulous and the affordable, to draw just the right kind of aspirational clientele, and should keep them lingering with a decent café and a food court – and on this, Raffles Mall scores the highest. Check out the *Fresh*

Everyday juice bar in the basement, and Novo Concept on the first floor for teen fashion. Daily 10am–10pm.

Times Square 时代豪庭 shídài háotíng 99 Huaihai Zhong Lu ☎63910691; map p.54. Times Square is particularly useful for expats, since its basement hosts an excellent English-language bookshop, Charterhouse (see p.131), a Western supermarket (see p.101), a Watsons chemist, and a pretty good sushi restaurant (see p.104). Daily 10am–10pm.

Xintiandi Style 新天地时尚 xīntiāndì shí shàng 245 Madang Lu ☎53820666, ⊛xintiandistyle.com; map p.62. Focuses on less well known luxury brands, and there are frequent events and happenings. Daily 10am–10pm.

ANTIQUES

There's no shortage of antique markets selling opium pipes, Cultural Revolution alarm clocks, carved screens, Mao's *Little Red Book*, silk paintings and the like – but never mind what the vendor tells you, always assume you're buying a modern copy. Still, it's all fairly cheap. The Dongtai Lu Market (see below) is the best place for this stuff, but barter hard. Genuine antiques are available at the reputable antique stores, but again most of their stock is reproduction. Anything over 100 years old will need authentication (see p.31).

Dongtai Lu Antique Market 东台路古玩市场 dōngtáilù gǔwán shìchǎng Dongtai Lu; ⓂLaoximen; map p.54. Scores of small stores sell all manner of portable knick-knacks along this street. It's at its biggest at weekends. Bargain hard, as starting prices are commonly twenty times what something is worth. Stalls generally operate around 8am–6pm.

Henry Antique Warehouse 亨利古典家具店 hēnglì gǔdiǎn jiājùdiàn 3rd Floor, Building 2, 359 Hongzhong Lu ☎64010831, ⊛h-antique.com. The English-speaking staff at this huge space show off antique Chinese furniture and furnishings; a carved Chinese bed costs around ¥13,000. Overseas shipping provided. It's in

the southern outskirts of the city, so you'll have to take a taxi. Mon–Sat 9am–7pm.

Shanghai Antique and Curio Store 上海文物商店 shànghǎi wénwù shāngdiàn 192–246 Guangdong Lu ☎63214697; map p.39. A little pricier than elsewhere, but the goods and staff at this government store can be relied on. Daily 9am–5pm.

Zhang's Textiles 绣花张 xiùhuā zhāng Shanghai Centre, 202A Nanjing Xi Lu ☎62798587, ⊛zhangstextiles.com; map pp.70–71. Genuine framed Qing-dynasty embroidery, jade bracelets and silk pillows. It's not cheap, though, at thousands of yuan for anything of any size. Daily 10am–9.30pm.

BARGAINING

In malls and high-street stores, prices are fixed, but there is always leeway for **bargaining** in small shops and markets. In touristy places such as the fake markets or Yuyuan, haggling is essential, as vendors can start at ten or even fifty times what they'll accept.

Always bargain good-naturedly, as confrontational behaviour will make the seller clam up. Feign complete disinterest in the object even if you've fallen in love with it. The seller (a girl, usually) will tap a price into a calculator. You then tap your best price in and she acts as if you just shot her puppy. After a little more discussion, walk away ruefully shaking your head, and she'll chase after you and give you a "last price". Then you start negotiating again.

The best way to get a reasonable price is to decide how much you want to pay for something and then keep obstinately repeating that figure, rather than getting drawn into incremental increases. Remember that in places like fake markets you are likely to see the same thing for sale in the next store along, so having got a price from one place, take it to another and ask if they will beat it. Remember, too, that you'll always get a better price if you buy several items.

13

FAKES

Quite a lot in China is not what it seems – 90 percent of the world's counterfeit goods originate here. It isn't just clothes, cigarettes and bags; you can buy counterfeit phones, medicine, computers, cars, fossils, eggs – there are even entire fake IKEA and Apple stores. In Shanghai there are several fake markets, though if you're buying a supposed antique, or just about anything from a backstreet market store, there's a good chance that it's a fake too.

You'll have to bargain harder here than anywhere else in the city; the pushy vendors commonly start at ten or twenty times the price they'll accept and it pays to shop around as plenty of people are selling the same thing. As a rough guide, a man's watch costs between ¥100 and ¥250, a woman's watch ¥50 to ¥150; "Converse" trainers can be had for ¥80, other brands for a little more. Handbags range from ¥80 to ¥130, a bit more for suitcases and backpacks. You can pick up fake computer games and software for ¥50 or so, and DVDs for ¥8. All clothes should cost less than ¥200, and sunglasses, pens and belts are all around ¥30. There's also golf gear on sale, and some stalls just hawk souvenirs.

Note that according to the customs laws of Western countries, you are only allowed to import one dubious item per brand; so one fake Armani watch is fine, but a dozen will be impounded.

Han City 假货市场 jiǎhuò shìchǎng 580 Nanjing Xi Lu; ⓜ People's Square; map pp.70–71. Not far from People's Square, this is a convenient fake market, with three storeys of dodgy shops – it's a little cheaper higher up. Daily 10am–9pm.

Qipu Lu Market 七浦路和河南北路 qīpǔlù hé hénán běilù 183 Qipu Lu, just off Henan Bei Lu, northeast of the Bund; map p.82. Giant stores here sell cheap local fashion among all the counterfeits. Generally, the higher the floor, the better the quality. Daily 9am–5.30pm.

Yatai Xinyang Fashion & Gift Market 亚太新阳服饰礼品市场 yàtài xīnyáng fúshì lǐpǐn shìchǎng ⓜ Science and Technology Museum (entrance close to the ticketing machines); map p.78. This is the city's biggest fake market, and conveniently located; the subway brings you up right next to the underground warren of stalls. It's divided up by zones, with maps on the walls. As well as the usual fake shoes, bags and clothes there are plenty of tailors (see p.127), and a whole zone for jewellery, notably pearls. Beware the tests that the stallholders do to show you their wares are genuine. Daily 10am–9pm.

CLOTHES AND SHOES

Sartorial elegance is something of a local obsession, and there's an old Chinese joke that Shanghai men would rather have oil for their hair than their wok. So you're spoilt for choice if you're looking for some glad rags. Name brands and chain stores will cost the same as at home or more, but there's a surfeit of great local shops and designers, and getting something tailor-made is a bargain.

Always try prospective purchases on as a Chinese large size is equivalent to a Western medium. Shops don't usually stock anything much bigger than that, and no shoes bigger than a (male) British size 10 (US size 10.5), so if you're looking for larger sizes you'll have to get something custom-made or head for one of the fake markets.

If you're after high-street fashions, try Raffles Mall, Nanjing Dong Lu or Huaihai Lu; if you just want something cheap and smart-looking head for a Giordano or a Uniqlo (there are branches of both at the eastern end of Nanjing Dong Lu).

Shanghai Fashion Week is no longer the joke it used to be, and draws some of the world's most famous names in fashion. It's held annually in October, with events held in Xintiandi and the parks nearby.

DESIGNER CLOTHES

If you want to see international designer clothes in showpiece stores head to Plaza 66 (see p.69), Xintiandi Style (see p.125) or the Bund. Alternatively, if you're after real designer gear on the cheap, make for the discount outlet stores (see p.128). Shanghai has produced some great local designers, who deserve your support; for stylish one-off fashions, browse the boutiques in Tianzifang and on Maoming Nan Lu and Shaanxi Nan Lu, or head up Fumin Lu.

34 Mary Ching Ferguson Lane, 376 Wukang Lu, near Hunan Lu ☎ 54652335, ⓦ mary-ching.com; map pp.60–61. Glamorous luxury footwear label crafting vampy heels, sometimes out of eye-catching material like snakeskin and lace, and starting at ¥1200. They've just branched out into bags and belts. Wed–Sun 11am–7pm.

38 Capital Joy 158 Jinxian Lu, near Maoming Nan Lu ☎ 62560134; map pp.60–61. Smart, affordable menswear from a Hong Kong designer. Off-the-peg suits start at ¥900. Daily 10am–6pm.

★ **Cha Gang** 茶缸 chágāng 70 Yongfu Lu, near Hunan Lu ☎ 64733104; map pp.60–61. Wang Yigang's unique but restrained unisex fashions and accessories, sold in a space that resembles an art gallery, are deservedly popular, though they're not cheap at around ¥800 for a top. Tues–Sun 11am–7pm.

Culture Matters CM飞跃回力国货鞋店 CM fēiyuè huílì guóhuò xiédiàn Shop 2, 15 Dongping Lu ☎ 13671882040, ⓦ fromsh.com; map pp.60–61. This is the main outlet store for two Chinese brands that have caught on with hipsters, Feiyue and Warrior sneakers: the cheap, comfortable and stylish shoes are available here in more than fifty designs, including high-top versions, and start at ¥65. They're *de rigueur* in clubs like *Shelter*. Daily 1–9pm.

Dong Liang Studio 栋梁的地图 dòngliáng de dìtú 184 Fumin Lu ☎34696926; map pp.60–61. This elegant converted house has three floors that showcase the best Chinese designers, with the more expensive and exclusive on the highest floor. Look out for evening wear by Na(too), Miss Mean and Shang Xia, and bags by Fan Fan. Plenty of artisanal jewellery on display too. Daily noon–10pm.

La Vie Courtyard 7, Lane 210, Taikang Lu ☎64453585, ⊕lavie.com.cn; map pp.60–61. A diverse collection of women's clothes, by local designer Jenny Li, that's worth rooting around for the odd gem. Prices start at around ¥300 for a top. Daily 10.30am–8.30pm.

Miss Mean 1462 Fuxing Zhong Lu ⊕missmean.cn; map pp.60–61. Floaty, Francophile dresses – girly but with an edge, from local designer Nio. Daily 11am–8.30pm.

★ **Nuomi** 糯米 nuòmǐ 196 Xinle Lu, near Donghu Lu ☎54034199; map pp.60–61; No. 12, Lane 274, Taikang Lu ☎64663952; map pp.60–61. Eco-conscious high fashion for women, made by a design collective from recycled materials; look out for the purses made from old billboard paper and elegant cotton evening dresses. Daily 10am–9pm.

Shanghai Tang 上海滩 shànghǎi tān Unit 15, Xintiandi North Block, Lane 181, Taicang Lu ☎63841601; map p.62; 868 Huaihai Zhong Lu ☎54030580; map pp.60–61; Shangri-La Hotel, 33 Fucheng Lu, Pudong ☎58776632; map p.76; ⊕shanghaitang.com. This is the only international Chinese luxury fashion brand, offering colourful, stylish chinoiserie such as silk pyjamas with embroidered dragons and the like. Home accessories and gifts are also on sale. Never mind that all their designers are foreign, and it's overpriced – it's still a lovely place to gawp. Xintiandi Mon–Thurs 11am–midnight, Fri–Sun 11am–2am; Huaihai Zhong Lu daily 10.30am–9.30pm; Shangri-La daily 10am–10pm.

Shiatzy Chen 夏姿陈 xiàzī chén 9 Zhongshan Dong Yi Lu ☎63219155, ⊕shiatzychen.com; map pp.60–61. Pleated skirts, tailored shirts and lavish evening gowns by Taiwanese designer Shiatzy Chen combine East and West with a dash of Hollywood glamour. Daily 10am–8pm.

Shirt Flag 衫旗帜 shān qízhì 1st Floor, Building 17, 50 Moganshan Lu ☎62986483, ⊕shirtflag.com; map pp.70–71. Retro, Cultural Revolution chic, casual wear and bags; so-called McStruggle images, such as lantern-jawed workers waving iPods rather than Little Red Books, predominate. This kind of stuff is regarded as pretty naff in China but it might look cool back home, and it's not too expensive, at ¥160 for a T-shirt. Tues–Sun 11am–6pm.

William the Beekeeper "养蜂人"的古着时装店 yǎngfēngrén de gǔzhuó shízhuāngdiàn 84 Fenyang Lu, near Fuxing Zhong Lu ☎131 6724 3796; map pp.60–61. This busy little store is a great place to

source distinctive vintage clothing and indie local designers, with dresses starting at ¥600. Sells honey too. Tues–Sun 11.30am–8pm.

Younik 2nd Floor, Bund 18 ☎63238688, ⊕bund18 .com; map p.40. A shiny boutique selling high-end clothes by Chinese designers. Look for Lu Lun's haute couture, Jenny Ji's embroidered textiles combined with modern shapes, and Shanghai Trio (see p.129). Daily 10am–10pm.

CHILDREN'S CLOTHES

Nihong Children's Clothing Market 霓虹儿童广场 níhóng értóng guǎngchǎng On Pu'an Lu at the junction with Jinling Lu; Ⓜ Huangpi Nan Lu; map pp.60–61. Check out this cheap underground market that has hundreds of stalls and a playground to leave the little darlings in (¥15). You can get a fancy dress costume and a sweater for your dog while you're at it. Daily 9.30am–8pm.

Rouge Baiser 299 Fuxing Xi Lu ☎64318019; map pp.60–61. Stylish children's clothing, made to order, with embroidered lotus flowers and the like. Also embroidered tunics, bedspreads and pyjamas. Mon–Sat 10.30am–6.30pm.

TAILORS AND COBBLERS

Getting some clothes or shoes made up is a recommended Shanghai experience, as it will cost so much less than at home and the artisans are skilled (provided you're clear about exactly what you are after) and quick. Either head to the South Bund Fabric Market and barter, or play it safe and spend more at one of the established places, which line Moaming Nan Lu, just south of Huaihai Lu.

Billy Shoes 比利王制作鞋工作室 bǐlìwáng zhìzuòxié gōngzuòshì 1238 Changle Lu, near Huashan Lu ☎62484881, ⊕billyshoes.com; map pp.60–61. This is *the* Shanghai cobbler. Plenty of samples, or turn up with a picture from a magazine. You won't get much change from ¥1000, and you'll have to wait up to three weeks for your shoes to be finished. Daily 10.30am–8pm.

Dave's Custom Tailoring 上海不列颠西服 shànghǎi bùlièdiān xīfú Lane 6, 288 Wuyuan Lu ☎54040001, ⊕tailordave.com; map pp.60–61. The men's dress shirts and wool suits made here are certainly not the cheapest in town (suits start at ¥4000) but English-speaking staff make it popular. Items require at least ten days and two fittings to complete. Daily 10am–7pm.

Hanyi Cheongsam 瀚艺旗袍店 hànyì qípáodiàn 221 Changle Lu ☎54042303; map pp.60–61. This *cheongsam* store isn't cheap, but it's regarded as the best; prices start at ¥1800. Daily 9.30am–9.30pm.

Silk King 真丝大王 zhēnsī dàwáng 66 Nanjing Dong Lu ☎63211869; map p.39; 1226 Huaihai Zhong Lu ☎62821533; map pp.60–61; 819 Nanjing Xi Lu ☎62150706; map pp.70–71; ⊕silkking.com. The top silk retailers in Shanghai can tailor a silk or wool suit or a

13

qipao in as little as 24 hours. Silk starts around ¥120 per metre, while cashmere is almost ten times that. All branches daily 9.30am–10pm.

★ **South Bund Fabric Market** 南外滩轻纺面料市场 nānwàitān qīngfǎng miànliào shìchǎng 399 Lujiabang Lu; map p.54. Never mind the run-down area, this market is great, with a huge choice of textiles – from denim and corduroy to bouclé and gold lamé – that can be bargained down to ¥20–50 per metre, a little more for cashmere or silk (be wary though as some of the silk is fake). In addition, most shops also have an on-site tailor (Eric Chang at no. 310 speaks English; shops that enjoy some kind of reputation include Mr Bing at 305, Jennifer at 237 and Xia Ron at 326). Come with a good idea of what you want – a photo from a fashion magazine will do, but you'll get much better results if you ask them to directly copy something you give them. If you're interested in a man's suit they'll show you a catalogue of styles. Don't be talked into buying more material than you need: a man's suit requires about 5m of material, a shirt about 1.5m. Prices vary, but expect to pay roughly ¥100 for a linen shirt, ¥120 for wool trousers, and ¥250 for a man's lined corduroy blazer. If you've bartered sharply, the total price for a man's wool suit with a spare pair of trousers will be around ¥600 – less than half what you'd pay in a local shop. It will take them around a week to make. Daily 10am–7pm.

Suits de Heart 真挚服 zhēnzhì fú Shop 1–3, 59 Maoming Nan Lu, near Huaihai Zhong Lu ☎34060822, ⓦ sh-zff.com; map pp.60–61. The experienced tailors here are known for a fanatical eye for detail and knowledge of Japanese styles. A suit here costs around ¥5000. Daily 10am–8pm.

Suzhou Cobblers 苏州鞋匠 sūzhōu xiéjiàng Room 101, 17 Fuzhou Lu ☎63217087, ⓦ suzhou-cobblers .com; map pp.60–61. Hand-embroidered slippers, bags and hand-knitted children's clothing in charming traditional designs. A pair of embroidered slippers is around ¥500. Daily 10am–6.30pm.

XY Creations Room 302, 667 Changping Lu ☎130 02195532; map pp.70–71. Stylish eveningwear from cool young tailor Lu Xiao Yu. A suit or cocktail dress will cost around ¥1000. Mon–Sat 11am–7pm.

Yanye Shoe Studio 言业制鞋 yányè zhìxié 1363 Fuxing Zhong Lu, near Baoqing Lu ☎1316 2705506; map pp.60–61. This tiny store does made-to-order shoes, starting at ¥600 or so. Choose the material from a range of leathers and plastics, and details such as depth of heel and finish. You'll have to wait twenty days before they're finished. Daily 8am–6pm.

KNICKS-KNACKS, JEWELLERY AND ACCESSORIES

Shanghai does curios, accessories and knick-knacks much better than it does antiques, with something of a craft renaissance going on. There is also some very well-designed mass-market homeware and porcelain that's worth investigating. The place to start looking is Tianzifang (see p.64), where you'll find a conveniently dense cluster of stores.

Annabel Lee 安梨家居 ānlí jiājū Unit 3, North Block, Xintiandi, 181 Taicang Lu ☎63200045, ⓦannabel-lee .com; map p.62. Chic boutique selling cashmere scarves and blankets, silk underwear and pricey souvenirs such as tissue holders. Daily 10am–8pm.

Bai Sher 摆什 bǎishè 866 Yan'an Zhong Lu, near

THE REAL DEAL

Forget the bad-quality counterfeit designer gear in the fake markets – if you know where to look, you can get **the real thing** for not much more. Just about all the world's textile production has moved to China, and it's common practice for Chinese factories to make a little more than was ordered and sell the overstock out the back door. This grey market gear makes its way, together with factory seconds, to backstreet stores, which sell it on at not much over cost price. Sometimes the label is cut or defaced, as a legal requirement, but never in such a way that it's not easy to work out.

These shops will be unpromising from the outside, quite possibly won't have a name, and will usually carry their own lines in the window, with the good stuff hung rather negligently on a rail at the back. The place to start is at Ruijin Er Lu, at the intersection with Huaihai Zhong Lu. Head south down the street then turn onto Nanchang Lu; look in any clothes shop that's busy on the way. A second concentration of these stores is on Fuxing Zhong Lu, east of Baoqing Lu. You won't find much in the way of men's clothes and you'll need patience. For a rather more regulated experience, head out of town to the outlet mall below.

Foxtown 富客斯国际购物中心 fùkèsī guójì gòuwù zhōngxīn 5885 Yexin Lu, Xinbang Town ☎57899500, ⓦ foxtown.cn. This mall of factory outlet stalls has discounts running up to about 50 percent. It's out in the suburbs, in the far west of town, so you'll need to get a cab here or pick up their shuttle bus from Xujiahu (see their website for timetable; trip takes about an hour). Daily 10am–8pm.

Shaanxi Bei Lu ☎ 13817778455; map pp.60–61. All sorts of affordable vintage, from Art Deco lamps to old doors and leather jackets. Look out for the jewellery made from old mah jong tiles, Mao badges and the like. Daily 10am–10pm.

Brocade Country 锦绣坊 jǐnxiùfǎng 616 Julu Lu ☎ 62792677; map pp.60–61. Hand-stitched tapestries (from ¥150) collected by owner Liu Xiao Lan in Miao villages, plus intricate Miao-made embroidery and handcrafted silver ornaments. Daily 10.30am–7pm.

Feicui Yuan 翡翠园 fěicuì yuán 514 Huaihai Zhong Lu, ☎ 53838099; map pp.60–61. A well-reputed jade jewellery store, much more reliable and better-value than the shops around touristy areas. Daily 10am–6pm.

Harvest Studio 盈稼坊工作室 yínjiàfǎng gōngzuòshì Room 118, No. 3, Lane 210, Taikang Lu, Tianzifang ☎ 64734566; map pp.60–61. Hand-embroidered clothing, soft furnishings, notebooks and wallets by eight resident Miao tribeswomen. Also offers embroidery classes. Daily 9.30am–8pm.

Jooi 2nd Floor, International Artist Factory, 210 Taikang Lu, Tianzifang ☎ 64736193, ⓦ jooi.com; map pp.60–61. Cute, chic bags, cushions and accessories in a diverse range of fabrics and often embroidered, all made by local artisans. Tues–Sun 10am–6pm.

Lan Yin Hua Bu Guan 蓝印花布馆 lányìnhuā bùguǎn Lane 637, 24 Changle Lu ☎ 54037947; map pp.60–61. Boutique selling handmade bags, waistcoats, tablecloths and the like made from a traditionally produced blue-and-white batik-style nankeen fabric. Daily 10am–7pm.

Madame Mao's Dowry 毛太设计 máotài shèjì 207 Fumin Lu ☎ 54033551, ⓦ madamemaosdowry.com; map pp.60–61. Cultural Revolution kitsch for the home, with Mao-related geegaws and knick-knacks aplenty. Propaganda posters from the Seventies will set you back at least ¥800; better value is the great Mao print wrapping paper (¥12 per metre). They have recently expanded into knowingly retro homeware, jewellery and clothes. Daily 10am–7pm.

Paddy Field 稻家居 dào jiā jū 30 Hunan Lu ☎ 64375567, ⓦ paddy-field.com.cn; map pp.60–61. This design emporium sells Southeast Asian-inspired homeware made from stone, leather and mother of pearl. Will also create custom furniture in about three weeks and ship internationally. Daily 10.30am–6.30pm.

Pilang Palang 噼呤啪啷 pīlíng pālāng Unit 220, Lane 210, Taikang Lu, Tianzifang ☎ 54202871,

ⓦ pilangpalang.com; map pp.60–61. China's best homeware brand now has an outlet store (admittedly tiny) in Tianzifang, and is worth seeking out for its bright and funky original porcelain, lacquer ware and cloisonné. Old Chinese forms are given a contemporary twist with modern designs, and a plate will cost around ¥100, a tray or snuffbox-shaped vase twice that. Mon–Thurs 10am–7pm, Fri–Sun 11am–9pm.

★ **Shanghai Trio** 上海组合家居店 shànghǎi zǔhé jiājūdiàn Unit 129, Xintiandi Style, 245 Madang Lu ☎ 53580188; map p.62; workshop/showroom at No. 6, Lane 37, Fuxing Xi Lu ☎ 64338901; map pp.60–61; ⓦ shanghaitrio.com.cn. Cotton and silk bags with traditional designs in vibrant colours. There's also a cute line of children's accessories, chic jewellery and wallets. Xintiandi Style Mon–Fri 10am–10pm, Sat & Sun 11am–11pm; workshop Mon–Fri 10am–7pm.

Simply Life 逸居生活 yìjū shēnghuó 159 Madang Lu, Xintiandi ☎ 63875100; map p.62; 9 Dongping Lu, ☎ 34060509; map pp.60–61; ⓦ simplylife-sh.com. One of the more affordable shops in the area, this is a good place for some speedy souvenir shopping, with Chinese-themed knick-knacks and homeware. Both branches Sun–Thurs 10.30am–10.30pm, Fri & Sat 10.30am–11.30pm.

★ **Spin** 旋陶艺 xuàn táoyì 360 Kanding Lu, near Shanxi Bei Lu ☎ 62792545; map pp.60–61. Modern ceramics from Jingdezhen – the capital of china in China, as it were. None of that chintzy "lovers on a willow bridge" stuff that your gran had, this is modern, chic and minimalist, sometimes playful. A dumpling-shaped paperweight will cost ¥60, a tulip-shaped candleholder is ¥200. Daily 11am–9.30pm.

Urban Tribe 城市山民 chéngshì shānmín 133 Fuxing Xi Lu ☎ 64335366; map pp.60–61. Ethnic clothing, pottery and jewellery, with a lovely café tucked away in the back (see p.111). Daily 9.30am–10pm.

Wholesale Pearl and Stone Market 城隍庙珍珠批发市场 chénghuángmiào zhēnzhū pīfā shìchǎng 3rd Floor, 288 Fuyou Lu, near Jiuxiachang Lu; map p.54. The stalls here sell lots of jewellery, mostly pearls. Remember to barter. Daily 10am–6pm.

Yatai Xinyang Fashion & Gift Market 亚太新阳服饰礼品市场 yàtàixīnyáng fúshì lǐpǐn shìchǎng Ⓜ Science and Technology Museum (entrance close to the ticketing machines); map p.76. For inexpensive jewellery and pearls, head here and remember to bargain (see p.78). Daily 10am–9pm.

SOUVENIRS

For souvenirs, you can't go wrong with teapots, fans, signature chops and chopsticks, and you can get them all at Yuyuan Bazaar (see p.55). But how about a tongue-in-cheek McStruggle T-shirt (Shirt Flag, see p.127); a calligraphy brush (art supply stores on Fuzhou Lu); a Peking opera costume (Nantai Costume Company, see p.130); silk slippers (Suzhou Cobblers, see p.128); Cultural Revolution picture postcards (Propaganda Poster Centre, see p.66); a replica of a ding pot

13

(Shanghai Museum shop, see p.49); a flashing Buddha (Yufo Temple, see p.72); or a model Oriental TV Tower (vendors in Huangpu Park, see p.41).

Cang Bao Lou Market 藏宝楼市场 cángbǎolóu shìchǎng 457 Fangbang Zhong Lu; map p.54. This chaotic five-storey mall is the wholesale market that supplies many of Yuyuan's shops, so everything should be a little cheaper than just outside – although you'll still have to barter hard. It's biggest at weekends and good for a souvenir blitz. Daily 8am-6pm.

Huangshan Tea Company 黄山茶业有限公司 huángshān cháyè yǒuxiàn gōngsī Basement, Hong Kong Plaza; map pp.60–61. Teapots from the famous factories at Yixing, as well as loose Chinese teas sold by weight. Vendors will let you sample all the wares. Daily 10am–10pm.

Nantai Costume Company 南泰戏剧服装用品有限公司 nántài xìjù fúzhuāng yòngpǐn yǒuxiàngōngsī 181 Henan Zhong Lu, near Fuzhou Lu ☎63238344; map p.39. With fake beards, tasselled hats and all manner of outlandish outfits, Nantai kits out both local opera troupes and expats looking for Halloween costumes. The shop mynah bird can say *ni hao*. Daily 9am–5pm.

Yaoyang Teahouse 尧阳茶行 yáoyáng cháháng Xintiandi North Block, 181 Taicang Lu ☎63556166; map p.62. Tiny shop selling speciality Chinese teas; pricier than elsewhere, but the packaging is excellent, making them good gifts. Go for Longjing from Hangzhou or Geow Yong from Fujian. Daily 10am–10pm.

ELECTRONICS, COMPUTER AND PHOTOGRAPHY EQUIPMENT

There's not much point buying big-name-brand electronics here, or anything that's near the top of the range; prices are the same as in the West, and you'll get less after-sales support. But it is worth checking out the local brands that you've probably never heard of (Lenovo is the biggest) and mid-range brands from Japan, Korea and Taiwan such as Acer.

A basic Chinese laptop costs as little as ¥2500, though it may well have build-quality issues. For twice that you can pick up one from a Korean company that will usually have an international warranty and will still cost two-thirds what it would cost in the West. But the best value is in gadgets and add-ons such as memory sticks, USB fans, webcams and the like.

Apple Store 300 Nanjing Dong Lu ☎23131800, ⓦapple.com; map p.39. The Chinese have gone nuts for the shiny fruit, with students in particular feeling social pressure to turn up to college with an "Apple three set" – Mac, iPad and iPhone. This is Asia's biggest Apple store – you'll see plenty of parents blanching at the prices. Daily 10am–10pm.

Huanlong Department Store 黄龙百货 huánglóng bǎihuò 3rd floor, 360 Meiyuan Lu, by the train station; map pp.70–71. Prices for photography equipment are not as good as in Hong Kong but still cheaper than the West. Plenty of the stores sell second-hand and studio gear, but don't get anything printed here as you can't be sure of the quality. Daily 9am–6pm.

Pacific Digital Plaza 太平洋数码广场 tàipíngyáng shùmǎ guǎngchǎng 117 Zhaojiabang Lu ☎54905900; ⓂXujiahui; map pp.86–87. A huge, three-storey mall of stalls selling international and local electronics. There is some leeway for bargaining – always compare prices. Test everything and remember that for the majority of this stuff the warranty is not valid internationally. Daily 10am–8pm.

FURNITURE

Middle-class locals might be flocking to the new IKEA, but foreign expats, it would seem, just can't get enough retro Chinese furniture, with four-poster beds, carved screens, and lacquered chairs the most popular of many lines. All shops will arrange shipping home. The majority is, of course, reproduction. See also Henry Antique Warehouse (p.125) and Paddy Field (p.129).

★ **Kava Kava Home** 吉木坊 jímù fāng 167 Anfu Lu ☎54043873, ⓦkavakavahome.com; map pp.60–61. Traditional Ming-dynasty furniture designs (including lovely medicine chests and bedframes) jazzed up with bright colours and simple lines. Daily 10am–5.30pm.

Pusu 朴素生活 púsù shēnghuó Number 15, Alley 188, Changhsu Lu ☎34619855, ⓦinpusu.com; map pp.60–61. Elegant and well-crafted wooden furniture. The lines are distinctly Chinese but there's no twiddly ornamentation. A chair will cost ¥1800, a bed ten times that. They also sell ceramics and will give a calligraphy class (¥150 for two hours). Daily 10am–10pm.

Shanghai Art Deco 阿帝克私藏家私 ādìkè sīcáng jiāsī 107 Zizhong Lu, near Jinan Lu ☎137 0164 6397; map pp.60–61. A wide choice of sleek, stylish Art Deco furniture, real and reproduction. Daily 9am–8pm.

BOOKS, CDS AND DVDS

It's not hard to find books in English in Shanghai. You can pick up those printed by local presses – usually dryly written guides, or classics – for around ¥20, though imported books are expensive at over ¥100. Fuzhou Lu is known to locals as "Book Street", but there's not much English-language material in its huge bookshops.

You can buy fake CDs and DVDs from roadside stalls in just about any backstreet. They cost ¥8 (Westerners might have to barter the vendors down) and quality is unreliable; new releases almost never work, or are grainy prints filmed in a cinema. In addition, many Western films will be dubbed into Russian – because of anti-pirating measures in the West, the counterfeiters are now copying the Russian releases. The Shanghai Grand Theatre Shop and the Foreign Language Bookstore stock plenty of authentic DVDs.

Charterhouse Basement, Times Square, 93 Huaihai Zhong Lu ☏ 63918237; map p.54; 68 Superbrand Mall, 168 Lujiazui Lu ☏ 50495155; map pp.86–87. A good English-language bookstore with an excellent selection of modern novels, nonfiction and magazines. Times Square daily 10am–9pm; Superbrand Mall 10am–10pm.

Foreign Language Bookstore 上海外文书店 shànghǎi wàiwén shūdiàn 390 Fuzhou Lu ☏ 23204994, ⓦ sbt.com.cn; map p.39. Though it's no longer the main source of English-language material, there's still a good range of books in English about China, plus audiovisual material and textbooks for those learning Chinese, maps, old film DVDs and classic fiction. Daily 9.30am–7pm.

★ **Garden Books** 韬奋西文书局 tāofèn xīwén shūdiàn 325 Changle Lu, near Shanxi Nan Lu ☏ 54048728, ⓦ gardenbooks.cn; map pp.60–61. One of the city's mellowest spaces, this is not just a good place to browse; the attached coffee shop is a great place to cast a discreet eye over both your new acquisitions and the other customers, while sampling some tasty ice cream. Fiction, art and coffee-table books. Daily 10am–10pm.

Shanghai Grand Theatre Shop Shanghai Grand Theatre, 300 Renmin Dadao, People's Square; ☏ 63728701, ⓦ shgtheatre.com; map p.49. Good selection of genuine DVDs, mostly documentaries and old films, from ¥12 to ¥30. An excellent place to complete your Hitchcock or Kurosawa collections. Daily 10am–5pm.

Around Shanghai

Shanghai being the polluted, hectic, crowded urban jungle it is, it would be a rare visitor who never felt the urge at some point to escape to fresh air, trees, and a bit of peace and quiet. Though you'll find no wilderness in the flat, wet and heavily populated outskirts, the nearby cities of Suzhou and Hangzhou are two of the most pleasant in China, and their landscaped gardens and parks will certainly restore stretched nerves; both are ideal for a two- or three-day break. A bus ride north of Hangzhou will bring you to the up-and-coming hill resort of Moganshan, which despite being only a couple of hours from Shanghai feels a world away in spirit. You'll get an even more comprehensive change of scene on the Buddhist island of Putuo Shan, a night's ferry ride from the city, with temples set in charmingly leafy surroundings. Both are great places to while away a few days.

There are a couple of worthwhile attractions closer to the city which make for ideal day-trips. At barely a hundred metres high, **She Shan**, about 30km south of Shanghai, might not be much of a hill but it does feature some interesting historic buildings. And the **canal towns** of Zhouzhuang, Tongli, Wuzhen and Xitang are attractive places to wander, though they are firmly on the tourist circuit. If at all possible, visit all these places on a weekday; on weekends, they can get crowded.

GETTING AROUND   AROUND SHANGHAI

BY TRAIN

Trains are the most efficient way of getting to the larger nearby cities. Most leave from the main railway station in the north of Shanghai (on subway lines #1, #3 and #4), though some for Hangzhou also leave from Shanghai South (on subway lines #1 and #3). Super-fast G-class trains to Beijing, Suzhou and Hangzhou leave from Hongqiao Station in the west (on subway lines #2 and #10).

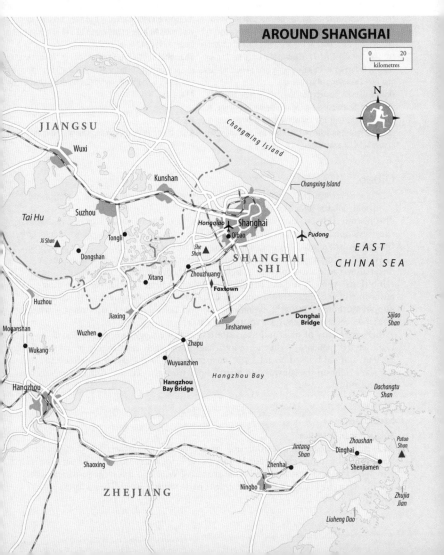

14

BUYING TRAIN TICKETS

Usually, tickets can be bought six days in advance, but they can be available as many as ten or as few as two days ahead. Advance bookings are certainly worthwhile at peak times, such as over the Spring Festival, or during the public holidays that begin on 1 May and 1 October. Most hotels will sort tickets out for you for a small fee. Note that you'll need your passport to buy a ticket.

At the station Foreigners can't use the automatic machines, so you'll have to join the queues – often long, but at least orderly – at the station ticket office.

Booking offices You can book tickets from a number of booking offices around town, for a ¥5 fee – you almost certainly won't have to queue, but no English will be spoken by the usually rather brusque staff. Handy booking offices (daily 8am–noon & 1–5pm) are at 1057 Zhonghua Lu near the Old City; 77 Wanhangdu Lu (near Jing'an Temple) in Jing'an; 627 Nanjing Dong Lu; 124 Guizhou Lu; and 1071 Zhangyang Lu in Pudong.

Online Handily, tickets for the fast G-class trains to Hangzhou, Suzhou and Beijing can be booked online at ⓦ english.ctrip.com. You pay with a debit or credit card, or you can pay cash on delivery; the tickets will be dropped off at your hotel for a small fee.

BY BUS

For some destinations, such as the canal towns, you will need to take the bus.

Sightseeing Bus Centre Numerous buses for day-trippers depart from the Shanghai Stadium Sightseeing Bus Centre at 666 Tianyaoqiao Lu (ⓣ 64265555), on the south side of Shanghai Stadium, a 10min walk from ⓜ Shanghai Stadium. Tour buses leave frequently between 7am and 10.30am, returning in the afternoon. Often a guide is provided (non-English-speaking), though you're free to wander off on your own. Tickets are available up to a week in advance if you visit the office at the bus station. You can order tickets up to 3 days in advance on the phone (freephone ⓣ 400 8872626) and they'll deliver them to your hotel for a fee of between ¥10 and ¥30. Trips to the canal towns cost around ¥150.

Shanghai South Bus Station You can pick up buses to most destinations from the Shanghai South Bus Station, by the Shanghai South Railway Station which is on metro lines #1 and #3.

BY TAXI

A day-trip to any of the canal towns will cost in the region of ¥500.

Qibao

七宝, qībǎo · Attractions open 8.30am–4.30pm · ¥45, all-inclusive ticket · Shadow-puppet Museum 皮影艺术馆, píyǐng yìshù guǎn; performances 1pm & 3pm · ⓜ Qibao

This historical theme park in the western suburbs is essentially an area of canals and alleyways lined with olde-worlde souvenir shops, renovated buildings and snack stalls. **Qibao** is worth a look if you aren't visiting one of the larger canal towns (see opposite), or you're hoping to get all your souvenir shopping done at once. The all-inclusive ticket allows access to nine tourist sights (all of them historical buildings with small exhibitions), though you can choose to pay about ¥10 at each instead. The most rewarding of the sights are the cute old **Bell Tower** (钟楼, zhōnglóu) and the **Shadow-puppet Museum** (皮影艺术馆, píyǐng yìshùguǎn). A half-hour boat trip from the wharf (游船码头, yóuchuán mǎtóu) is a reasonable ¥10.

There are plenty of stalls and little eateries, with the biggest concentration along Nan Dajie (南大街, nándàjiē) – they serve local specialities such as smoked toad (熏癞蛤蟆, xūn làiháma) and red braised pork (红烧肉, hóng shāo ròu). As the easiest way to escape the city – it's right on the subway and just an hour from the centre – Qibao gets very busy at weekends.

She Shan

余山, shéshān · ⓜ She Shan

Such is the flatness of the surrounding land some 30km southwest of Shanghai that She Shan, which only rises about 100m, is visible for miles around. The park is divided into West Hill and East Hill; the more attractive West Hill has some historical sights and the adjacent Happy Valley amusement park, while East Hill has a forest park popular with families.

West Hill

Daily 8.30am–4.30pm • Free • Bike hire ¥1/hr, deposit ¥200 • Cable car ¥10 • **Observatory** Daily 8am–5pm; ¥12 • **Happy Valley** Daily 9am–6pm; ¥200, ¥100 for kids under 1.4m, free for kids under 1.2m • Free shuttle bus from Ⓜ She Shan stops at West Hill and Happy Valley, running every 20min 9am–3pm

It's a pleasant walk up West Hill at any time of year through dense bamboo forest, or you can hire a bike at the entrance (you will need your passport for ID). The less energetic can ride a cable car. The peak here is crowned by an impressive **basilica**, a legacy of nineteenth-century European missionary work – She Shan has been under the ownership of a Catholic community since the 1850s – though the present church was not built until 1925. Also on the hill are a meteorological station and an old **observatory**, the latter containing a small exhibition room displaying an ancient earthquake-detecting device – a dragon with steel balls in its mouth that is so firmly set in the ground that only movement of the earth itself, from the vibrations of distant earthquakes, can cause the balls to drop out. The more balls that fall, the more serious the earthquake.

Just behind West Hill is the enormous **Happy Valley amusement park**. It boasts six rollercoasters, including a kilometre-long wooden boneshaker. This place is a little ramshackle, but clean, and gets really busy at weekends and school holidays. Kids will love it.

East Hill

Daily 8am–6pm • ¥45 • Sculpture park ¥120, ¥50 for kids under 1.4m • Row boats ¥60/hr • 10min walk from Ⓜ She Shan

East Hill has been redeveloped as a woodland park and includes the artificial Moon Lake. A ten-minute walk west from the entrance brings you to a **sculpture park**. There's nothing particularly distinguished about the thirty or so works of art, but they serve as handy way-stations on a pleasant walk. With a long **beach**, manicured lawns and plenty of **playgrounds**, this makes a good retreat for kids and is busy with families at the weekend. If you would rather escape the crowds, just head uphill into the woods.

The canal towns

An extensive canal system once transported goods all around imperial China, and the attractive water towns that grew up around them – notably **Zhouzhuang**, **Xitang**, **Wuzhen** and **Tongli** – present some of eastern China's most distinctive urban environments. Whitewashed Ming and Qing timber buildings back onto the narrow waterways crossed by charming humpback stone bridges; travel is by foot or punt, as the alleys are too narrow for cars.

Today, these sleepy towns are a popular escape from the city, and each has become a nostalgia theme park for the urban sophisticate. They're fine as day-trips but don't expect much authenticity – there are far more comb shops than dwellings – and don't come on weekends, when they're overrun. All charge an **entrance fee**, which also gets you into the historical buildings, mostly the grand old houses of wealthy merchants.

Zhouzhuang

周庄, zhōuzhuāng • Entrance fee ¥100

Twenty kilometres southwest of the city, just across the border into Jiangsu Province, **ZHOUZHUANG** is the most accessible of the canal towns. It lies astride the large Jinghang Canal connecting Suzhou and Shanghai, and grew prosperous from the area's brisk grain, silk and pottery trade during the Ming dynasty. Many rich government officials, scholars and artisans moved here and constructed beautiful villas, while investing money into developing the stately stone bridges and tree-lined canals that now provide the city's main attractions.

The biggest mansion is the **Shen House** (沈厅, shěntīng; daily 8am–4.30pm) in the east of town, built in 1742. Over a hundred rooms (not all of them open) are

14

connected by covered colonnades, with grand public halls at the front and the more intimate family chambers at the back. Period furnishings help evoke a lost age of opulence, though it is all rather dark; the neat gardens offer a pleasant contrast. An exhibition of **folk instruments** in the Xiaotong Tower at the rear is worth seeking out, as is the nearby statue of the mansion's founder, Shen, looking rather pleased with himself.

Zhouzhuang's most highly rated views are of the pretty sixteenth-century twin **stone bridges** in the northeast of town. Also firmly on the itinerary are a **boat ride** round the canals (¥80/hr; you'll have to be firm if you don't want to be serenaded) and **lunch** – there is no shortage of restaurants, all offering the local specialities of pig's thigh, meatballs and clams as a set meal (around ¥60 per head).

ARRIVAL AND DEPARTURE	ZHOUZHUANG

By bus Buses depart from the Sightseeing Bus Centre (see p.134) at 7am, 8.30am, 9am, 9.30am and 10am and take 1hr 30min. They return between 4.30pm and 5.30pm.

Xitang

西塘, xītáng • Entrance fee ¥50; ¥100 including all sights; free entry on Sunday afternoon and Friday morning

XITANG, 60km southwest of Shanghai, was popularized by its appearance in *Mission Impossible III*, and you won't forget the fact – there are posters of Tom Cruise all over the place. Though short on specific sights, the lanes, canals and bridges are undeniably picturesque. And if it rains, at least you'll be dry: the locals, tired of the wet climate, built roofs over the main alleyways – the biggest is over a kilometre long, running alongside the central canal. Many of the buildings are now restaurants serving up local specialities such as pork with sweet potatoes. If you tire of walking, you can hire a cycle rickshaw – ¥100 for forty minutes.

ARRIVAL AND DEPARTURE	XITANG

By bus The bus from the Sightseeing Bus Centre (see p.134) leaves at 8.45am and returns at 4pm; the journey takes two hours. To get here under your own steam, take a bus from the South Bus Station (see p.134), to Jiashan (hourly; ¥28), then take one of the many minibuses for the short hop to Xitang.

ACCOMMODATION

Jinshui Lou Ge 近水 楼 阁 客 栈 jìnshuǐlóugé kèzhàn 10 Chaonan Dai ☎ 133 75731700. A small and cosy B&B whose rooms are full of repro Ming-dynasty furniture and have canal views. **¥570**

Xitang Youth Hostel 西塘国际青年旅舍 xītáng guójì qīngnián lǔshè 6 Tangjia Lane, off Xi Xia Jie ☎ 0512 65218885. Inexpensive accommodation can be found at this hostel on the west side of town, offering simple rooms and dorms. Dorm **¥50**, room **¥140**

Tongli

同里, tónglǐ • Entrance fee ¥80

Of all the canal towns, **TONGLI**, around eighty kilometres from Shanghai, has the best sights, and with more than forty humpback bridges (some more than a thousand years old) and fifteen canals it offers plenty of photo ops. The town's highlight is the UNESCO-listed **Tuisi Garden** on Beitu Lu (退思园, tuìsī yuán; daily 8am–6pm; ¥40), built by disillusioned retired official Ren Lansheng in 1886 as a place to retreat and meditate – though you'll have to come in the early morning, before the tour groups arrive, to appreciate the peacefulness of the place. With its harmonious arrangements of rockeries, pavilions and bridges, zigzagging over carp-filled ponds, it is comparable to anything in Suzhou. The nearby **Sex Museum** (中华性文化博物馆, zhōnghuá xìngwénhuà bówùguǎn; daily 8am–5.30pm; ¥20) has some intriguing exhibits – figurines of Tang-dynasty prostitutes, special coins for use in brothels, and a wide range of dildos. Some of the sex toys are over two thousand years old.

ARRIVAL AND DEPARTURE

By bus From Shanghai South Bus Station (see p.134), there are frequent buses to Tongli, which take two hours.

Also there are day-trips from the Shanghai Sightseeing Bus Centre which leave at 8:30am.

Wuzhen

乌镇, wūzhèn • Entrance fee to the west side ¥150 (¥80 after 6pm); entrance fee to the east side ¥80

Being a little further out from Shanghai than the other canal towns, **WUZHEN** is a little less busy and has also benefitted from recent restoration. The town is especially nice **at night**, when most of the visitors have left and the town is bathed in a romantic glow by lanterns – if you're planning to overnight in a water town, this is a good one to pick.

14

Wuzhen is divided into two areas, twenty minutes apart; the western section is the larger and more interesting, and is home to all the attractions described here. Prime draw is the cute little **Xiuzhen Taoist Temple** and its collection of folk art, including intricate wood-carvings and leather shadow-puppets which you can watch in action at the nearby playhouse (hourly shows 10am–5pm).

The town was once very well to do, and many of its grand residences have survived well and now act as museums or studios where local crafts such as silk painting or printing using dyes made from tea leaves are demonstrated. The **Xu Family Hall** on Dongzha Jie paints a vivid picture of genteel nineteenth-century Chinese country life with its darkly furnished, creaking interior and tables bearing tea cups as if the owners have just left. **The Bed Museum** (江南 百床馆, jiāngnán bǎichuángguǎn), also in a grand old house on Dongzha Jie, displays four-poster, enclosed antique beds that are extravagantly decorated though not very comfortable looking. The most lavish is the hyperbolic Qing-dynasty "bed of a thousand workers", which took dozens of craftsmen three years to make. Most of the carvings feature motifs that signify health and longevity – bats, turtles and double-happiness symbols.

The **Fanglu Pavilion** (访卢阁, fǎnglúgé), at 143 Changfeng Jie near the centre of town just to the south of Ying Bridge, is a teahouse with picturesque views over the canal, which makes a good place for a rest, though as ever in these places, you won't find it cheap (¥48 a pot).

ARRIVAL AND DEPARTURE
WUZHEN

By bus If you're coming on a day-trip, catch a sightseeing bus from Shanghai Stadium (see p.134); otherwise,

there are frequent buses from the South Bus Station (1hr 30min).

ACCOMMODATION

Wuzhen Guesthouse 乌镇民宿 wùzhèn minus Front desk at 137 Xizha Jie ☎573 88731230, ⊛wuzhen .com.cn. Quaint properties all over town, run in B&B style

by local families, who will cook your meals for you. It's worth paying a little extra for a riverside view. ¥380

Suzhou

苏州, sūzhōu

SUZHOU, about ninety kilometres west of Shanghai, is famous for its gardens, beautiful women and silk. The city is said to have been founded in 600 BC by He Lu, semi-mythical ruler of the Kingdom of Wu, as his capital, but it was the arrival of the **Grand Canal** more than a thousand years later that marked the beginning of its prosperity as a centre for the production of wood block and the weaving of silk. In the late thirteenth century, Marco Polo reported "six thousand bridges, clever merchants, cunning men of all crafts, very wise men called Sages and great natural physicians". These were the people responsible for carving out the intricate **gardens** that are now Suzhou's primary attractions.

Suzhou is an easy place in which to get your bearings. Renmin Lu, the main street, zooms south through the centre from the train station. The traditional commercial

14

> ## CHINESE GARDENS
>
> Gardens, above all, are what Suzhou is all about. They have been laid out here since the Song dynasty, a thousand years ago, and in their Ming and Qing heyday it is said that the city had two hundred of them.
>
> Chinese gardens do not set out to improve upon a slice of nature or to look natural. As with painting, sculpture and poetry, the aim is to produce for contemplation the **balance**, **harmony**, **proportion** and **variety** which the Chinese seek in life. Little pavilions and terraces are used to suggest a larger scale, undulating covered walkways and galleries to give a downward view, and intricate interlocking groups of rock and bamboo to hint at, and half conceal, what lies beyond. Almost everything you see has some symbolic significance – the pine tree and the crane for long life, mandarin ducks for married bliss, for example.

centre, **Guang Chedao**, lies around Guanqian Jie, halfway down Renmin Lu, the centre of an area of cramped, animated streets thronged with small shops, teahouses and restaurants.

The three most famous gardens – **Wangshi Yuan**, **Shizi Lin** and **Zhuozheng Yuan** – attract a stream of visitors to the city year-round, but many of the equally beautiful yet lesser-known gardens, notably **Canglang Ting** and **Ou Yuan**, are comparatively serene and crowd-free. Seasons make surprisingly little difference as the gardens can be appreciated at any time of year, although springtime brings more blossom and brighter colours. Suzhou also has some rather charming **temples** and **pagodas**, and a couple of decent **museums**.

Beisi Ta

北寺塔, běisì tǎ · Renmin Lu · Daily 7.45am–5pm · ¥25 · Bus #4 from the station

Just south of the train station, the sixteenth-century **Beisi Ta** (North Temple Pagoda) looms up unmistakeably. At 76m the pagoda is the tallest Chinese pagoda south of the Yangzi, though it retains only nine of its original eleven storeys. Climbing it gives an excellent view over some of Suzhou's more conspicuous features – the Shuang Ta, the Xuanmiao Guan, and, in the far southwest corner, the Ruiguang Ta. There's also a pleasant teahouse on site.

Suzhou Silk Museum

丝绸博物馆, sūzhōu bówùguǎn · 2001 Renmin Lu · Daily 9am–5pm · ¥15 · ☎ 0512 82112636, ⓦ szsilkmuseum · Buses #1, #102

This is one of China's better-presented museums, labelled in English throughout. Starting from the legendary inventor of silk, Lei Zu, the concubine of the equally legendary emperor Huang Di, it traces the history of silk production and its use from 4000 BC to the present day. There are displays of looms and weaving machines, and reproductions of early silk patterns, but the most riveting display – and something of a shock – is the room full of silkworms munching mulberry leaves and spinning cocoons, and copulating moths.

Suzhou Museum

苏州博物馆, sūzhōu bówùguǎn · 204 Dongbei Jie · Tues–Sun 9am–4pm · Free · ☎ 0512 67575666, ⓦ szmuseum.com

Suzhou seems very proud of the **Suzhou Museum**; you'll see plenty of pictures of it around town. It was designed by "starchitect" I.M. Pei, and is the most successful attempt at updating Suzhou's characteristic white-wall and black-beam building style. The collection is small but choice, and there are plenty of English captions. Some exquisitely delicate China and jade pieces are displayed in the first two galleries – look out for the ugly toad carved out of jasper – but the museum's highlight is the craft gallery which holds some fantastically elaborate bamboo-root carvings of Buddhist scenes. There are also temporary displays in the modern art gallery.

SUZHOU

SHOPS
The Antique Store	2
King Silk Store	1

RESTAURANTS & CAFÉS
Bookworm	4
Mingtown	2
Songhelou Caiguan	3
Waterfront Teahouse	1
Xinjiang Yakexi	5

ACCOMMODATION
Archi Garden	1
Bamboo Grove	4
Mingtown Suzhou Youth Hostel	2
Pan Pacific	5
Pingjiang Lodge	3

Train Station

Train Ticket Office

XIHUI LU

North Bus Station

Tourist Boat Jetty

PINGQI LU

Zhouzhuang & Shanghai

Bike Rental

Suzhou Silk Museum

Beisi Ta

Bike Rental

XIBEI JIE

QIMEN LU

Zhuozheng Yuan

Suzhou Museum

DONGBEI JIE

Shizi Lin

YUANLIN LU

PINGJIANG LU

BAITA DONG LU

RENMIN LU

BAITA XI LU

LINDUN LU

DONG ZHONGSHI

CANG JIE

Ou Yuan

ZHONGJIE LU

Bank of China

Xuanmiao Guan

Museum of Opera & Theatre

ZHONGZHANGJIA XIANG

JINGDE LU

GUANQIAN JIE

GONG XIANG

TAIJIAN LANE

Cang Jie

GANJIANG DONG LU

CITS

Yi Yuan

Renmin Lu

Lundun Lu

Shuang Ta

Yangyu Xiang

GANJIANG XI LU

Renmin Lu

FENGHUANG JIE

No. 1 Hospital

YANGYU XIANG

PSB

WUZHOU LU

SHIZI JIE

@

DAOQIAN JIE

GUNXIU FANG

SIQUAN JIE

DONG DAJIE

RENMIN LU

Canglang Ting

SHIQUAN JIE

DAICHENGQIAO LU

Wangshi Yuan

Bike Rental

ZHUHUI LU

PANMEN LU

XINSHI LU

Ruiguang Ta

Pan Men

Nanmen Dock

NANYUAN NAN LU

Guang Chadao and Ligong Di

Wumen Qiao

NANMEN LU

RENMIN NAN LU

DONG QING LU

Tongli

NANHUAN DONG LU

South Bus Station

0   500
metres

BAR
Goodfellas	1

N

The **Prince Zhong Residence**, adjacent to the museum and included in the same ticket, is a traditional courtyard house turned exhibition hall. The small rooms show Ming and Qing furniture, rare books, and a display on the Taiping Rebellion, in which the house's original owner was involved. The most engrossing display is on Chinese opera, and includes a little theatre and costumes.

Zhuozheng Yuan

拙政园, zhuózhèng yuán • Dongbei Jie • Daily 7.30am–5.30pm • ¥70 • ☏ 0512 67537002, Ⓦ szzy.cn

At forty thousand square metres, the **Zhuozheng Yuan** (Humble Administrator's Garden) is the largest garden in the city. It is based on water and set out in three linked sections: the eastern part (just inside the entrance) consists of a small lotus pond and pavilions; the centre is largely water, with two small islands connected by zigzag bridges; while the western part has unusually open green spaces. Built at the time of the Ming by an imperial censor, Wang Xianchen, who had just resigned his post, the garden was named by its creator as an ironic lament on the fact that this was now all he could administer.

Shizi Lin

狮子林, shīzi lín • 23 Yuanling Lu • Daily 7.30am–5.30pm • ¥30 (¥20 Nov–March) • Buses #2, #4, #5

One of Suzhou's must-see gardens, **Shizi Lin** (Lion Grove) was laid out by monk Tian Ru in 1342 and largely consists of rocks that are supposed to resemble lions. Part of the rockery takes the form of a convoluted labyrinth, from the top of which you emerge occasionally to gaze down at the water reflecting the trees and stones.

Xuanmiao Guan

玄妙观, xuánmiàoguān • At the start of Gong Chedao on Guanqian Jie • Mon–Fri 7.30am–4.30pm • ¥20 • Buses #1, #2, #20, #101 to Guanqian Jie from where it's a short walk

The **Xuanmiao Guan** (Taoist Temple of Mystery) stands rather incongruously at the heart of the modern city's consumer zone. Founded during the Jin dynasty in the third century AD, the temple has been destroyed, rebuilt, burnt down and put back together many times during its history. Nowadays the attractive complex basically consists of a vast entrance court full of resting locals with, at its far end, a hall of Taoist deities and symbols – the whole thing encircled by a newly constructed park.

Yi Yuan

怡园, yíyuán • 1265 Renmin Lu • Daily 7.30am–midnight • ¥4 • Buses #1, #8, #32, #38, #502

A few minutes south of Guanqian Jie is one of the lesser gardens, **Yi Yuan** (Joyous Garden), laid out in the late Qing dynasty by official Gu Wenbin. Considerably newer than the others, it is supposed to encompass all the key features of a Chinese garden; unusually, it also has formal flowerbeds and arrangements of coloured pebbles.

The Museum of Opera and Theatre

戏曲博物馆, xìqǔ bówùguǎn • 14 Zhongjia Chedao • Daily 8.30am–4.30pm • Free • Performances Sun 2pm; ¥30 • ☏ 0512 67275338 • Buses #202, #204

A ten-minute walk along narrow lanes due east from the end of Guanqian Jie, the unusual **Museum of Opera and Theatre** stands on Zhongzhangjia Xiang. The rooms are filled with costumes, masks, musical instruments, and even a full-sized model orchestra, complete with cups of tea, though the building itself is the star, a Ming-dynasty theatre made of latticed wood. The Suzhou area is the home of the 5000-year-old **Kun opera** style, China's oldest operatic form. Kun is distinguished by storytelling and ballad singing but can be hard to follow (even if you speak Chinese) as it is performed in the obscure Suzhou dialect. Performances, which last an hour and a half, can be seen in the classical building; just turn up and buy a ticket before the show.

Ou Yuan

耦园, ǒuyuán • 5–9 Xiaoxinqiao Chedao • Daily 8am–5pm • ¥20 • Buses #301, #305, #701

Abutting the outer moat and along a canal, the **Ou Yuan** is a quiet garden, free from tour groups. Here a series of hallways and corridors opens onto an intimate courtyard, with a pond in the middle surrounded by abstract rock formations and relaxing teahouses.

Shuang Ta

双塔, shuāng tǎ • 22 Dingshui Chedao • Daily 7am–4.30pm • ¥4 • Buses #2, #5, #27, #68

Several blocks east of Renmin Lu and immediately south of Ganjiang Dong Lu, the **Shuang Ta** (Twin Pagodas) are matching slender towers built during the Song dynasty by a group of successful candidates in the imperial examinations who wanted to honour their teacher. The teahouse here is crowded in summer with old folk fanning themselves against the heat.

Canglang Ting

沧浪亭, cānglàng tíng • 3 Canglangting Jie • Daily 7.30am–5.30pm • ¥20 • ☎ 0512 65293190 • Buses #1, #14, #28, #701

South of Shiquan Jie, the intriguing **Canglang Ting** (Dark Blue Wave Pavilion) is the oldest of the major surviving gardens. Originally built by scholar Su Zimei around 1044 AD, it's approached through a grand stone bridge and ceremonial marble archway. The curious Five Hundred Sage Temple in the south of the garden is lined with stone tablets recording the names and achievements of Suzhou's statesmen, heroes and poets.

Wangshi Yuan

网师园, wǎngshī yuán • 11 Touxiang Chedao • Daily March–Nov 7am–10pm; Dec–Feb 7.30am–5.30pm • ¥30, ¥80 in the evening including performance • ☎ 051 265293190 • Buses #2, #4, #14

The intimate **Wangshi Yuan** (Master of the Nets Garden) lies down a narrow alleyway on the south side of Shiquan Jie. The garden, so named because the owner, a retired official, decided he wanted to become a fisherman, was started in 1140, but was later abandoned and not restored to its present layout until 1770. Considered by garden connoisseurs to be the finest of them all, it boasts an attractive central lake, minuscule connecting halls, pavilions with pocket-handkerchief courtyards and carved wooden doors – and rather more visitors than it can cope with. The garden is said to be best seen on moonlit nights, when the moon can be seen three times over from the Moon-watching Pavilion – in the sky, in the water and in a mirror. Other features include its delicate latticework and fretted windows. Between March and November, Wangshui Yuan also plays host to nightly performances of Chinese performing arts, from Beijing opera to folk dancing and storytelling.

Pan Men and around

盘门, pánmén • 1 Dong Dajie • Daily 8am–4.45pm • ¥25 • Bus #7 from the train station passes the southern edge of the moat

In the far southwestern corner of the moated area is one of the city's most pleasant areas, centred around **Pan Men** (Coiled Gate) and a stretch of the original city wall, built in 514 BC; the gate is the only surviving one of eight that once surrounded Suzhou. The best approach is from the south, via **Wumen Qiao** (吴门桥, wúmén qiáo), a delightful high-arched bridge (the tallest in Suzhou) with steps built into it; it's a great vantage point for watching the canal traffic. Just inside Pan Men sits the dramatic **Ruiguang Ta** (瑞光塔, ruìguāng tǎ), a thousand-year-old pagoda now rebuilt from ruins, once housing a rare Buddhist pearl stupa (since moved to the Suzhou Museum).

ARRIVAL AND DEPARTURE **SUZHOU**

By train From Shanghai Hongqiao train station, frequent and fast G-class trains (hourly) make the run to Suzhou in 40min. Normal trains are more frequent, and take an hour. From the train station, you can get into town on buses #1 and #20.

By bus Buses to Suzhou leave every half-hour from Shanghai South Bus Station and Hengfeng Lu Station by

14

the main train station, and take almost two hours. In Suzhou, the North Bus Station (北公共汽车站 běi gōnggòng qìchēzhàn), which has half-hourly connections with Shanghai, is directly to the east of the train station (which is where buses from Hengfeng Station arrive). The South Bus Station (南公共汽车站 nán gōnggòng qìchēzhàn), which sees arrivals from points south including Hangzhou and Zhouzhuang, is at the junction between Nanyuan Dong Lu and Yingchun Lu. Buses #29 and #101 run into town, or it's ¥11 in a cab.

GETTING AROUND

By bus Buses are a cheap way to get around though as ever watch your pockets. There are no English announcements or signs. Note the *pinyin* for your stop – written on the timetable at the bus stop – and listen out for the onboard announcement.

By bike The best way to get around is by rented bike, which'll cost around ¥30 for a day with a deposit of a few hundred yuan. There are many bike rental places along Shiquan Jie and a couple on Renmin Lu.

INFORMATION, TOURS AND BOAT TRIPS

CITS Next to the Lexiang Hotel on Dajing Lu ☎0512 65155207. Various city tours can be arranged by CITS. Mon–Sat 8.30am–5.30pm.

Boat trips Canal boat tours of the city cost from ¥120 and can be arranged at Nanmen dock and booths just south of Zhuozheng Yuan. Trips last an hour and include a performance of traditional Suzhou singing. Enterprising boatmen will also offer you a ride – it's around ¥100 per boat for a 40min trip.

Minibus tours Tours of the city, on which you get ferried to all the sights (without commentary), depart from the train station square at 7.30am and return at 4.30pm. Just turn up or book in advance at the tourist office (¥15 exclusive of admission charges).

ACCOMMODATION

The main hotel area, and the heaviest concentration of gardens and historic buildings, is in the south of the city, around Shiquan Jie. Out of season (Oct–May), you should be able to get a discount of at least 20 percent if you ask.

★ **Archi Garden** 筑园 zhúyuán 31 Pingjiang Lu ☎0512 65810618, ⓦarchi-garden.com. A place for Suzhou's artier visitors, featuring just four spartan but immaculate rooms – think sliding doors, white linen and an atmosphere so quiet you could hear a pin drop. The lobby also functions as a café, gallery and style-book library. Highly recommended. **¥450**

Bamboo Grove 竹辉饭店 zhúhuī fàndiàn 168 Zhuhui Lu ☎0512 65205601, ⓦbg-hotel.com. A tour-group favourite, this efficient if rather old-fashioned Japanese-run four-star imitates local style with black and white walls and abundant bamboo in the garden. There are a couple of good restaurants on site. **¥988.**

Mingtown Suzhou Youth Hostel 28 Pingjiang Lu ☎0512 65816869. An attractive courtyard and local-style buildings make this the most appealing budget option in town. Doubles are very stylish for the price though dorms can be stuffy. Bike rental for ¥30 a day. Dorm **¥60**, double **¥205**

Pan Pacific 吴宫喜来登酒店 wúgōng xǐláidēng jiǔdiàn 259 Xinshi Lu, near Pan Men in the southwest of town ☎0512 65103388, ⓦpanpacific.com. This pastiche Chinese mansion sprawls over two city blocks and, though the building is old, it is still the most attractive choice in its range thanks to the large rooms and charming gardens. Indoor and outdoor swimming pools are a plus. Heavy discounts available online. **¥880**

Pingjiang Lodge 平江客栈 píngjiāng kèzhàn 33 Pingjiang Lu ☎0512 65233888, ⓦthe-silk-road.com. This appealingly rustic venue seeks to re-create the charm of old Suzhou, with traditionally styled rooms. It's popular with Chinese families. **¥450**

RESTAURANTS AND CAFÉS

Suzhou cooking, with its emphasis on fish from the nearby lakes and rivers, is justly renowned; specialities include *yinyu* ("silver fish") and *kaobing* (grilled pancakes with sweet filling). The town is well stocked with restaurants for all budgets. There are a number of restaurants of repute on Taijian Lane, each claiming more than one hundred years of history and good for a splurge on local dishes – *Songhelou Caiguan* (see below) is the best.

Bookworm 老书虫 lǎoshū chóng 77 Gunxiu Fang, at the corner and round the back of Shiquan Jie ☎0152 50074471, ⓦsuzhoubookworm.com. Like the original in Beijing, this place is ground zero for local expats, and popular with locals too. Just pop by for coffee or an evening drink, or take part in the many events that they organize such as art and literary festivals, open mics, and pub quizzes. Daily 9am–midnight.

Mingtown 明堂 míngtáng 28 Pingjiang Lu ☎0512 65816869. Just down the road from the youth hostel (see opposite), *Mingtown* is popular with backpackers on account of its tasty food, decent coffee and only-slightly-wonky pool table. Good for a Western breakfast (¥20–28). Turns into a bar of sorts in the evening. Daily 8am–11pm.

Songhelou Caiguan 松鹤楼菜馆 sōnghèlóu càiguǎn Taijian Lane, just south of Xuanmiao Guan ☎ 0512 67700688. The most famous restaurant in town, it claims to be old enough to have served Qing Emperor Qianlong, who reigned 1736–95. The menu is elaborate and long on fish and seafood (crab, eel, squirrel fish and the like), though not cheap at around ¥150 a head. There are four more good places nearby on Taijian Lane (see p.139).

Daily 11am–2pm & 5–8.30pm.

Waterfront Teahouse 运河茶馆 yùnhé cháguǎn 36 Pingjiang Lu. Traditional canal-side venue. Get a seat on the outside veranda, and take in the local canal life over a latte or herbal tea. Daily 8am–8pm.

Xinjiang Yakexi 新疆亚克西酒楼 xīnjiāng yǎkèxī jiǔlóu 768 Shiquan Jie ☎ 0512 65291798, ⓦ szyakexi .com. Xinjiang comfort food – pulled noodles with vegetables (*latiaozi*) and *naan* bread, among others – in a bright dining room bustling with local Uyghurs and tourists (mains ¥20–30). Also sells lamb kebabs cooked on a grill outside for just ¥4. Daily 9am–midnight.

BARS, CLUBS AND ENTERTAINMENT

The town is developing a vibrant nightlife, with the oldest bars (as well as the oldest profession) along Shiquan Jie. However, the Ligong Di area (especially the 1912 Bar Street) on the southeastern corner of Jinji Lake is fast overtaking it as the nightlife centre of the city, especially with the expat community, due to its many new bars, clubs and various international restaurants. The *Bookworm* and *Mingtown* (see p.142) are good for a drink too. There's a nightly opera extravaganza at *Wangshi Yuan* (see p.141).

Goodfellas 菲拉主题吧 fēilā zhǔtíba A9, 1912 Bar Street ☎ 0512 62962789, ⓦ southerncrosssz.com. The best of the foreigner-friendly bars in this area, *Goodfellas* has live music (Tues–Sat 9pm–1am) on its ample stage, as

well as pool and darts, and dancing later in the night. Has a good range of foreign drafts as well as some fine cocktails. Daily 6.30pm–2am.

SHOPPING

There are numerous opportunities to shop for silk, paintings and embroidery in Suzhou, although be aware of outrageous prices, especially in the boutiques along Shiquan Jie and Guanyin Jie, and the night market on Shi Lu. Bargain hard, as these sellers can quote prices up to ten times the going rate.

King Silk Store 丝绸博物馆 sīchóu bówùguǎn 2001 Renmin Lu. This silk shop next to the Silk Museum has a good selection, including great duvets starting at just over ¥300. Daily 9am–5pm.

The Antique Store 1208 Renmin Lu ☎ 0512 65233851. Sells jade, jewellery and reproduction antique furniture; there's some room for bargaining. Daily 9am–5pm.

DIRECTORY

Banks and exchange The Bank of China head office (daily 8.15am–5.15pm) is at 1450 Renmin Lu, in the centre of town, just north of Guanqian Jie and has money exchange and international ATMs.

Hospital The best hospital in the city for foreigners is the Suzhou Kowloon Hospital (上海交通大学医学院苏州九龙医院, shànghǎi jiāotōng dàxué yīxuéyuàn sūzhōu jiǔlóng yīyuàn) at 118 Wangsheng Jie about a ¥60 taxi-ride from the centre in

the Suzhou Industrial Park Zone.

Internet The best place to find internet cafés is on Moye Lu, at the east end of Shiquan Jie; an hour costs about ¥2.50. Most cafés, bars and hotels will have wi-fi and often have computers you can use.

Mail Suzhou's main post office (daily 9am–6pm) is at the corner of Renmin Lu and Jingde Lu.

PSB At 201 Renmin Lu, at the junction with the small lane Dashitou Xiang.

Hangzhou
杭州, hángzhōu

HANGZHOU, one of China's most established tourist attractions, lies in the north of Zhejiang Province at the head of Hangzhou Bay, two hours by train from Shanghai South Station. The modern city is not of much interest in itself, but **Xi Hu** – the lake around which Hangzhou curls – and its shores still offer wonderful Chinese vistas of trees, hills, flowers, old causeways over the lake, fishing boats, pavilions and pagodas.

14

14

With the building of the Grand Canal at the end of the sixth century, Hangzhou became the centre for trade between north and south China, and the Yellow and Yangzi river basins. During the **Song dynasty**, it was made the **imperial capital**, setting off a boom in all the trades that waited upon the court, particularly silk. Marco Polo, writing of Hangzhou towards the end of the thirteenth century, spoke of "the City of Heaven, the most beautiful and magnificent in the world." Though its role as imperial capital ceased when the Southern Song dynasty was overthrown by the Mongols in 1279, it remained an important centre of commerce. **Ming** rulers repaired the city walls and deepened the Grand Canal so that large ships could go all the way from Hangzhou to Beijing, and two great **Qing** emperors, Kangxi and Qianlong, built villas, temples and gardens by the lake. Although largely destroyed in the Taiping Rebellion (see p.160), it recovered quickly, and the **foreign concessions** that were established towards the end of the century – followed by the building of rail lines from Shanghai and Ningbo – stimulated the growth of new industries alongside traditional silk and brocade manufacturing.

Orientation

Broadly, the city has two halves; to the east and north of the lake is **downtown**, with its shops and tourist facilities, while to the west and south you'll find greenery and scenic spots. The commercial centre of town is the area around the Jiefang Lu/Yan'an Lu intersection, where you'll find accommodation, restaurants and shops; buses around the lake also leave from here.

Within the lake are various **islands** and causeways, while the shores are home to endless **parks** holding Hangzhou's most famous individual sights. These range from the extravagant and historic **Yuefei Mu** (Tomb of Yuefei) to the ancient hillside Buddhist carvings of **Feilai Feng** and its associated temple, the **Lingyin Temple**, one of China's largest and most renowned. Farther afield, beautiful tea plantations nestle around the village of **Longjing**, while south down to the **Qiantang River** are excellent walking opportunities.

Xi Hu

西湖, xīhú

Xi Hu forms a series of landscapes with rocks, trees, grass and lakeside buildings all reflected in the water and backed by luxuriant wooded hills. The lake itself stretches just over 3km from north to south and just under 3km from east to west, though the surrounding parks and associated sights spread far beyond this. On a sunny day the colours are brilliant, but even with grey skies and choppy waters, the lake views are soothing and tranquil; for the Chinese they are also laden with literary and historic associations. Although the crowds and hawkers are sometimes distracting, the area is so large that you can find places to escape the hubbub.

As early as the Tang dynasty, efforts were made to control the waters of the lake using dykes and locks, and the two **causeways** that now cross sections of the lake, **Bai Di** across the north and **Su Di** across the west, originated in these ancient embankments. Mainly used by pedestrians and cyclists, the causeways offer instant escape from the noise and smog of the built-up area to the east. The western end of Bai Di supposedly offers the best vantage point over the lake.

Bai Di and Gu Shan

白堤, báidī · 孤山, gūshān · **Zhejiang Provincial Museum** 浙江博物馆, zhèjiāng bówùguǎn · 25 Gushan Lu · Tues–Sun 8.30am–4.30pm · Free · ☎ 0571 87980281, ⓦ zhejiangmuseum.com · **Xiling Seal Engravers' Society** 西泠印社, xīlíng yìnshè · Gushan Lu · Daily 9am–5pm · ¥5 · Bus #850

Bai Di is the shorter and more popular of the two causeways, about 1500m in length. Starting in the northwest of the lake near the *Shangri-La* hotel, it runs along the outer edge of Gu Shan before crossing back to the northeastern shore, enclosing a small strip known as Beili Hu (North Inner Lake).

The little island of **Gu Shan** in the middle of the causeway is one of Hangzhou's highlights, a great place to relax under a shady tree. Dotted with pavilions and pagodas, this tiny area was originally landscaped under the Tang, but the present style dates from the Qing, when Emperor Qianlong built himself a palace here. Part of the palace itself, facing south to the centre of the lake, is now the **Zhejiang Provincial Museum**, a huge place with English captions throughout. The main building in front of the entrance houses historical relics, including some superb bronzes from the eleventh to the eighth century BC. Another hall centres on coin collections and has specimens of the world's first banknotes, dating to the Northern Song; you'll get an appreciation of the deep conservatism of Chinese society from its coinage, which remained fundamentally unchanged for two thousand years from the Han to the Qing dynasties. Other galleries outside hold displays of painting and Tibetan Buddha statues.

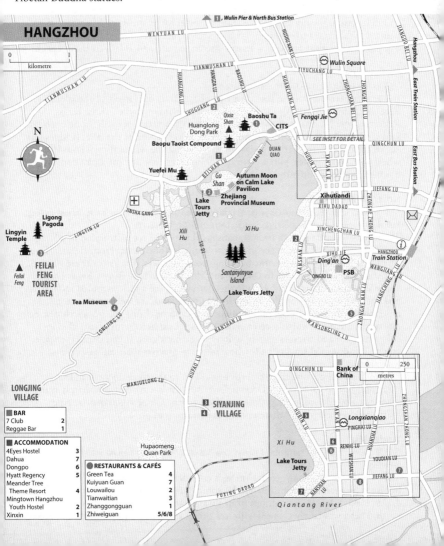

14

The curious **Xiling Seal Engravers' Society**, founded in 1904, occupies the western side of Gu Shan, next to the *Louwailou Restaurant*. Its tiny park encloses a pavilion with a pleasant blend of steps, carved stone tablets, shrubbery, and nearby a small early Buddhist stupa. On the southeastern side of the hill by the water is another of Qianlong's buildings, the **Autumn Moon on a Calm Lake Pavilion**, which is the perfect place to watch the full moon. It's a teahouse now, very popular after sunset and full of honeymooners. The low stone **Duan Qiao** (Broken Bridge), at the far eastern end of the causeway, gets its name because winter snow melts first on the hump of the bridge, creating the illusion of a gap.

Su Di

苏堤, sūdī

The longer causeway, **Su Di**, named after the Song-dynasty poet-official Su Dong Po, who was governor of Hangzhou, starts from the southwest corner of the lake and runs its full length to the northern shore close to Yuefei Mu. Consisting of embankments planted with banana trees, weeping willows and plum trees, linked by six stone arch bridges, the causeway encloses a narrow stretch of water, **Xili Hu** (West Inner Lake).

Santanyinyue Island

三潭印月, sāntán yìnyuè • ¥20 (included in tourist boat fees)

In the southern part of the lake, just east of Su Di, is the largest of the islands, Xiaoying, built up in 1607. It's better known as **Santanyinyue** (Three Flags Reflecting the Moon) after the three "flags" in the water – actually stone pagodas, said to control the evil spirits lurking in the deepest spots of the lake. Bridges link across from north to south and east to west so that the whole thing seems like a wheel with four spokes, plus a central hub just large enough for a pavilion, which doubles as a shop and a restaurant.

North of the lake

栖霞山, qīxiá shān • **Baopu Taoist Compound** 包朴道院, bāopǔ dàoyuàn; Daily 7am–5pm; ¥5 • **Huanglong Dong Park** 黄龙洞公园, huánglóngdòng gōngyuán; Daily 6.30am–4pm; ¥15; Bus #Y3

The seven-storey **Baoshu Ta** (保淑塔, bǎoshū tǎ) is a 1933 reconstruction of a Song-dynasty tower, and a nice place to walk to along hillside paths. From Beishan Lu a small lane leads up behind some buildings to the pagoda. Tracks continue beyond, and you can climb right up to **Qixia Shan** (Mountain Where Rosy Clouds Linger) above the lake. About halfway along this path you'll see a yellow-roofed monastery, lurking below to your left the **Baopu Taoist Compound**. It's well worth a stop, especially in the late afternoon, if only because you might be able to watch discreetly one of the ancestral worship ceremonies that are held here, with priests clad in colourful garb and widows clutching long black necklaces. If you climb the stairs, you will find several smaller halls where old men practise their calligraphy and young women play the *pipa*.

From here, a short uphill walk north brings you to the charmingly secluded **Huanglong Dong Park** (Yellow Dragon Cave Park). It is sunk between sharply rising hills with a pond, teahouses, a shrine to Yue Lao (the Chinese god of arranging marriages) and a pavilion where musicians perform traditional music.

Yuefei Mu

岳飞墓, yuèfēi mù • 80 Beishan Lu • Daily 7.30am–5.30pm • ¥25 • ☎ 0571 8798 6653 • Buses #K7, #Y1, #Y2, #Y3 run from the train station

The twelfth-century Song general Yuefei is considered a hero in modern China thanks to his unquestioning patriotism, and his tomb, **Yuefei Mu**, is one of Hangzhou's big draws. Having emerged victorious from a war against barbarian invaders from the north, Yuefei was falsely charged with treason by a jealous prime minister, and executed at the age of 39. Twenty years later, the subsequent emperor annulled all charges against him and had him reburied here with full honours. Walk through the temple to reach the tomb itself – a tiny bridge over water, a small double row of stone men and animals, steles, a mound with old pine trees and four cast-iron statues of the villains, kneeling in shame with their hands behind their backs. The calligraphy on the front wall of the tomb reads, "Be loyal to your country".

Feilai Feng

飞来峰, fēilái fēng • Daily 5.30am–5.30pm • ¥45 • Buses #Y1, #Y2, #Y4, #7, #807

Three kilometres west of the lake, some of Hangzhou's most famous sights are scattered around **Feilai Feng**, "The Hill that Flew Here". The hill's name derives from the tale of an Indian Buddhist named Hui Li who, upon arrival in Hangzhou, thought he recognized the hill from one back home, and asked when it had flown here. Near the entrance is the **Ligong Pagoda**, constructed for him. If you turn left shortly after entering the site, you'll come to a surprisingly impressive group of fake rock carvings, replicas of giant Buddhas from all over China. To the right of the entrance you'll find a snack bar and beautiful views over the neighbouring tea plantations up the hill.

The main feature of Feilai Feng is the hundreds of **Buddhist sculptures** carved into its limestone rocks. These date from between the tenth and fourteenth centuries and are the most important examples of their type to be found south of the Yangzi. Today the little Buddhas and other figurines are dotted about everywhere, moss-covered and laughing among the foliage. It's possible to follow trails right up to the top of the hill to escape the tourist hubbub.

Lingyin Temple

灵隐寺, língyǐn sì • Daily 7am–5.30pm • ¥30 • ☎ 0571 87968665 • Buses #Y1, #Y2, #Y4, #7, #807

Deep inside the Feilai Feng tourist area you'll eventually arrive at **Lingyin Temple** (Temple of the Soul's Retreat), one of the biggest temple complexes in China. Founded in 326 AD by Hui Li, who is buried nearby, it was the largest and most important monastery in Hangzhou and once had three thousand monks, nine towers, eighteen pavilions and 75 halls and rooms. Today it is an attractive working temple with daily services, usually in the early morning or after 3pm.

The temple was so badly riddled with woodworm that in the 1940s the main crossbeams collapsed onto the statues; the eighteen-metre-high Tang statue of Sakyamuni is a replica, carved in 1956 from 24 pieces of camphorwood. Elsewhere in the temple, the old frequently brushes against the new – the **Hall of the Heavenly King** contains four large and highly painted Guardians of the Four Directions made in the 1930s, while the Guardian of the Buddhist Law and Order, who shields the Maitreya, was carved from a single piece of wood eight hundred years ago.

Tea Museum

茶博物馆, chá bówùguǎn • 88 Longjing Lu • Tues–Sun 8.30am–4.30pm • Free • ☎ 0571 87964221 • Bus #27 or #Y3 from Pinghai Lu in the town centre to the former Zhejiang Hotel, where both buses stop, then walk southwest to the museum along a small lane just to the north of, and parallel to, the main road

Down in the southwestern quarter of the city, in the direction of the village of Longjing, the dominant theme is tea production: gleaming green tea bushes sweep up and down the land, and old ladies pester tourists into buying fresh tea leaves. Fittingly, this is where you'll find the Tea Museum, a smart place with lots of captions in English, covering themes such as the history of tea and the etiquette of tea drinking. There are displays on different varieties of tea, cultivation techniques, the development of special teaware, and finally, reconstructed tearooms in various ethnic styles, such as Tibetan and Yunnanese.

Longjing

龙井, lóngjǐng · Bus #K27 from the northwestern lakeshore, near the Tomb of Yuefei or #Y3

The village of **Longjing** (Dragon Well), with tea terraces rising on all sides behind the houses, is famous as the origin of **Longjing Tea**, perhaps the finest variety of green tea produced in China. Depending on the season, a stroll around here affords glimpses of leaves in different stages of processing – being cut, sorted or dried. You'll be hassled to sit at an overpriced teahouse or to buy leaves when you get off the bus – have a good look around first, as there is a very complex grading system and a huge range in quality and price. The **Dragon Well** itself is at the end of the village, a group of buildings around a spring, done up in a rather touristy fashion.

Hupaomeng Quan

虎跑梦泉, hǔpǎomèng quán · Daily 8am–5pm · ¥15 · Bus #504 or #Y5 from the city centre, down the eastern shore of the lake; bus #Y3 from Longjing passes close by

East of Longjing and south of Xi Hu, the area extending down to the Qiantang River is full of trees and gentle slopes. Of all the parks in this part of the city, perhaps the most attractive is the **Hupaomeng Quan** (Tiger Running Dream Spring). The spring here – according to legend, originally found by a ninth-century Zen Buddhist monk with the help of two tigers – is said to produce the purest water around, which serious connoisseurs use for brewing the best Longjing teas. For centuries, this has been a popular site for hermits to settle; now largely forested, it is dotted with teahouses, shrines, waterfalls and pagodas.

ARRIVAL AND DEPARTURE

HANGZHOU

BY TRAIN

The easiest way to get to Hangzhou is by train from Shanghai Hongqiao Station. The fast G- and D-class trains are frequent and take 1hr to –1hr 30min and cost around ¥80 one way.

Hangzhou East Station (杭州东站, hángzhōu dōngzhàn) Most fast trains stop at this new high-speed hub, 5km out of the centre. The easiest way to get to the northeastern lakefront from here is on the metro or by bus #K28. The last fast train back to Shanghai is at 9.51pm.

Hangzhou Station (杭州火车站, hángzhōu huǒchēzhàn) This station is more convenient, just 2km east of Xi Hu. D-class trains that terminate here leave from Shanghai Hongqiao Station every hour. Reaching the lake on foot takes about 20min; otherwise, take bus #7, #K7 or #Y2 direct to the lake. The last fast train back to Shanghai from here is at 8.34pm.

BY BUS

Buses from Shanghai take just over two hours.

Public bus from Shanghai Most services leave from Shanghai South Bus Station and pull in at the North Bus Station (汽车北站, qìchē běizhàn) – buses #K15, #K67 and #K290 run the 9km to the centre – or at the East (Jiubao) Bus Station (九堡汽车站, jiǔbǎo qìchēzhàn) in the northeast of town at 3339 Desheng Dong Lu, and connected by metro to the centre of town.

Private bus from Shanghai Private buses which leave from outside Shanghai main train station drop off at the square in front of Hangzhou main station.

From Suzhou Buses drop off at the square in front of the main train station.

GETTING AROUND

By bus There are some useful "Y" tourist bus routes around the lakeshore; ask for information at any of the many tourist booths. Regular buses cost ¥1–1.5, a/c buses ¥2, and "Y" buses ¥3–5.

By metro The new metro system currently only has one line, but it does very usefully connect all the train stations with the lake area and costs ¥2–8 (5.30am–11pm).

By boat It would be a shame to leave Hangzhou without taking a boat ride on Xi Hu. Tourist boats (¥45) depart from jetties all around the lake; the trip takes 90min and includes a jaunt around Santanyinyue (entrance fees included in the ticket price). You can also rent a four-person boat for ¥80/hr.

By bike Renting a bike to race around the lake is also an option. All hostels rent them for around ¥10 per day, but the city authorities have laid on an astonishing 50,000 bikes at the same rate, available outside all tourist booths for a deposit of ¥200. An electronic card costs ¥300 and the time you spend on the bike is deducted from the remaining ¥100. Only a few special booths, including one in Hangzhou train station, will redeem your credit and return your deposit. The bikes are free for the first hour, and young Chinese travellers

14

have cottoned on to the fact that they don't have to pay at all if they simply change bikes every 55min.

By taxi Taxis are a convenient way to get around town with the meter starting at ¥11 for the first 3km.

INFORMATION

Hangzhou Tourist Centre In front of the train station, between the public bus stops ☎0571 96123; 3 Huanglong Lu ☎0571 87961729, ⓦgotohz.gov.cn. The tourist centre runs one-day tours of Hangzhou and surrounding canal towns and cities, as well as shuttles to Shanghai's Pudong airport. Pick up a free, annually updated guide in English to the city which contains many maps and useful information. There are also offices at the airport and on Yan'an Lu with several visitor information booths dotted around town. Daily 8am–8pm.

CITS North shore of the lake, on a hillock above the junction of Beishan Lu and Baoshu Lu ☎0571 85059033, ⓕ0571 85059052. Nearly all Hangzhou hotels have their own travel desks, usually more helpful than CITS. Daily 8.30am–5pm.

More Hangzhou ⓦmorehangzhou.com. For handy restaurant and nightlife recommendations, check the expat listings magazine *More Hanghzhou* – you'll find the print edition in expat-oriented restaurants, and it's online too.

ACCOMMODATION

There are some excellent hotels in Hangzhou, particularly on the lakefront, and a handful of hostels have opened in recent years. Rooms fill quickly in the spring and autumn, so you would be wise to book in advance.

4Eyes Hostel 四眼睛青年旅舍 sìyǎnjīng qīngnián lǚshè 66 Siyanjing Village ☎0571 86435731, ⓦhostelhangzhou.com. Tucked away in a tranquil village, this place has clean dorms and rooms as well as a cosy outdoor seating area where you can sup draft beer or coffee and enjoy reasonably priced cook-ups. Dorm ¥40, double ¥166

Dahua 大华饭店 dàhuá fàndiàn 171 Nanshan Lu ☎0571 87181888, ⓦdh-hotel.com. On the lakeside, several blocks south of Jiefang Lu. Spacious grounds with comfortable rooms and attentive service justify the prices – this hotel is actually better value than many of its competitors. Mao Zedong and Zhou Enlai stayed here whenever they were in town. Also has a good and reasonably priced restaurant overlooking the lake. ¥1380

Dongpo 东坡宾馆 dōngpō bīnguǎn 52 Renhe Lu ☎0571 28973333, ⓦnewdongpo.com. Smart rooms, a beautiful six-storey central atrium and friendly staff make this hotel just about the best deal in Hangzhou as rooms are often half the listed price, but those at the front can get noisy. ¥888

★ **Hyatt Regency** 凯悦酒店 kǎiyuè jiǔdiàn 28 Hubin Lu ☎0571 87121234, ⓦhangzhou.regency .hyatt.com. Bill Clinton's abode of choice when he came to town, this hotel offers lake views for the ¥1000 more expensive deluxe rooms (even from the bathtubs, if you're in a suite), which have been decorated with splashes of red and gold, and boast stylish furniture. There are excellent restaurants on site, as well as a swimming pool which

makes you feel like you're paddling in Xi Hu. ¥2300

Meander Tree Theme Resort 漫居主题度假酒店 mànjū zhǔtí dùjià jiǔdiàn 58 Siyanjing Village ☎0571 87979158, ⓦmanju58.com. Candidate for the most psychedelic hotel in China. The exterior and grounds of this resort are decorated with dozens of colourful mosaics and sculptures à la Gaudí's Park Güell in Barcelona. The themed rooms are individually decorated, some with bright primary colours, others in eclectic or ethnic styles; some are more recently renovated than others, but all have very comfy beds. Also has a couple of restaurants, but the staff speak no English. ¥350

Mingtown Hangzhou Youth Hostel 明堂国际青年 旅舍 míngtáng guójì qīngnián lǚshè 101 Nanshan Lu ☎0571 87918948, ⓔmingtown@foxmail.com. A pleasant range of rooms, including a few with a view of the lake or a private bathroom. Has all the hostel facilities you'd expect, plus a nice bar/restaurant and a very pleasant rooftop overlooking the lake. Discounts for YHA members. Take bus #Y2 from the train station or it's about 1km south-west of Dingban Lu metro stop. Dorm ¥70, double ¥375

Xinxin 新新饭店 xīnxīn fàndiàn 58 Beishan Lu ☎0571 87999090, ⓦthenewhotel.com. Recently refurbished rooms in this grand old building with antique furniture and wood panelling at one of the nicest locations in town, overlooking the northern shore of the lake. Many rooms have lake views (for an extra ¥200), as does the ground-floor restaurant which serves high-class local dishes. Also called *The New Hotel* in English. ¥1180

EATING AND DRINKING

As a busy resort for local tourists, Hangzhou has plenty of good places to eat. The wedge-shaped neighbourhood between Hubin Lu and Yan'an Lu is home to a number of Chinese restaurants and fast-food joints, while touristy Hefang Jie is also a good spot for Chinese restaurants and snacks. Lastly, the area between Shuguang Lu and the park has its own little cultural microclimate – downmarket and sometimes downright seedy, but fascinating nonetheless.

TOWER, SKY, MOUNTAIN

Many Chinese tourists make it a point to visit one of the famous **historical restaurants** in town: both *Louwailou* – Tower Beyond Tower (see below) – and *Tianwaitian* – Sky Beyond Sky (see below) – serve local specialities at reasonable prices, while a third, *Shanwaishan* (Mountain Beyond Mountain), has garnered a bad reputation over the years. All three were named after a line in Southern Song poet Lin Hejin's most famous poem: "Sky beyond sky, mountain beyond mountain and tower beyond tower/Could song and dance by West Lake be ended anyhow?"

14

Green Tea 绿茶 lǜchá 83 Longjing Lu ☎0571 87888022. Sitting amid tea plantations and next door to the Tea Museum itself, this out-of-the-way yet very popular restaurant – a rickety pine structure sitting lakeside above the lily pads – is quite a treat. Its collection of dishes is extensive but the barbecued beef deserves a special mention. Mains start at around ¥40. Packed most evenings, so book ahead. Daily 11am–10pm.

Kuiyuan Guan 奎元馆 kuíyuán guǎn 154 Jiefang Lu, just west of Zhongshan Zhong Lu ☎0571 87029012. Specializing in more than forty noodle dishes for all tastes, from the mundane (beef noodle soup) to the acquired (pig intestines and kidneys). It also offers a range of local seafood delicacies. A little tricky to find – go through the entrance with Chinese lanterns hanging outside, and it's on the left, upstairs. Daily 8am–9pm.

Louwailou 楼外楼 lóuwài lóu Gu Shan Island ☎0571 87969023. The best-known and seemingly most popular restaurant in Hangzhou, whose specialities include *dongpo* pork, fish-shred soup, and beggar's chicken (a whole chicken cooked inside a ball of mud, which is broken and removed at your table). Lu Xun and Zhou Enlai, among others, have dined here. Surprisingly, standard dishes cost as little as ¥45. Daily 11am–11pm.

Tianwaitian 天外天 tiānwài tiān 2 Lingzhu Lu at the gate to Feilai Feng and Lingyin Si ☎0571 87960599.

Chinese tourists flock here to sample the fresh seafood, supposedly caught from Xi Hu. Not as good as *Louwailou*, though, but a great location by the lake under some immense trees. Dishes are local cuisine and mains cost around ¥50 – the pricier West Lake Vinegar Carp is great if you can afford it. Daily 7am–9pm.

Zhanggongguan 张功馆 zhānggōng guǎn 3 Baoshu Lu ☎0571 86586609. Rustic, local cookery – actually very rustic as despite its stylish interior, a room full of live fish and even chickens replaces the conventional menu card. Choose your beast (or select a more prosaic dish from the picture menu on the wall) and they'll dispatch and cook it for you. The fresh fish is quite pricy, but the regular dishes start at ¥25 and include a very fine *dongpo* pork. There are two branches on this street, the first you come to only serves inexpensive local noodle dishes for under ¥20. Daily 10am–11pm.

Zhiweiguan 知味观 zhīwèi guān Downtown: 71 Gaoyin Jie or 156 Jiafang Lu; southwest of the lake: 10 Yanggongdo ☎0571 87010200, ⓦzhiweiguan.com.cn. In a very urbane atmosphere, with piped Western classical music, you can enjoy assorted *dianxin* (*dim sum*) by the plate, including *xiaolong bao* (small, fine steamed dumplings) and *mao erduo* (fried, crunchy stuffed dumplings). The *huntun tang* (wonton soup) and *jiu miao* (fried chives) are also good. At least ¥100 per person. Daily 11am–10pm.

NIGHTLIFE

For nightlife, Shuguang Lu and the north end of Nanshan Lu are the best bar strips in the Xi Hu area, but they tend to be a bit touristy; the local hangouts are slightly outside the centre especially in the area north of Shuguang Lu. For up-to-date information, check ⓦmorehangzhou.com.

7 Club 7号酒吧 qīhàojiǔbā ba 43 Shuguang Lu (behind the florist) ☎0571 86431517. Intimate and friendly basement bar with mostly local, but some expat customers. An outstanding selection of Belgian and British bottled beers, as well as cocktails and single-malt scotch, though prices for all of them start at ¥50. Very laidback, and the eclectic mix of music is kept at a reasonable volume. Some English spoken. Daily 6pm–2am.

Reggae Bar 黑根酒吧 hēigēn jiǔbā 131 Xue Yuan Lu ☎0571 86575749. About 3km north of Shuguang

Lu, this happy, three-storey bar is a favourite among local and foreign students, and sees plenty of action at the weekend; it's also a good place to find out about happening events. Decor is arty/squat party, but drinks are quality with many imported beers at reasonable prices (bottles ¥20–45). The track selection goes beyond reggae, with DJs working to get the dancefloor moving and student bands playing live Tues–Sun 8.30–10pm. Daily 6pm–5am (or later).

SHOPPING

The most touristy concentration of souvenir outlets – selling silk, tea and crafts – is along Hefang Jie. An L-shaped night market bends around the western end of Renhe Lu, with street sellers peddling a proletarian jumble of wares, ranging from watches to DVDs to Little Red Books. The ritziest brand names are all on Hubin Lu, right on the waterfront.

Ten Fu Tea 天福茗茶 tiānfú míngchá B1 132 Shuguang Lu ☎ 0571 8763063. Handy branch of a chain that sells tea and tea-related souvenirs; stock up on local varieties, Longjing and chrysanthemum. Daily 10am–5pm.

China Silk Town 中国丝绸城 zhōngguó sīchóu chéng 127 Xinhua Jie ☎ 0571 85100192. Maybe avoid the clothes, which are a little gaudy, and go for pyjamas, umbrellas and fans at this venerable store. Daily 10am–5pm.

DIRECTORY

Banks and exchange The Bank of China head office is at 140 Yan'an Bei Lu (daily 8am–5pm), immediately north of Qingchun Lu.
Hospital Sir Run Run Shaw Hospital at 3 Qingchun Dong Lu (☎ 0571 86006613, ⊛ english-srrsh.com) is the best

equipped and has English-speaking staff.
PSB For visa extensions, enquire at the PSB in the centre of town, just south of Dingban Lu metro stop at 35 Huaguang Lu (Mon–Fri 8.30am–noon & 2.30–5pm; ☎ 0571 87280561, ⊛ hzcrj.gov.cn).

Moganshan

莫干山, mògān shān · ¥80 per day (ticket office is at the gate to the village; daily 8am–6.30pm)

The hill station of **MOGANSHAN**, 60km north of Hangzhou, was popular before World War II with the fast foreign set and has recently reprised its role as a resort to escape the stifling summer heat. The old European-style villas and po-faced communist-style sanatoriums are being restored and turned into guesthouses, bars and cafés. There's little to do here but wander the incongruously European-looking village, hike in the bamboo forest with its many pagodas to rest in, and enjoy the views. It's lovely, but get here sooner rather than later, before it all gets overdeveloped. The centre of the village is already getting spoiled, and it's overly busy at weekends and in the summer, but a thirty-minute walk in any direction will take you into peace and quiet.

ARRIVAL AND DEPARTURE   MOGANSHAN

There is no direct route to Moganshan – you have to first head either to Deqing (德清, déqīng) or Wukang (武康, wǔkāng) at the bottom of the mountain. Then once you're there, a taxi or minivan the rest of the way up the mountain costs ¥80–100. Do not get tempted to save pennies by getting one of the three-wheelers – they're slow and often cheat tourists. Note that there are no ATMs in Moganshan, so arrive with enough money to last your stay.

FROM SHANGHAI

By bus Buses from Shanghai South Bus Station run to Deqing at 7.50am, 9am, 1.25pm and 3pm. The trip takes 3hr 30min.

FROM HANGZHOU

By train Regular trains depart Hangzhou's central train

station day and night for the 40–60min trip to Deqing.
By bus Buses leave hourly from Hangzhou's North Bus Station for the 1hr run to Wukang.
By taxi A taxi all the way from Hangzhou to Moganshan will cost around ¥250.

ACCOMMODATION

Moganshan has a surfeit of faded, Chinese-style two-star accommodation (from ¥200); fine if you just want a bed, but a slightly more expensive room in one of the old villas listed below is more atmospheric. For a real retreat, stay in one of the forest villas (from ¥380) operated by the *Moganshan Lodge* (see below).

Du Yuesheng Villa 杜月笙别墅 dùyuèshēng biéshù ☎ 0572 3033601. Once owned by the gangster himself (see p.161), the *Du Yuesheng Villa* is now operated by Radisson. Exteriors are period and rather lovely, but the rooms themselves are ordinary, so it feels a little overpriced. ¥900

House 23 and 25 ☎ 0572 8033822, ⊛ moganshan house23.com. The best place to stay in the price range, *House 23* is a foreign-owned, converted 1930s villa at the top of the hill. They also run *House 25*, a cottage retreat fifteen minutes' walk away in the woods and will arrange

transport from Shanghai or Hangzhou. **¥900**
Naked Retreats 62 Gao'an Lu, Shanghai ☎021
64318901, ⓦnakedretreats.cn. If you really want to
get back to nature, try one of *Naked Retreat*'s cosy, rustic
eco-lodges tucked away in bamboo forest. Despite the
name, there's no naturism involved, and the lodges are
very civilized (although a 20min drive from the nearest

shop), with wood fires, jacuzzis and fitted kitchens, and a
maid on hand to do your cooking. Mountain biking,
horseriding, fishing and of course plenty of hiking,
guided if you like, are also on offer. Booking ahead is a
must; they'll arrange for you to be picked up from
Deqing/Wukang or Hangzhou (from ¥350). Weekdays
¥350, weekends **¥450**

EATING AND DRINKING

Moganshan Lodge 莫干山旅馆 mògānshān lǚguǎn
Yin Shan Jie ☎0572 8033011, ⓦmoganshanlodge.com.
A bar and restaurant in a wing of at the southern end of
the main street. Foreign-owned bar-cum-café-cum-restaurant
in an old lodge – the *Songliang Shanzhuang Hotel*
(松梁山庄, sōngliáng shānzhuāng) – with fantastic
coffee and even better views from the patio. The food, all

Western staples including pukka British breakfasts and set
dinners (¥125–145), is excellent, though you have to order in
advance so that they can buy supplies. The helpful foreign
owners will point you in the right direction for walks. It's also
the best place for a drink in the evening. Check out their
helpful website before you arrive for accommodation options
and to get a feel for the town.

Putuo Shan

普陀山, pǔtuó shān

Putuo Shan, an island dotted with ancient monasteries and one of the four holy
mountains of Chinese Buddhism, has been at the centre of a cult of Guanyin, the
Buddhist Goddess of Mercy, for centuries. During the goddess's birthday celebrations in
early April, thousands of pilgrims and sightseers crowd onto the island for chanting and
ceremonies. Improved transport links mean it is busy with local tourists at weekends and
in summer, but still, catch it at the right time and it's a seductive retreat from the bustle
of the city. The best times to come are April, May, September and October.

The main **temples** have been recently renovated, with yellow-ochre walls offsetting
the deep green of the mature trees in their forecourts. They're squarely geared up for
tourism, each charging around ¥10 to get in, though they are also frequented by plenty
of pilgrims. As well as temples, two **caves** are firmly on the pilgrim circuit and there are
even a couple of **beaches**.

The island is long and thin, with the **ferry jetty**, where all visitors arrive and pay an
entrance fee, in the far south. All the temples are connected by minibuses which depart
from the bus stop just southeast of the central square in town. The best way to get
around, however, is to walk; you can cover most of the island in a day.

The town

About 1km north of the jetty is the main **town**, a tiny collection of hotels, shops and
restaurants. The town itself is unremarkable, but it does hold one of the island's star
attractions, the **Puji Temple** (普济寺, pǔjì sì; daily 6am–9pm; ¥5), built in 1080 and
enlarged by successive dynasties. Standing among magnificent camphor trees, it boasts
a bridge lined with statues and an elegantly tall pagoda with an enormous iron bell.
The town's second major religious structure is the five-storey **Duobao Pagoda** (多宝塔,
duōbǎo tǎ). It was built in 1334 using stones brought over from Tai Hu in Jiangsu
Province, and has Buddhist inscriptions on all four sides.

Qianbu Sha and Baibu Sha

Qianbu Sha 千步沙, qiānbù shā; ¥12 until 5pm, free afterwards • **Baibu Sha** 百步沙, bǎibù shā; ¥10 until 5pm, free
afterwards • **Zizhu Temple** 紫竹寺, zǐzhú sì; daily 6am–6pm; ¥5, which includes admission to Chaoyin Dong

A short walk from town, two decent beaches line the eastern shore, **Qianbu Sha**
(Thousand Step Beach) and **Baibu Sha** (Hundred Step Beach). The beaches are separated
by a small headland hiding the **Chaoyang Dong** (潮阳洞, cháoyáng dòng), a little cave
inside which there's a teahouse and a seating area overlooking the sea. At the southern

end of Baibu Sha is a second cave, **Chaoyin Dong** (潮音洞 cháoyīn dòng), which is frequented by pilgrims who stand with their ears cupped; the din of crashing waves is thought to resemble the call of Buddha. The neighbouring **Zizhu Temple** (Purple Bamboo Temple) is one of the less-touristed temples on the island and, for that reason alone, a good spot to observe the monks' daily rituals.

Guanyintiao

观音跳, guānyīn tiào • Daily 7am–5pm • ¥6 • Bus #2

Lying on a headland on the island's southernmost tip, is the **Guanyintiao** (Guanyin Leap), Putuo's most prominent sight: a spectacular 33-metre-high bronze-plated statue of the Goddess of Mercy visible from much of the island. In her left hand, Guanyin holds a steering wheel, symbolically protecting fishermen (not to mention travelling monks) from violent storms at sea. The pavilion at the base of the statue houses a small exhibit of wooden murals recounting how Guanyin has aided Putuo villagers and fishermen over the years, while in a small room directly underneath the statue sit four hundred statues representing the various spiritual incarnations of the goddess. The view from the statue's base is sublime, especially on a clear day.

Huiji Temple

慧济寺, huìjì sì • Daily 6.30am–5pm • ¥5 • Cable car: Daily 7am–5pm; ¥25 up, ¥15 down

It's a bracing, three-kilometre uphill walk north from town to **Huiji Temple**, on the summit of **Foding Shan** (佛顶山 fódǐng shān) though once there you'll be rewarded with great views of the sea and surrounding temples. You'll likely be walking alone, as pilgrims take the bus or the **cable car** from the minibus stand. The temple itself, built mainly between 1793 and 1851, occupies a beautiful site, surrounded by green tea plantations. Its halls stand in a flattened area between hoary trees and bamboo groves, the greens, reds, blues and gold of their enamelled tiles gleaming magnificently in the sunshine. There's also a vegetarian restaurant here.

From Huiji Temple to Fayu Temple

From Huiji Temple, head down a marked path towards the island's third major temple, Fayu Temple (see below). Shortly after setting off, you'll see a secondary track branching away to the east. The **Ancient Buddha Cave** is a delightfully secluded spot by a sandy beach on the northeastern coast of the island; give yourself a couple of hours to get there and back. Back on the main path, the steep steps bring you to the **Xiangyun Pavilion**, where you can rest and drink tea with the friendly monks. A twenty-minute walk south from here will bring you to the Fayu Temple.

Fayu Temple

法雨寺, fǎyǔ sì • Daily 6.30am–5.30pm • ¥5 • Bus #2

The **Fayu Temple** is a superb collection of over two hundred halls amid huge trees, built up in levels against the slope during the Ming. With the mountain behind and the sea just in front, it's a delightful place to sit in peaceful contemplation. The Daxiong Hall has been well restored, while the Dayuan Hall has a unique beamless arched roof and a dome, around the inside of which squirm nine carved wooden dragons. This hall is said to have been moved here from Nanjing by Emperor Kangxi in 1689. Its great **statue of Guanyin**, flanked by monks and nuns, is the focal point of the goddess's birthday celebrations in early April, when thousands of pilgrims and sightseers crowd onto the island for chanting and ceremonies lasting all evening.

ARRIVAL AND DEPARTURE   PUTUO SHAN

BY PLANE

You can fly from Hongqiao Airport in Shanghai to Putuoshan Airport on the neighbouring Zhujiajian Island. From here, take a taxi or bus to Wugongzhi Dock, from where frequent ferries make the 10min crossing to Putuo Shan.

BY BUS

Until recently, the ferry from Shanghai was the most common way to reach Putuo Shan, but thanks to a couple of new bridges it is now possible to travel by bus to the island of Shenjiamen, a short ferry ride away from Putuo Shan (10min; ¥22). Tour buses leave daily 7–9am from Shanghai Stadium Sightseeing Bus Centre (see p.134) and return the following morning from Shenjiamen. Regular buses from Shanghai South Bus Station take 4hr and cost ¥138.

FERRY

Tickets for all boats can be bought in advance from Shanghai CITS (see p.37) or from the booking office at 59 Jinling Dong Lu (⊙56575500; daily 7am–5.30pm). You can buy tickets back to Shanghai from any of the island's hotels or at the jetty office. The slow service is worth considering – chugging back into the city just after sunrise, it provides a memorable view of the awakening metropolis.

Fast ferry A fast ferry departs from Luchaogang dock at 9.30am, 10am and 3.30pm (2hr 30min; ¥190–260). The dock is more than an hour south of Shanghai; your ticket includes the bus journey there from a pick-up point at 1588 Waima Lu, near Nanpu Bridge. There are several fast ferries back each morning.

Overnight boat A slow overnight boat departs Shanghai daily at 8pm, arriving at Putuo Shan at 7am the next morning. Boats leave from Wusong Dock (251 Songbao Lu ⊙021 56575500), which you can reach by bus #51 from Hongkou Stadium. The cheapest tickets (¥109) are for the large common room, but you're better off in second class (¥235), where you'll get a berth in a four-bunk cabin with a washbasin; travelling first class (¥500) gets you a two-bed cabin but doesn't offer much more comfort. One or two overnight departures leave the island 4.30pm. Bring some food as the meals on board aren't up to much.

14

GETTING AROUND AND INFORMATION

Entrance fee A ¥160 entry fee is payable when you set foot on dry land. Temples charge around ¥10 for admission.

Minibuses There are only a few roads, travelled by a handful of minibuses (¥4–6) which connect the port with Puji Temple and other sights farther north.

Getting to town Upon arrival, you can reach the town by following either the road heading west or the one east

from the jetty, or by picking up a bus from the car park just east of the arrival gate. The westerly route is slightly shorter and takes you past most of the modern buildings and facilities on the island, including the Bank of China (daily 8–11am & 1–4.30pm) and the CITS office. A little farther north is the post office.

ACCOMMODATION

★ **Putuoshan Hotel** 普陀山大酒店 pǔtuóshān dàjiǔdiàn ⊙0580 6092828, ⊚putuoshanhotel.com. Very easy to spot on the main west road between the jetty and town thanks to its spacious grounds and opulent design, this is the best hotel in the south of the island, and it's cheaper than some less-salubrious competitors. Traditional Chinese furniture in the classier rooms, and a vegetarian restaurant. **¥1568**

Xiang Sheng Grand Hotel 祥生大酒店 xiángshēng dàjiǔdiàn ⊙0580 669 6666, ⊚xsdjhotel.com. Perched up on a headland overlooking the sea by Fuding Mountain in the north, this new 5-star has big, comfortable rooms and most have balconies with fantastic views. Staff are

friendly, the service is good and there are three restaurants serving seafood, Cantonese and Southeast Asian cuisine. It has all the facilities you'd expect, and runs a private minibus fleet for getting around the island. By far the best hotel on Putuo Shan. **¥1880**

Xiang Yuan 翔园宾馆 xiángyuán bīnguǎn ⊙0580 6095298, ⊚ptsxybg.com. In the little square on the western road from the jetty before the Bank of China. *Xiang Yuan* is one of the cheapest hotels on the island – the midweek price is about a third of the standard rate. Its rooms are fairly comfortable and clean, if slightly old and decrepit. There are three other marginally more expensive places nearby, where rooms are similar, but a little less worn. **¥580**

EATING

Most food must be brought in from the mainland and is, therefore, expensive. The lane running northeast away from Puji Si, as well as the road between the jetty departure and arrival points, both have some dingy-looking places specializing in seafood (fish, molluscs, eel) though they also do standard dishes and noodles starting at around ¥40. All the main temples have simple vegetarian restaurants which serve breakfast (5.30–6.30am), lunch (10.30–11.30am), and supper (4.30–5.30pm) for just ¥2.5–10 a person.

★ **Putuoshan Hotel** 普陀山大酒店 pǔtuóshān dàjiǔdiàn ⊙0580 6092828. Upscale vegetarian

restaurant, serving mostly fake meat dishes, attached to the *Putuoshan Hotel*. Daily 11am–2pm & 5–9pm.

SHANGHAI WORLD FINANCIAL CENTRE

Contexts

History

Shanghai's history as a metropolis is distinct from that of the nation as a whole, as the machinations of thousands of years of imperial dynasties have not much influenced its destiny. In fact, it's a young city (for China) whose story is dominated by trade rather than politics, and by international forces as much as domestic ones.

The port on the Yangzi

Contrary to Western interpretations, Shanghai's history did not begin with the founding of the foreign concessions. Located at the head of the **Yangzi River**, Shanghai grew from a fishing village (Shanghai simply means "on the sea") into a major commercial port during the Song dynasty. By the time of the Qing dynasty, huge **mercantile guilds** dealing in lucrative local products – silk, cotton and tea – often organized by trade and bearing superficial resemblance to their Dutch counterparts, had established economic and, to some extent, political control of the city. The Yangzi basin reaches half of China, and this formidable route to the interior was bolstered by almost a million kilometres of **canals** – vital trade routes in a country with very few roads. It was this unprecedented accessibility, noted by its first Western visitor, Hugh Lindsay of the British East India Company, that was to prove so alluring to the foreign powers, and set the city off down its unique, tempestuous path. The story of **foreign intervention** in China began in morally murky waters (and, some would say, remained there): it started with a dispute over drugs and money.

Ocean barbarians

The **Qing dynasty**, established in 1644, followed the pattern of China's long and repetitive history; a rebellion, in this case by the Manchus from the north, overthrew the emperor and established a new dynasty which ran, as usual, on a feudal, Confucian social model – everyone from peasant to emperor knew their place in a rigid hierarchy. By the eighteenth century the Qing had lost their early vigour and grown conservative and decadent, the out-of-touch royal court embroiled in intrigue. As with all previous dynasties, they were little troubled by outsiders. For thousands of years, China had remained alone and aloof, isolated from the rest of the world; the only foreigners in the Chinese experience were nomadic tribesmen at the fringes of the empire – savages to be treated with disdain.

So when the **British East India Company** arrived in the early seventeenth century the Manchu officials were not much interested. The "ocean barbarians" began trading in Canton in the far south, China's only open port – they sold English textiles to India, took Indian cotton to China, and bought Chinese tea, porcelain and silk. The Chinese wanted no British manufacturing in return, only silver.

1644	1832	1839
Qing dynasty established	British East India Company arrives in Shanghai	First Opium War

Even this much trade was begrudged by the Qing, whose policies ensured that the East India Company always bought more than it sold, with the result that the British exchequer reluctantly made up the balance with hard currency. The Company's infamous solution to this trade imbalance was to get the country hooked. **Opium** grown in India was exported to China, and proved a great success; in 1760 more than a thousand chests, each weighing more than a hundred pounds, were imported; fifty years later, this had grown to more than forty thousand. Stupefied addicts numbered more than two million and now the trade imbalance was firmly in the other direction.

In 1839, fearing a crippled economy, Emperor Daoguang abruptly declared the trade illegal and British merchants were forced to watch their opium cargo hurled overboard their ships. It was a typically ill-judged response. The British countered by **seizing Hong Kong** (then a minor outpost) and sending an expeditionary force to attack Canton, triggering the **First Opium War**. Chinese tactics such as sending monkeys with fireworks to set enemy ships alight were inventive but hardly effective; the superior technology of the British meant that the result was never in doubt.

In 1842 the defeated Manchus were forced to sign the unequal **Treaty of Nanjing**, which ceded Hong Kong to the British and opened Shanghai, then a small fortified town, as well as four other ports (Fuzhou, Xiamen, Guangzhou and Ningbo), to foreign trade. This, the first of many unequal treaties, marks the beginning of modern Chinese history, on a sour note of national humiliation.

The concession era

Of the new open ports, Shanghai was the most ideally situated – at the midpoint of China's coast, close to established trading routes between the West and Japan, and offering a route straight into the heart of China. The town was soon booming, and other nations scrambled to get a foothold in the alluring new market that the British had prised open. France, Belgium, Norway and Russia all began to make their own demands on the Qing administration, but it was the **Americans** who proved most influential. An envoy sent by President Tyler "to save the Chinese from being an exclusive monopoly of England" managed, in the 1844 Treaty of Wangxia, to hack out the principle that was to prove vital to Shanghai's development, the idea of "**extra-territoriality**"; foreigners resident in the treaty ports would be subject to the laws of their own nation rather than those of China. This guaranteed the safety and property of traders – and of course, set them completely apart from the local population.

Shanghai was divided up between trading powers, with each claiming a riverside frontage: the British along the Bund and the area to the north of the Chinese city, the **French** in an area to the southwest, centred on the site of a cathedral a French missionary had founded two centuries earlier. Later the Americans, in 1863, came to tack their own areas onto the British Concession, which expanded into the so-called **International Settlement**. Each section was a mini-state, with its own police force, and a municipal council voted in by prominent traders. The borders of these states had not been fixed, so the foreigners used every excuse to extend them. It was colonialism in all but name; but whereas in other colonial territories, such as British India, a degree of mixing occurred between people, in Shanghai the Chinese and the foreigners lived in isolation from each other, in a state of mutual contempt.

1842	**1844**	**1863**
Defeated Manchus sign the Treaty of Nanjing with the British	Sino-American Treaty of Wangxia allows for extra-territoriality	Americans join the British Concession, creating the International Settlement

The Huangpu riverfront swelled as the **great trading houses** such as Jardine Matheson and Swire from Hong Kong rushed to open godowns (warehouses) and offices. Silk, tea and opium (still technically illegal) remained important but insurance and banking proved lucrative new moneymakers. Behind the river, homesick merchants built mansions in imitation of the ones they had left behind in Europe, with large gardens. By 1853 there were several hundred foreign ships making regular trips into the Chinese interior, and almost a thousand resident foreigners, most of them British. Still, even the largest firms had only a dozen or so foreign staff. It would take a catastrophic civil war to kick the city's development into a much higher gear.

The Taiping Rebellion and beyond

China's humiliation by foreigners, and the corruption and decadence of her ineffectual overlords, caused instability in Shanghai's giant, mysterious hinterland. Between 1740 and 1840 the Chinese population tripled, and vast numbers of peasantry became poverty-stricken and rootless. Arbitrary taxes and lawlessness compounded their plight. Resentment crystallized around the unlikely figure of charismatic cult leader **Hong Xiuquan**, a failed scholar who declared himself the younger brother of Jesus Christ. His egalitarian philosophy proved wildly popular, and he attracted millions of followers. Declaring their intention to build a Taiping Tianguo, or "Heavenly Kingdom of Great Peace", with Hong as its absolute ruler, these **Taipings** stormed across southern China, capturing Nanjing in 1854 and making it their capital. They abolished slavery, redistributed the land and replaced Confucianism with a heretical form of Christianity.

A sister organization, the **Small Sword Society**, took over the Chinese quarter at the centre of Shanghai. Alarmed by these fanatical revolutionaries, the city's foreign residents joined forces with the armies of the Qing against them. The fighting devastated the countryside around Shanghai, and more than twenty million are thought to have died (more than a hundred million if natural disasters and famine are added) – making this obscure rebellion, little known in the West, the world's bloodiest-ever civil war. Hong retreated into the sensual distractions of his harem, and the drive of the Taiping faltered; the final blows were administered with the help of foreign mercenaries in 1865.

For Shanghai, the crisis proved an opportunity. Chinese **refugees** from the conflict swarmed, for safety, into the city's foreign concessions. Previously, foreigners had banned Chinese from living in their exclusive enclaves, but plenty of the new arrivals had gold enough to make them overcome any scruples. Now Shanghai's greatest asset became land, as the average price of an acre in the foreign concessions shot up from £70 to more than £10,000 in less than a decade. The merchants demolished their spacious villas, sold their grounds, and annexed local farms in a feverish **real-estate boom**. The city's Chinese population exploded from fewer than a thousand souls in 1850 to more than 70,000 by 1870.

A pattern was set: as Manchu misrule continued and warlords blighted millions of lives, Shanghai profited by offering haven under the racist but at least orderly rule of the foreigners. This is when the city began to take its modern shape, with Nanjing Lu emerging as the busiest shopping street, and the French Concession providing the most desirable residences. The Chinese were not allowed any say in running the city, though their taxes paid for improvements such as gas lighting, electricity and tarmacked roads.

1854	**1865**	**1895**
Taiping Rebellion begins	Taiping Rebellion defeated	Japanese win the right to start manufacturing in Shanghai

The seeds of revolution

It was the arrival of a new foreign power, who played by different rules to the old colonial nations, that caused Shanghai's next spurt of growth. For the **Japanese**, dealings with the West had proved much more positive than for the Chinese and by the mid-nineteenth century Japan had successfully transformed itself into a modern industrial nation. Following their defeat of the Qing in a conflict over the vassal state of Korea in 1895, the Japanese copied the Western tactic of extracting unequal treaties, and won for themselves the right to start **manufacturing** in Shanghai. It was a clever move; coal and electricity were cheap, and, with the city stuffed with desperate refugees, labour even cheaper. The Western powers followed, factories replaced the godowns along the Huangpu and the city grew from a trading port into an industrial powerhouse.

Squalid living conditions, outbreaks of unemployment and glaring abuses of Chinese labour by foreign investors made the city a natural breeding ground for **revolutionary ferment**. But just as influential was first-hand experience of foreign technology, ideologies and administration. To Shanghai's urban intellectuals, especially those who had been educated abroad, it became clear that the old imperial order had to be overthrown. Just as clearly, the foreigner had to be expelled – from now on, far from being aloof from China's political life, the city was about to be thrown into the centre of it.

By the early twentieth century, mass **civil disorder** had broken out across the country. Attempts to reform the administration had been quashed by the conservative Dowager Empress Cixi, and her death in 1908 further destabilized the country. In 1911, the dynasty finally collapsed, in large part due to the influence of the Shanghai intellectual, **Sun Yatsen**, leader of the Nationalists and a champion of Chinese self-determination. Steeped in international culture, this ex-medical student was a fine product of the city's intellectual foment. Yet against men such as this, who understood the need to modernize, warlords maintained China's old ideological model, and fought to establish a new dynasty. No one succeeded, and with the absence of central government, chaos reigned.

In 1921, the **Chinese Communist Party** (**CCP**) was founded in Shanghai. Four years later, in protest at the indiscriminate killing of protesting students by settlement police, the CCP organized China's first strike. Two hundred thousand workers downed tools; some even marched under the slogan "No taxation without representation!" Much to

LADISLAV HUDEC

The most notable exponent of Shanghai's Art Deco architecture was Hungarian architect **Ladislav Hudec** (1893–1958), who more than anyone else, created the city's distinctive Art Deco stamp. In 1918, he fought for the Hungarian army and was captured by the Russians; en route to a prison camp in Siberia, he jumped the train – and ended up in Shanghai. Having set up in practice here, he built dozens of buildings, most famously the *Park Hotel* (which was the city's tallest building well into the 1980s; see p.49), what is now the Arts and Crafts Museum (see p.66); the lovely Grand Theatre (see p.51), and the striking, flatiron-style Wukang Mansions (also known as the Normandie Apartments, on the corner of Wukang Lu and Huaihai ZHong Lu).

Hudec fans might want to track a couple more classics down in the backstreets behind the Bund: you'll find the Savings and Loan Building (though it's sadly rather dilapidated) at 259 Sichuan Zhong Lu, the Christian Literature Society building at 128 Huqiu Lu and, directly behind it at 209 Yuanmingyuan Lu, the China Baptist Publication Building.

1908	**1911**	**1921**
Dowager Empress Cixi dies	Qing Dynasty collapses	Chinese Communist Party founded in Shanghai

the chagrin of Shanghai's foreign overlords, the Chinese were beginning to develop political consciousness.

Nationalists versus Communists

The most powerful of the new groups, however, was the **Nationalist Party**, now led by the wily **Chiang Kaishek**. In 1927 he attempted to unite the country in an alliance with the Communists. Curfews and labour unrest froze the city as the Nationalists and Communists fought Shanghai's own warlords. Having won that battle, Chiang promptly turned on his allies and launched a surprise attack against the Communists, with the help of the city's ruthless criminal mastermind, **Du Yuesheng**. In what came to be known as the White Terror, Du's hoods, dressed in Nationalist uniforms, rampaged across the city, killing anyone with any association with communism; at least twelve thousand died, most of them executed in cold blood.

But even during the chaos, the party continued, and the foreign concessions remained an enclave of privilege. Foreign Shanghai was at its decadent height in the 1920s and 1930s, and it was during this age of inequality and decadence that Shanghai got its reputation as the "**Paris of the East**" or, less politely, "whore of the Orient". A visiting missionary sniffed, "If God allows Shanghai to endure, he owes Sodom and Gomorrah an apology." For foreigners, no visa or passport was needed and every new arrival, it was said, had something to hide. White Russian *émigrés* (see p.65) filled the chorus lines at the Paramount and the Majestic, and their unluckier sisters joined the Chinese girls at the only institutions more popular than the cabaret, the brothels. The traps that a destitute woman could fall into were many, yet only in Shanghai could a Chinese girl receive an education, reject an arranged marriage, or carve out a career. Film stars such as Ruan Lingyu, China's Garbo, personified the new independent spirit, in both her roles and her life – though the latter ended in tragedy, with her suicide.

Inevitably, the show could not last. By 1928 Chiang Kaishek had defeated enough warlords to form a tentative **National Government**, with its capital in Nanjing. Now he courted the Western powers and, partly to prove that he was a modernizer, converted to Christianity and married Song Meiling, whose father had been a close ally of Sun Yatsen. Though he was explicit about his desire to rid China of the foreigners, the powers in Shanghai backed him as the man to control the country. They were forced to renege on some of the more outrageous racist policies, such as the ruling that kept the Chinese out of Shanghai's parks; more importantly, Chinese were allowed to vote in municipal elections.

But Chiang had not rooted out all of Shanghai's Communists; by 1931 they had regrouped, and a messy civil war began. To compound the nation's woes, the same year the **Japanese snatched Manchuria** (China's northeastern province, present-day Dongbei) and Chiang found himself fighting two conflicts. Believing the Communists to be the more serious threat, he fled west with his government to avoid a showdown that he feared losing. The Japanese now struck against the interior, and in 1937 succeeded in occupying the valley of the Yangzi River, thus cutting off river trade, and depriving Shanghai of its source of wealth. Hobbled by the depression at home, weary of fighting losing battles against China's resurgent nationalism, the Western powers lost their appetite for interference in the country's chaotic affairs, and Shanghai was left to decline. By the time the Japanese marched in 1941, the life had already drained from the metropolis.

1928	**1931**	**1937**
Chiang Kaishek forms National Government in Nanjing	Civil war between Nationalists and Communists begins, Manchuria lost to the Japanese	Japanese occupy the valley of the Yangzi River

Shanghai under the Communists

It took nearly a decade for China to become once more united, this time under the Communist Party, led by **Mao Zedong**. Communism might have come from abroad, but the manner of its triumph and rule – shrewd charismatic leader leads a peasants' revolt, then becomes an all-powerful despot – were a rerun of dynastic models. They might have been born there, but the Communists distrusted Shanghai; associating it with imperialism, squalor and bourgeois individualism, they deliberately ran the city down. The worst slums were replaced by apartments, the gangsters and prostitutes were taken away for "re-education", and foreign capital was ruthlessly taxed if not confiscated (although Chiang Kaishek did manage to spirit away the gold reserves of the Bank of China to Taiwan, leaving the city broke). For 35 years Western influences were forcibly suppressed.

Perhaps eager to please its new bosses, the city became a centre of radicalism, and Mao, stifled by Beijing bureaucracy, launched his **Cultural Revolution** here in 1966 – officially a campaign to rid China of its counter-revolutionaries, but really a way to

ARCHITECTURE IN SHANGHAI

Shanghai has a great mix of striking buildings, all rather jumbled together, with traditional Chinese temples abutting Art Deco classics in the shadow of looming, brutalist skyscrapers. It isn't always pretty or coherent – a "Shanghai skyline" is architects' slang for a poorly planned mess – but, at least in the centre, there is always some marvel, oddity or bizarre juxtaposition to appreciate. The city's **architectural wonders** date from two distinct periods: 1900 to the 1930s, when colonial powers were making their mark, and the late twentieth century to today, when formidable new commercial powers were making theirs.

THE COLONIAL PERIOD

Shanghai's first building boom began at the start of the twentieth century, when the foreigners set their stamp on their new concession. For their public buildings, they picked a style then much in vogue: Neo-Classicism, which consciously echoes ancient Greek and Roman archetypes, implying that the new colonial powers were modern heirs to those ancient empires. The finest examples were built by the British firm Palmer and Turner, including the **HSBC building**, the **Yokohama Specie Building** and the **Customs House**, all on the Bund. The French take on the rather po-faced style was lighter; known as Beaux Arts, the best example in Shanghai is the **Okura Garden Hotel**.

More intimate in scale were the villas which the new European merchant class built as luxurious reminders of home. These were in all kinds of European styles, from Spanish hacienda to German castles, but the most popular was the Tudor half-timbered mansion. Though generally neglected in the twentieth century, many have been restored and reopened as offices, restaurants or hotels; striking examples include the **Hengshan Moller Mansion** and **Ruijin Hotel**.

It is fortuitous that the city's biggest colonial building boom, in the 1920s, coincided with the rise of one of the modern era's most elegant styles: Art Deco. Its design principles of streamlining, exuberance and assertive modernity created masterworks that still look contemporary, despite being dwarfed by newly built skyscrapers. Notable examples include the **Park Hotel**, **Broadway Mansions**, **Grosvenor House** and the **Fairmont Peace Hotel**.

1941	**1949**	**1966**
Japanese occupy Shanghai	Communists take over China	Mao Zedong launches the Cultural Revolution

regain control of the party after a string of economic failures. Fervent Red Guards even proclaimed a Shanghai Workers' Commune, modelled on the Paris Commune, but the whole affair quickly descended into wanton destruction and petty vindictiveness. After Mao's death in 1976, Shanghai was the last stronghold of hardcore Maoists, the Gang of Four, in their struggle for the succession, though their planned coup never materialized.

The Shanghainese never lost their ability to make waves for themselves; their chance came when following the death of Mao – and the failure of his experiment – China's communists became **one-party capitalists**. Its economic renaissance dates from 1990 when Shanghai became an autonomous municipality and the paddy fields of Pudong were designated a "Special Economic Zone". The pragmatic leader **Deng Xiaoping** declared an end to the destructiveness of ideological politicking by declaring "It doesn't matter if the cat is black or white, as long as it catches mice" – though the dictum of his that Shanghai has really taken to heart is "To get rich is glorious".

MODERN ARCHITECTURE

Since the early 1990s Shanghai has been growing faster than anywhere else in the world, ever – at one point, a quarter of the world's cranes were in use here. In the rush to globalize, the city has become something of a construction free-for-all, a playground for some of the most celebrated names in architecture. The result has been some of the world's most ambitious building projects – from spectacular high-rises to brand-new futuristic cities.

With Shanghai attempting to become a global power, thirty percent of new projects were awarded to foreign architects. They usually attempted at least a nod towards Chinese culture; one recurring theme has been the use of circles atop squares, as a reference to the Chinese idea that the earth is square, heaven round – this is notable in French architect Jean-Marie Charpentier's **Shanghai Grand Theatre** (see p.51). The most effectively Sinicized building has to be the **Jinmao Tower**, whose proportions are built around the number eight – associated with prosperity in Chinese culture – and whose tiered form constantly references pagoda design.

Construction continues at a frantic pace. Work has just started on Pudong's most ambitious skyscraper yet, the enormous **Shanghai Tower**. This twisted cylinder, set to be finished in 2014, is planned to be over 600m high, which will make it the second tallest building in the world. To get a taste of what this and other grand projects will look like, head to the Shanghai Urban Planning Exhibition Hall (see p.51).

SHANGHAI'S SATELLITES

Developments within the city are certainly eye-catching, but the most ambitious projects are happening outside the city centre. With its population set to double over the next twenty years, and a population density four times greater than that of New York, Shanghai cannot simply build upwards – it needs to spread outwards too. Accordingly, nine new **satellite cities** have been built from scratch, providing homes for half a million souls. Designed to appeal to the affluent and increasingly Westernized Chinese middle class, they are all pastiches of European cities and towns. **Pujiang** has an Italian flavour; **Fencheng** focuses on an adaptation of Barcelona's Ramblas; **Anting** is a German-themed town designed by Albert Speer, the son of Hitler's favourite architect. And **Thames Town**, the faux-English centre to Song Jiang new town, features cobbled streets, half-timbered mock Tudor houses and a parish church.

1976	1990	2003
Mao Zedong dies	Shanghai becomes an autonomous municipality, Pudong designated a "Special Economic Zone"	China puts a man into space

Shanghai today

Having opened for business, **Shanghai's growth** has never dipped below ten percent a year. The city has been torn up and built anew (locals quip that its new mascot is the crane), and now has more skyscrapers than New York. In twenty years the population has almost doubled to 23 million people. Per capita incomes have risen from US$1000 per year in 1977 to US$13,000 in 2013. Accounting for a third of China's foreign imports and attracting a quarter of all foreign investment into the country, the city is the white-hot core of the nation's astonishing boom.

As well as batteries of skyscrapers, there has been massive investment in **infrastructure projects**, most notably the Maglev train, five new subway lines, the US$2 billion Pudong International Airport, Hongqiao Station and the high-speed lines that emanate from it. Prestige ventures such as the Oriental Arts Centre and Mercedes Benz Arena have joined high-profile projects such as the Shanghai Centre in expressing the city's breezy new swagger. In 2010 Shanghai also garnered global attention with the glitzy **World Expo**, which brought more than 50 million visitors to the city; the beano was an excuse for yet more huge construction projects, including the regeneration of the Bund. With a booming new stock exchange, its next target is to become Asia's biggest financial centre.

Of course there are problems. Shanghai's destiny is still controlled by outside forces, today in the form of the technocrats of Beijing. Until recently, many key modernizing officials in the central government were from the Shanghai area; Jiang Zemin and Zhu Rongji were both former mayors. But the arrest in 2007 of Shanghai's Mayor Han Zheng and Party Secretary Chen Liangyu on corruption charges represented an attempt by Beijing to rein in the influential "Shanghai clique". Despite huge gains economically, China remains **politically stagnant**. Corruption is rife – more than US$15 billion is embezzled annually from state coffers. And thanks to China's uniquely opaque business environment, government connections have replaced entrepreneurial spirit as the necessary prerequisite for high achievement.

Simply dealing with the products of success has become a considerable headache. The city is almost four times as dense as New York and the flow of new arrivals is constant, many of them poor migrant workers from the countryside in search of work. Not unionized, they are often exploited, and – though the majority are family men who send their wages home – widely resented.

Shanghai's attitude to the **environment**, along with the rest of China, is that the clean-up will start just as soon as the city gets rich; the result is that the air quality is poor, and the rivers filthy – five million tonnes of untreated sewage and industrial waste are deposited in the mouth of the Yangzi every day. Finally, the city is becoming a victim of its own success – all those skyscrapers are causing it to **sink** at the rate of about a centimetre and a half a year, so the city government has had to cap new buildings.

Never mind; Shanghai is a natural survivor, and will surely cope with whatever new vicissitudes history throws – it's not as if it hasn't had practise. As the business heart of the world's newest superpower, it's booming in all directions, and the sheer buzz of a city on the make is intoxicating. It might not have had much of a past, but it's guaranteed a future.

2008	2010	2014
Beijing hosts the Olympic Games	Shanghai hosts the World Expo	Shanghai Tower built

Books

Don't expect too much variety in English-language reading material in Shanghai, and what is available will mostly be expensive imports. You will, though, find cheap editions of Chinese and Western classics published in English by Chinese publishers. In the reviews below, titles marked with a ★ are particularly recommended.

HISTORY

Robert Bickers *Empire Made Me: An Englishman Adrift in Shanghai* (Allen Lane, UK). This readable but carefully researched tale humanizes the concession era by focusing on one English policeman who is both toughened and corrupted by his experiences.

Nien Cheng *Life and Death in Shanghai* (Flamingo, UK; Penguin, US). One of many "my years of hell in the Cultural Revolution" books, but better than most, with absorbing descriptions of life in Shanghai in the bad old days of dour ideological purity.

★ **Stella Dong** *Shanghai: The Rise and Fall of a Decadent City 1842–1949* (HarperCollins, UK; Harper Perennial, US). Excellent popular history, vivid and readable, though with rather an anti-foreigner bias. Plenty of salacious stories of opium, flower girls, squalor and debauchery.

Harriet Sargeant *Shanghai* (John Murray, UK). Academic and broad-ranging exploration of the city during the concession era, giving equal weight to both Chinese and foreign inhabitants, and particularly good on their interrelations.

SOCIETY AND BUSINESS

★ **Tim Clissold** *Mister China* (Constable & Robinson, UK). Engaging and eye-opening real-life horror story of how a Western venture capitalist lost US$400 million in China, thanks largely to fraud and malfeasance by his local partners. It's not Shanghai-specific but is a must for anyone thinking of tackling China's "eccentric" business environment.

James Farrer *Opening Up: Youth Sex Culture & Market Reform in Shanghai* (University of Chicago Press, US). An original and engrossing piece of social anthropology, based on interviews, that uses an examination of Shanghai's sexual revolution to make some telling points.

★ **Sun Tzu** *The Art of War.* "Lure them with the prospect of gain, then take them by confusion"; this classic treatise on military strategy is as relevant now as it was when it was written, nearly three thousand years ago. Short and to the point, it's full of pithy maxims that can be applied to many aspects of life, particularly business.

Pamela Yatsko *New Shanghai* (John Wiley). This journalistic introduction to the vagaries of the twenty-first-century's new metropolis is an expat essential, as it's breezy and well informed on both business and culture.

FICTION

★ **JG Ballard** *Empire of the Sun* (Flamingo, UK; Simon & Schuster, US). This, the best literary evocation of old Shanghai, is a compelling tale of how the gilded life of expat Shanghai collapsed into chaos with the onset of war, based on the author's own experience (see box, p.166). It was subsequently made into a pretty decent film by Steven Spielberg.

Tom Bradby *The Master of Rain* (Corgi, UK; Anchor, USA). A breathless if overlong novel of murder and betrayal in 1920s Shanghai.

★ **Hergé** *The Blue Lotus* (Mammoth, UK; Casterman Editions, US). One of the best Tintin yarns, a tale of drugs and derring-do set in Shanghai during the Sino–Japanese conflicts of the 1930s.

Kazuo Ishiguro *When We Were Orphans* (Faber & Faber, UK). Ishiguro is a great writer but this postmodern detective story set in Shanghai between the wars is a little too clever and doesn't quite deliver.

Mian Mian *Candy* (Back Bay, US). Salacious if meandering *roman-à-clef,* with plenty of sex, drugs and rock and roll, by one of China's modern *enfants terribles*. Though set in the 1980s and 90s, it already seems very dated.

Neal Stephenson *The Diamond Age* (Penguin, UK; Bantam Spectra, US). A brilliant and inventive science fiction reinvention of concession-era Shanghai, set in a future where the world has been transformed by nanotechnology.

★ **Qiu Xiaolong** *When Red is Black; Death of a Red Heroine; A Case of Two Cities; A Loyal Character Dancer; The Mao Case* (Sceptre, UK; Soho Crime, US). Procedural detective fiction, featuring the poetry-loving Inspector Chen of the Shanghai PSB. Though Qiu sometimes seems more interested in examining Shanghai society and morals than in weaving a mystery, his stories of corrupt officials, sharp operators and compromised cops are the best

COCKTAILS AND ATROCITIES: JG BALLARD IN SHANGHAI

The most interesting foreign novelist associated with Shanghai is **JG Ballard** (1930–2009), whose work was formed by his experience in the city. Ballard was born and raised in the French Concession, where he experienced a childhood of great privilege, living in a villa on what is now Panyu Lu, then, following the Japanese invasion in 1941, a nightmare of total privation – he spent much of the war in a Japanese internment camp near the Longhua Temple. The rest of his life was lived in comfortable suburban obscurity in England.

As a writer he was known for visionary fiction concerning the psychological effects of technological developments and mass media; *Crash* (1973), for instance, is about a gang of car crash fetishists, *Concrete Island* (1974) a Robinson Crusoe story set on a traffic roundabout. His apocalyptic imagination was clearly formed by his experience of war as a teenager: as he wrote in his autobiography *Miracles of Life* (2008), "The memories of Shanghai that I had tried to repress had been knocking at the floorboards under my feet, and had slipped quietly into my fiction."

Late in his career, he finally dealt with the subject head on, in the semiautobiographical *Empire of the Sun* (1984); it was described as "the best British novel about the Second World War" by *The Guardian* and made into a film by Stephen Spielberg. Its description of wartime Shanghai's cocktail parties and atrocities feels very distant from the city today; on the other hand, his dystopian fiction about alienating urban environments – such as *High Rise* (1975), in which tower block residents descend into tribal savagery – feel strangely prescient in the Shanghai of Pudong and Thames Town.

evocations of the city and its people written in English.

Wei Hui *Shanghai Baby* (Constable & Robinson). Infamous chick-lit, banned in China for its louche moral tone, concerning a girl torn between her impotent Chinese boyfriend and married Western lover – though her true love is for designer labels. Self-absorbed, over-hyped, with rather more style than substance – very Shanghai.

Zhang Henshui *Shanghai Express* (University of Hawaii Press, US). A pulp novel from the 1930s, very popular in its day. Lots of incidental detail enlivens a melodramatic tale of seduction and betrayal set on a train ride from Beijing to Shanghai.

Chinese

Though you'll certainly hear the local Shanghai dialect being spoken, Mandarin Chinese, derived from the language of officialdom in the Beijing area, is the city's primary tongue. It's been systematically promoted over the past hundred years as the official, unifying language of the Chinese people, much as modern French, for example, is based on the original Parisian dialect. It is known in mainland China as putonghua, "common language".

Chinese **grammar** is delightfully simple. There is no need to conjugate verbs, decline nouns or make adjectives agree – Chinese characters are immutable, so Chinese words simply cannot have different "endings". Instead, context and fairly rigid rules about word order are relied on to make those distinctions of time, number and gender that Indo-European languages are so concerned with. Instead of cumbersome tenses, the Chinese make use of words such as "yesterday" or "tomorrow" to indicate when things happen; instead of plural endings they simply state how many things there are. For English speakers, Chinese word order is very familiar, and you'll find that by simply stringing words together you'll be producing perfectly grammatical Chinese. Basic sentences follow the subject-verb-object format; adjectives, as well as all qualifying and describing phrases, precede nouns.

From the point of view of foreigners, the main thing that distinguishes Mandarin from familiar languages is that it's a **tonal language**. In order to pronounce a word correctly, it is necessary to know not only the sounds of its consonants and vowels but also its correct tone – though with the help of context, intelligent listeners should be able to work out what you are trying to say even if you don't get the tones quite right.

Pinyin

Back in the 1950s it was hoped eventually to replace Chinese characters with an alphabet of Roman letters, and to this end the **pinyin system**, a precise and exact means of representing all the sounds of Mandarin Chinese, was devised. It comprises all the Roman letters of the English alphabet (except "v"), with the four tones represented by diacritical marks, or accents, which appear above each syllable. The old aim of replacing Chinese characters with *pinyin* was abandoned long ago, but in the meantime *pinyin* has one very important function, that of helping foreigners pronounce Chinese words. However, there is the added complication that in *pinyin* the letters don't all have the sounds you would expect, and you'll need to spend an hour or two learning the correct sounds (see p.168).

You'll often see *pinyin* in Shanghai, on street signs and shop displays, but only well-educated locals know the system very well. The Chinese names in this book have been given both in characters and in *pinyin*; the pronunciation guide below is your first step to making yourself comprehensible. For more information, see the *Rough Guide Mandarin Chinese Phrasebook* or *Pocket Interpreter* (FLP, Beijing; it's available at Shanghai's Foreign Language Bookstore).

Pronunciation

There are four possible **tones** in Mandarin Chinese, and every syllable of every word is characterized by one of them, except for a few syllables, which are considered toneless. In English, to change the tone is to change the mood or the emphasis; in Chinese, to change the tone is to change the word itself. The tones are:

First or "high" *ā ē ī ō ū*. In English this level tone is used when mimicking robotic or very boring, flat voices.

Second or "rising" *á é í ó ú*. Used in English when asking a question showing surprise; for example "*eh?*"

Third or "falling-rising" *ǎ ě ǐ ǒ ǔ*. Used in English when echoing someone's words with a measure of incredulity; for example, "John's dead." "*De-ad?!*"

Fourth or "falling" *à è ì ò ù*. Often used in English when counting in a brusque manner – "*One! Two! Three! Four!*"

Toneless A few syllables do not have a tone accent. These are pronounced without emphasis, such as in the English **u**pon.

Note that when two words with the third tone occur consecutively, the first word is pronounced as though it carries the second tone. Thus nǐ (meaning "you") and hǎo ("well, good"), when combined, are pronounced ní hǎo, meaning "how are you?"

CONSONANTS

Most consonants, as written in *pinyin*, are pronounced in a similar way to their English equivalents, with the following exceptions:

c as in ha**ts**

g is hard as in **g**od (except when preceded by "n", when it sounds like sa**ng**)

q as in **ch**eese

x has no direct equivalent in English, but you can make the sound by sliding from an "s" to an "sh" sound and stopping midway between the two

z as in su**ds**

zh as in fu**dge**

VOWELS AND DIPHTHONGS

As in most languages, the vowel sounds are rather harder to quantify than the consonants. The examples below give a rough description of the sound of each vowel as written in *pinyin*.

a usually somewhere between **fa**r and m**a**n

ai as in **eye**

ao as in c**ow**

e usually as in f**ur**

ei as in g**ay**

en as in hyph**en**

eng as in s**ung**

er as in b**ar** with a pronounced "r"

i usually as in b**ee**, except in *zi, ci, si, ri, zhi, chi* and *shi*, when *i* is a short, clipped sound, like the American military "sir".

ia as in **ya**k

ian as in **yen**

ie as in **yeah**

o as in s**aw**

ou as in sh**ow**

ü as in the German **ü** (make an "ee" sound and glide slowly into an "oo"; at the mid-point between the two sounds you should hit the *ü*-sound.

u usually as in f**oo**l, though whenever *u* follows *j, q, x* or *y*, it is always pronounced **ü**

ua as in s**ua**ve

uai as in **wh**y

ue as though contracting "you" and "air" together, **you**'air

ui as in **wa**y

uo as in w**ore**

Useful words and phrases

When writing or saying the name of a Chinese person, the surname is given first; thus Mao Zedong's family name is Mao.

BASICS

I	我	wǒ	No, I don't want...	我不要	wǒ bú yào...
You (singular)	你	nǐ	Is it possible...?	可不可以...	kěbù kěyǐ...?
He	他	tā	It is (not) possible	(不)可以...	(bù)kěyǐ
She	她	tā	Is there any/Have you got any...?	你有没有...	nǐ yǒuméiyǒu...?
We	我们	wǒmen			
You (plural)	你们	nǐmen	There is/I have	有...	yǒu...
They	他们	tāmen	There isn't/I haven't	没有...	méiyǒu
I want...	我要	wǒ yào...			

Please help me	请帮我忙...	qǐng bāng	Mr...	.....先生	xiānshēng
		wǒ máng	Mrs...	.....太太	tàitai
			Miss...	.....小姐	xiǎojiě

COMMUNICATING

I don't speak Chinese	我不会说中文	wǒ búhuì shuō zhōngwén
Can you speak English?	你会说英语吗?	nǐ huì shuō yī ngyǔ ma?
Can you get someone who speaks English?	请给我找一个会说英文的人？	qǐng gěi wǒ zhǎo yī gè huì shuō yīngyǔ de rén?
Please speak slowly	请说得慢一点	qǐng shuōde mànyīdiǎn
Please say that again	请再说一遍	qǐng zài shuō yībiàn
I understand	我听得懂	wǒ tīngdedǒng
I don't understand	我听不懂	wǒ tīngbùdǒng
I can't read Chinese characters	我看不懂汉字	wǒ kànbùdǒng hànzì
What does this mean?	这是什么意思？	zhè shì shénme yìsi?
How do you pronounce this character?	这个字怎么念？	zhègè zì zěnme niàn?

GREETINGS AND BASIC COURTESIES

Hello/How do you do/How are you?	你好	nǐhǎo
I'm fine	我很好	wǒhěnhǎo
Thank you	谢谢	xièxie
Don't mention it/You're welcome	不客气	búkèqi
Sorry to bother you...	麻烦你	máfán nǐ
Sorry/I apologize	对不起	duìbùqǐ
It's not important/No problem	没关系	méi guānxì
Goodbye	再见	zài jiàn
Excuse me	对不起	dùibùqǐ

CHITCHAT

What country are you from?	你是哪个国家的？	nǐ shì nǎgè guójiā de?
Britain	英国	yīngguó
England	英国/英格兰	yīngguó/yīnggélán
Scotland	苏格兰	sūgélán
Wales	威尔士	wēi'ěrshì
Ireland	爱尔兰	ài'ěrlán
America	美国	měiguó
Canada	加拿大	jiānádà
Australia	澳大利亚	àodàliyà
New Zealand	新西兰	xīnxīlán
South Africa	南非	nánfēi
China	中国	zhōngguó
Outside China	外国	wàiguó
What's your name?	你叫什么名字？	nǐ jiào shénme míngzi?
My name is...	我叫....	wǒ jiào...
Are you married?	你结婚了吗？	nǐ jiéhūn le ma?
I am (not) married	我(没有)结婚(了)	wǒ (méiyǒu) jiéhūn (le)
Have you got (children)?	你有没有孩子？	nǐ yǒu méiyǒu háizi?
Do you like...?	你喜不喜欢.....？	nǐ xǐ bù xǐhuān....?
I (don't) like...	我不喜欢....	wǒ (bù) xǐhuān...
What's your job?	你干什么工作？	nǐ gàn shénme gōngzuò?
I'm a foreign student	我是留学生	wǒ shì liúxuéshēng
I'm a teacher	我是老师	wǒ shì lǎoshī
I work in a company	我在一个公司工作	wǒ zài yígè gōngsī gōngzuò
I'm retired	我退休了	wǒ tuìxiūle

Clean/dirty	干净/脏	gānjìng/zāng
Hot/cold	热/冷	rè/lěng
Fast/slow	快/慢	kuài/màn
Good/bad	好/坏	hǎo/huài
Big/small	大/小	dà/xiǎo
Pretty	漂亮	piàoliàng
Interesting	有意思	yǒuyìsi

NUMBERS

Zero	零	líng
One	一	yī
Two	二/两	èr/liǎng*
Three	三	sān
Four	四	sì
Five	五	wǔ
Six	六	liù
Seven	七	qī
Eight	八	bā
Nine	九	jiǔ
Ten	十	shí
Eleven	十一	shíyī
Twelve	十二	shíèr
Twenty	二十	èrshí
Twenty-one	二十一	èrshíyī
One hundred	一百	yībǎi
Two hundred	二百	èrbǎi
One thousand	一千	yīqiān
Ten thousand	一万	yīwàn
One hundred thousand	十万	shíwàn
One million	一百万	yībǎiwàn
One hundred million	一亿	yīyì
One billion	十亿	shíyì

* 两/liǎng is used when enumerating, for example "two people" (liǎnggè rén). 二 /èr is used when counting.

TIME

Now	现在	xiànzài
Today	今天	jīntiān
(In the) morning	早上	zǎoshàng
(In the) afternoon	下午	xiàwǔ
(In the) evening	晚上	wǎnshàng
Tomorrow	明天	míngtiān
The day after tomorrow	后天	hòutiān
Yesterday	昨天	zuótiān
Week/month/year	星期/月/年	xīngqī/yuè/nián
Next/last week/month/year	下/上 星期/月/年	xià/shàng xīngqī/yuè/nián
Monday	星期一	xīngqī yī
Tuesday	星期二	xīngqī èr
Wednesday	星期三	xīngqī sān
Thursday	星期四	xīngqī sì
Friday	星期五	xīngqī wǔ
Saturday	星期六	xīngqī liù
Sunday	星期天	xīngqī tiān
What's the time?	几点了?	jǐdiǎn le?
Morning	早上	zǎoshàng

Afternoon	中午	zhōngwǔ
10 o'clock	十点钟	shídiǎn zhōng
10.20	十点二十	shídiǎn èrshí
10.30	十点半	shídiǎn bàn

TRAVELLING AND GETTING AROUND TOWN

North	北	běi
South	南	nán
East	东	dōng
West	西	xī
Airport	机场	jīchǎng
Ferry dock	船码头	chuánmǎtóu
Left-luggage office	寄存处	jìcún chù
Ticket office	售票处	shòupiào chù
Ticket	票	piào
Can you sell me a ticket to…?	可不可以给我买到 ….的票?	kěbùkěyǐ gěi wǒ mǎi dào….de piào?
I want to go to…	我想到…..去	wǒ xiǎng dào … qù
I want to leave at (8 o'clock)	我想(八点钟)离开	wǒ xiǎng (bā diǎn zhōng) líkāi
When does it leave?	什么时候出发?	shénme shíhòu chūfā?
When does it arrive?	什么时候到?	shénme shíhòu dào?
How long does it take?	路上得多长时间?	lùshàng děi duōcháng shíjiān?
CITS	中国国际旅行社	zhōngguó guójì lǚxíngshè
Train	火车	huǒchē
(Main) train station	主要火车站	(zhǔyào) huǒchēzhàn
Bus	公共汽车	gōnggòng qìchēzhàn
Bus station	汽车站	qìchēzhàn
Long-distance bus station	长途汽车站	chángtú qìchēzhàn
Express train/bus	特快车	tèkuài chē
Fast train/bus	快车	kuài chē
Ordinary train/bus	普通车	pǔtōng chē
Timetable	时间表	shíjiān biǎo
Map	地图	dìtú
Where is…?	……在 哪里?	…zài nǎlǐ?
Go straight on	往前走	wǎng qián zǒu
Turn right	往右走	wǎng yòu zǒu
Turn left	往左拐	wǎng zuǒ guǎi
Taxi	出租车	chūzū chē
Please use the meter	请打开记价器	qǐng dǎkāi jìjiàqì
Underground/subway station	地铁站	dìtiě zhàn
Bicycle	自行车	zìxíngchē
Which bus goes to…?	几路车到……去?	jǐlù chēdào … qù?
Number (10) bus	(十)路车	(shí) lù chē
Does this bus go to…?	这车到……去吗?	zhè chē dào … qù ma?
When is the next bus?	下一班车几点开?	xiàyìbānchē jǐdiǎn kāi?
The first bus	头班车	tóubān chē
The last bus	末班车	mòbān chē
Please tell me where to get off	请告诉我在哪里下车	qǐng gàosù wǒ zài nǎlǐ xiàchē?
Museum	博物馆	bówù guǎn
Temple	寺庙	sìmiào
Church	教堂	jiàotáng

ACCOMMODATION

Accommodation	住宿	zhùsù
Hotel (upmarket)	宾馆	bīnguǎn

Hotel (cheap)	招待所, 旅馆	zhāodàisuǒ, lǚguǎn
Hostel	旅社	lǚshè
Do you have a room available?	你们有房间吗？	nǐmén yǒu fángjiān ma?
Can I have a look at the room?	能不能看一下房间？	néngbùnéng kànyíxià fángjiān?
I want the cheapest bed you've got	我要你这里最便宜的床位	wǒ yào nǐzhèlǐ zuìpiányi
Single room	单人房	dānrén fáng
Twin room	双人房	shuāngrén fáng
Double room with a big bed	双人房间带大床	shuāngrén fángjiān dài dàchuáng
Three-bed room	三人房	sānrén fáng
Dormitory	多人房	duōrén fáng
Suite	套房	tàofáng
(Large) bed	(大) 床	(dà) chuáng
Passport	护照	hùzhào
Deposit	押金	yājīn
Key	钥匙	yàoshi
I want to change my room	我想换一个房间	wǒ xiǎng huàn yígè fángjiān

SHOPPING AND MONEY

How much is it?	这是多少钱？	zhè shì duōshǎo qián?
That's too expensive	太贵了	tàiguìle
I haven't got any cash	我没有现金	wǒ méiyǒu xiànjīn
Have you got anything cheaper?	你没有便宜一点的？	yǒu méiyǒu piányì yìdiǎn de?
Do you accept credit cards?	可不可以用信用卡	kě bù kěyǐ yòng xìnyòngkǎ?
Department store	百货商店	bǎihuò shāngdiàn
Market	市场	shìchǎng
¥1 (RMB)	一块 (人民币)	yíkuài (rénmínbì)
US$1	一块美金	yíkuài měijīn
£1	一个英镑	yígè yīngbàng
Change money	换钱	huànqián
Bank	银行	yínháng
ATM	提款机	tíkuǎn jī
PSB	公安局	gōng'ān jú

COMMUNICATIONS

Post office	邮电局	yóudiàn jú
Envelope	信封	xìnfēng
Stamp	邮票	yóupiào
Airmail	航空信	hángkōng xìn
Surface mail	平信	píngxìn
Telephone	电话	diànhuà
Mobile phone	手机	shǒujī
SMS message	短信	duǎnxìn
International telephone call	国际电话	guójì diànhuà
Reverse charges/collect call	对方付钱电话	duìfāngfùqián diànhuà
Telephone card	电话卡	diànhuà kǎ
I want to make a telephone call to (Britain)	我想给 (英国) 打电话	wǒ xiǎng gěi (yīngguó) dǎ diànhuà
Internet	网吧	wǎngbā
Email	电邮	diànyóu

HEALTH

Hospital	医院	yīyuàn
Pharmacy	药店	yàodiàn
Medicine	药	yào

Chinese medicine	中药	zhōngyào
Diarrhoea	腹泻	fùxiè
Vomit	呕吐	ǒutù
Fever	发烧	fāshāo
I'm ill	我生病了	wǒ shēngbìng le
I've got flu	我感冒了	wǒ gǎnmào le
I'm (not) allergic to…	我对…..(不)过敏	wǒ duì … (bù) guòmin
Antibiotics	抗生素	kàngshēngsù
Condom	避孕套	bìyùntào
Tampons	卫生棉条	wèishēng miántiáo

Menu reader

GENERAL

Restaurant	餐厅	cāntīng
House speciality	拿手好菜	náshǒu hǎocài
How much is that?	多少钱?	duōshǎo qián?
I don't eat (meat)	我不吃(肉)	wǒ bù chī (ròu)
I would like…	我想要….	wǒ xiāng yào…
Local dishes	地方菜	dìfāngcài
Snacks	小吃	xiǎochī
Menu/set menu/English menu	菜单/套菜/英文菜单	càidān/tàocài/yīngwén càidān
Small portion	少量	shǎoliàng
Chopsticks	筷子	kuàizi
Knife and fork	刀叉	dāchā
Spoon	勺子	sháozi
Waiter/waitress	服务员	fúwùyuán
Bill/cheque	买单	mǎidān
Cook these ingredients together	一快儿做	yíkuài'r zuò
Not spicy/no chilli please	请不要辣椒	qīngbúyào làjiāo
Only a little spice/chilli	一点辣椒	yìdiǎnlàjiāo
50 grams	两	liǎng
250 grams	半斤	bànjīn
500 grams	斤	jīn
1 kilo	公斤	gōngjīn

DRINKS

Beer	啤酒	píjiǔ
Coffee	咖啡	kāfēi
Milk	牛奶	niúnǎi
(Mineral) water	(矿泉)水	(kuàngquán) shuǐ
Wine	葡萄酒	pútáojiǔ
Tea	茶	chá
Black tea	红茶	hóngchá
Green tea	绿茶	lǜchá
Jasmine tea	茉莉花茶	mòlìhuā chá

STAPLE FOODS

Aubergine	茄子	qiézi
Bamboo shoots	笋尖	sǔnjiān
Bean sprouts	豆芽	dòuyá
Beans	豆	dòu
Beef	牛肉	niúròu

Black bean sauce	黑豆豉	hēidòuchǐ
Bread	面包	miànbāo
Buns (filled)	包子	bāozi
Buns (plain)	馒头	mántou
Carrot	胡萝卜	húluóbo
Cashew nuts	腰果	yāoguǒ
Chicken	鸡	jī
Chilli	辣椒	làjiāo
Crab	蟹	xiè
Cucumber	黄瓜	huángguā
Duck	鸭	yā
Eel	鳝鱼	shànyú
Eggs (fried)	煎鸡蛋	jiān jīdàn
Fish	鱼	yú
Fried dough stick	油条	yóutiáo
Garlic	大蒜	dàsuàn
Ginger	姜	jiāng
Green pepper (capsicum)	青椒	qīngjiāo
Green vegetables	绿叶蔬菜	lùyè shūcài
Jiaozi (dumplings, steamed or boiled)	饺子	jiǎozi
Lamb	羊肉	yángròu
Lotus root	莲心	liánxīn
MSG	味精	wèijīng
Mushrooms	蘑菇	mógū
Noodles	面条	miàntiáo
Omelette	摊鸡蛋	tānjīdàn
Onions	洋葱	yángcōng
Oyster sauce	蚝油	háoyóu
Pancake	摊饼	tānbǐng
Peanut	花生	huāshēng
Pork	猪肉	zhūròu
Potato (stir-fried)	(炒)土豆	(chǎo) tǔdòu
Prawns	虾	xiā
Preserved egg	皮蛋	pídàn
Rice, boiled	白饭	báifàn
Rice, fried	炒饭	chǎofàn
Rice noodles	河粉	héfěn
Rice porridge (aka congee)	粥	zhōu
Salt	盐	yán
Shuijiao (dumplings in soup)	水饺	shuǐjiāo
Sichuan pepper	四川辣椒	sìchuān làjiāo
Soup	汤	tāng
Soy sauce	酱油	jiàngyóu
Squid	鱿鱼	yóuyú
Sugar	糖	táng
Tofu	豆腐	dòufu
Tomato	蕃茄	fānqié
Vinegar	醋	cù
Water chestnuts	马蹄	mǎtí
Yogurt	酸奶	suānnǎi

COOKING METHODS

| Boiled | 煮 | zhǔ |
| Casseroled | 焙 | bèi |

Deep-fried	油煎	yóujiān
Fried	炒	chǎo
Poached	白煮	báizhǔ
Red-cooked (stewed in soy sauce)	红烧	hóngshāo
Roast	烤	kǎo
Steamed	蒸	zhēng
Stir-fried	清炒	qīngchǎo

SHANGHAI SPECIALITIES

Beggars' chicken (baked)	叫花鸡	jiàohuā jī
Braised pig trotters	蹄膀	tí pang
Brine duck	盐水鸭	yánshuǐ yā
Crab soup	蟹肉汤	xièròu tāng
Crispy eel	香酥脆	xiāngsū cuì
Crystal prawns	水晶虾仁	shuǐjīng xiārén
Dongpo pork casserole (steamed in wine)	东坡焙肉	dōngpō bèiròu
Drunken chicken (chicken cooked in wine)	醉鸡	zuìjī
Drunken prawns	醉虾	zuìxiā
Fish-shred soup	鱼丝汤	yúsī táng
Five-flower pork (steamed in lotus leaves)	五花肉	wǔhuā ròu
Fried crab with eggs	蟹肉鸡蛋	xièròu jīdàn
Hairy crab	大闸蟹	dàzhá xiè
Pearl balls (rice grain-coated, steamed rissoles)	珍珠球	zhēnzhū qiú
Shaoxing chicken	绍兴鸡	shàoxīng jī
Shengjian dumplings	生煎包	shēnjiān bāo
Smoked fish	熏鱼	xún yú
Soup dumplings (steamed, containing jellied stock)	汤包	tāngbāo
Sour and hot soup with eel and chicken	龙凤酸辣汤	lóngfèng suānlà tāng
Steamed "lionshead" (mincemeat)	清蒸狮子头	qīngzhēng shīzitóu
Steamed sea bass	清蒸鲈鱼	qīngzhēng lúyú
Stuffed green peppers	馅青椒	xiàn qīngjiāo
Sweet and sour spare ribs	糖醋小排	tángcù xiǎopái
West Lake fish (braised in a sour sauce)	西湖醋鱼	xīhú cùyú
White-cut beef (spiced and steamed)	白切牛肉	báiqiē niúròu
Xiaolong dumplings	小笼包	xiǎolóng bāo
Yangzhou fried rice	杨州炒饭	yángzhōu chǎofàn

EVERYDAY DISHES

Braised duck with vegetables	炖鸭素菜	dùnyā sùcài
Cabbage rolls (stuffed with meat or vegetables)	卷心菜	juǎnxīncài
Chicken and sweetcorn soup	玉米鸡丝汤	yùmǐ jīsī tāng
Chicken with cashew nuts	腰果鸡片	yāoguǒ jīpiàn
Claypot/sandpot (casserole)	沙锅	shāguō
Crispy aromatic duck	香酥鸭	xiāngsūyā
Egg flower soup with tomato	蕃茄蛋汤	fānqié dàn tāng
Egg fried rice	蛋炒饭	dànchǎofàn
Fish casserole	焙鱼	bèiyú
Fried shredded pork with garlic and chilli	大蒜辣椒炒肉片	dàsuàn làjiāo chǎoròupiàn
Kebab	串肉	chuànròu
Noodle soup	汤面	tāngmiàn
Pork and mustard greens	芥末肉片	jièmò ròupiàn
Pork and water chestnut	马蹄猪肉	mǎtí zhūròu
Prawn with garlic sauce	大蒜炒虾	dàsuàn chǎoxiā
Pulled noodles	拉面	lāmiàn

Roast duck	烤鸭	kǎoyā
Scrambled egg with pork on rice	滑蛋猪肉饭	huádàn zhūròufàn
Steamed rice packets wrapped in lotus leaves	荷叶蒸饭	héyè zhēngfàn
Stewed pork belly with vegetables	回锅肉	huíguōròu
Stir-fried chicken and bamboo shoots	笋尖炒鸡片	sǔnjiān chǎojīpiàn
Sweet bean paste pancakes	赤豆摊饼	chìdòu tānbǐng
Wonton soup	馄饨汤	húntun tāng

VEGETABLES AND EGGS

Aubergine with chilli and garlic sauce	大蒜辣椒炒茄子	dàsuàn làjiāo chǎoqiézi
Bean curd and spinach soup	菠菜豆腐汤	bōcài dòufutāng
Egg fried with tomatoes	蕃茄炒蛋	fānqié chǎodàn
Fried bean curd with vegetables	豆腐蔬菜	dòufu shūcài
Fried bean sprouts	炒豆芽	chǎo dòuyá
Spicy braised aubergine	香茄子条	xiāngqiézitiáo
Stir-fried bamboo shoots	炒冬笋	chǎo dōngsǔn
Stir-fried mushrooms	炒鲜菇	chǎo xiāngū
Vegetable soup	蔬菜汤	shūcài tāng

REGIONAL DISHES

NORTHERN

Aromatic fried lamb	炒羊肉	chǎo yángròu
Beijing (Peking) duck	北京烤鸭	běijīng kǎoyā
Fish with ham and vegetables	火腿蔬菜鱼片	huǒtuǐ shūcài yúpiàn
Fried prawn balls	炒虾球	chǎo xiāqiú
Hotpot	火锅	huǒguō
Lion's head (pork rissoles casseroled with greens)	狮子头	shīzitóu
Red-cooked lamb	红烧羊肉	hóngshāo yángròu

SICHUAN WESTERN CHINESE

Boiled beef slices (spicy)	水煮牛肉	shuǐzhǔ niúròu
Crackling-rice with pork	爆米肉片	bàomǐ ròupiàn
Crossing-the-bridge noodles	过桥面	guòqiáo miàn
Double-cooked pork	回锅肉	huíguōròu
Dry-fried pork shreds	油炸肉丝	yóuzhá ròusi
Gongbao chicken (with chillies and peanuts)	公保鸡丁	gōngbǎo jīdīng
Hot and sour soup (flavoured with vinegar and white pepper)	酸辣汤	suānlà tāng
Hot-spiced bean curd	麻婆豆腐	mápó dòufu
Smoked duck	熏鸭	xūnyā
Stuffed aubergine slices	馅茄子	xiàn qiézi

FRUIT

Honeydew melon	哈密瓜	hāmìguā
Lychee	荔枝	lìzhī
Mango	芒果	mángguǒ
Orange	橙子	chéngzi
Peach	桃子	táozi
Pear	梨	lí
Plum	李子	lǐzi
Pomegranate	石榴	shíliú
Watermelon	西瓜	xīguā

Glossary

Arhat Buddhist saint

Bei North

CCP Chinese Communist Party

Concession A section of Shanghai under the control of a foreign power during the nineteenth and twentieth centuries; a colonial territory in all but name

Cultural Revolution Ten-year period beginning in 1966 and characterized by destruction, persecution and fanatical devotion to Mao

Dagoba Another name for a stupa

Ding An ancient three-legged vessel, used for cooking and ceremonial purposes

Dingpeng Literally a nail shed, the cheapest kind of brothel in concession-era Shanghai

Dong East

Dougong Ornate, load-bearing bracket used in temple roofs

Fen Smallest denomination of Chinese currency – there are one hundred fen to the yuan

Feng Peak

Feng shui A system of geomancy used to determine the positioning of buildings

Gong Palace

Gongyuan Park

Guan Temple

Guanyin The ubiquitous Buddhist Goddess of Mercy, who postponed her entry into paradise in order to help ease human misery. Derived from the Indian deity Avalokiteshvara, she is often depicted with up to a thousand arms

Guomindang (GMD) The Nationalist Peoples' Party. Under Chiang Kaishek, the GMD fought Communist forces for 25 years before being defeated and moving to Taiwan in 1949, where it remains a major political party

Han Chinese The main body of the Chinese people, as distinct from other ethnic groups such as Uigur, Miao, Hui or Tibetan

Hu Lake

Jiao (or mao) Ten fen

Jie Street

Little Red Book A selection of "Quotations from Chairman Mao Zedong", produced in 1966 as a philosophical treatise for Red Guards during the Cultural Revolution

Longtang A narrow lane lined with *shikumen* houses

Lu Street

Maitreya Buddha The Buddha of the future, at present awaiting rebirth

Men Gate/door

Miao Temple

Ming Chinese dynasty that ruled from 1368 to 1644, before being overthrown by the Manchus from the north

Nan South

PLA The People's Liberation Army, the official name of the Communist military forces since 1949

PSB Public Security Bureau, the branch of China's police force which deals directly with foreigners

Pagoda Tower with distinctively tapering structure

Pipa A traditional string instrument

Pinyin The official system of transliterating Chinese script into Roman characters

Putonghua Mandarin Chinese; literally "Common Language"

Qiao Bridge

Qing The last of the great Chinese dynasties (1644–1911), administered from Beijing

Qipao The characteristic Chinese long fitted dress.

Red Guards The unruly factional forces unleashed by Mao during the Cultural Revolution to find and destroy brutally any "reactionaries" among the populace

Renmimbi Literally "people's money"; the official Chinese term for the Chinese currency

Renmin The people

Shikumen Terraced housing created in the nineteenth century by the British

Shuyu A high-class courtesan, like a geisha, skilled in singing and dancing as well as love

Si Temple, usually Buddhist

Song A Chinese dynasty (960–1279 AD) administered first from Kaifeng and later from Hangzhou, regarded as mercantilist and progressive

Stele Freestanding stone tablet carved with text

Stupa Multi-tiered tower associated with Buddhist temples that usually contains sacred objects

Ta Tower or pagoda

Tang Arguably the greatest Chinese dynasty (618–907 AD). The Tang was outward looking and stable. The era also represented a high-water mark for the Chinese arts

Taxi girls Girls who danced for money in concession-era Shanghai

Tai ji A discipline of physical exercise, characterized by slow, deliberate, balletic movements

Tea dances Organized dances in concession Shanghai, rather less innocent than the name implies

Tian Heaven or the sky

Xi West

Yuan China's unit of currency. Also a courtyard or garden

Zhou Villa or manor

Small print and index

Rough Guide credits

Editors: Eleanor Aldridge, Kathryn Lane
Layout: Jessica Subramanian
Cartography: Swati Handoo
Picture editor: Marta Bescos
Proofreader: Diane Margolis
Managing editor: Keith Drew
Assistant editor: Prema Dutta
Production: Charlotte Cade

Cover design: Nicole Newman, Pepi Bluck, Jessica Subramanian
Editorial assistant: Rebecca Hallett
Senior pre-press designer: Dan May
Programme manager: Helen Blount
Publisher: Joanna Kirby

Publishing information

This third edition published July 2014 by
Rough Guides Ltd,
80 Strand, London WC2R 0RL
11, Community Centre, Panchsheel Park,
New Delhi 110017, India
Distributed by Penguin Random House
Penguin Books Ltd,
80 Strand, London WC2R 0RL
Penguin Group (USA)
345 Hudson Street, NY 10014, USA
Penguin Group (Australia)
250 Camberwell Road, Camberwell,
Victoria 3124, Australia
Penguin Group (NZ)
67 Apollo Drive, Mairangi Bay, Auckland 1310,
New Zealand
Penguin Group (South Africa)
Block D, Rosebank Office Park, 181 Jan Smuts Avenue,
Parktown North, Gauteng, South Africa 2193
Rough Guides is represented in Canada by Tourmaline
Editions Inc. 662 King Street West, Suite 304, Toronto,
Ontario M5V 1M7
Printed in Singapore by Toppan Security Printing Pte. Ltd.

MIX
Paper from
responsible sources
FSC™ C018179

Help us update

We've gone to a lot of effort to ensure that the third
edition of **The Rough Guide to Shanghai** is accurate
and up-to-date. However, things change – places get
"discovered", opening hours are notoriously fickle,
restaurants and rooms raise prices or lower standards. If
you feel we've got it wrong or left something out, we'd like
to know, and if you can remember the address, the price,
the hours, the phone number, so much the better.

Please send your comments with the subject line
"**Rough Guide Shanghai Update**" to ✉ mail
@uk.roughguides.com. We'll credit all contributions and
send a copy of the next edition (or any other Rough Guide
if you prefer) for the very best emails.

Find more travel information, connect with fellow
travellers and plan your trip on ⊕ roughguides.com

ABOUT THE AUTHOR

Simon Lewis is a novelist and screenwriter. His crime novel *Bad Traffic* has been translated into seven languages and was shortlisted for the *LA Times* Book of the Year 2012. His produced feature film scripts include thrillers *Tiger House* and *The Anomaly*.

Acknowledgements

Thanks to Kat, Mark, Xiao Song, Noe, Tim, Harkin, Dana, Ryan, Pan Yin, Sitang, Maggie, Kelly, Callum, Shane, Zoe.

Readers' updates

Thanks to all the readers who have taken the time to write in with comments and suggestions (and apologies if we've inadvertently omitted or misspelt anyone's name):

Kirk T. McDonald, Benjamin L. Monshor, Steinar Saethre, Wiard Sterk, Anthony Steward, Paul Takla, Wilfried Viebahn and Rob Zwaga

Photo credits

All photos © Rough Guides except the following:
(Key: a-above; b-below/bottom; c-centre; f-far; l-left; r-right; t-top)

p.1 Dreamstime.com: Dominikschmidt
p.2 Robert Harding Picture Library: age fotostock/Robert Harding
p.4 Dreamstime.com: Jackmalipan
p.7 Alamy: Alex Segre
p.9 LOOK Die Bildagentur der Fotografen GmbH (t); Alamy: Hemis (c); Getty Images: Wei Fang (b)
p.11 123RF.com: Philip Lange (tl); Robert Harding Picture Library: Lucas Vallecillos (c)
p.12 Getty Images: EIGHTFISH (t)
p.13 Dreamstime.com: Pixattitude (tr); Robert Harding Picture Library: LOOK/Karl Johaentges (c)
p.14 Photoshot: Tibor Bognar (t); Robert Harding Picture Library: Xinhua (b)
p.15 T8 Restaurant & Bar (c)
p.16 Alamy: kpzfoto
p.38 Getty Images: China Span RM/Keren Su
p.53 Dreamstime.com: Mikhail Nekrasov
p.70 Dreamstime.com: William Perry

p.83 Dreamstime.com: Ktree
p.87 Dreamstime.com: Bartlomiej Magierowski
p.91 Fairmont Peace Hotel
p.100 M on the Bund
p.111 Alamy: Mr&Mrs Bund (bl); Kevin Foy (br)
p.114 Alamy: LOOK Die Bildagentur der Fotografen GmbH
p.124 Alamy: Planetpix
p.133 Alamy: JTB MEDIA CREATION, Inc.
p.151 Dreamstime.com: Badoff (t); Alamy: dbimages (bl); Robert Harding Picture Library: Tao Images (br)
p.158 Getty Images: Flickr RF

Front cover Nanjing shopping street © Getty Images: Grant Faint
Back cover Shopping in the Yu Yuan Bazaar, Yu Gardens, Nanshi © Robert Harding Picture Library: Amanda Hall (t); Tourists visit the West Lake in Hangzhou © Photoshot: Xinhua (bl); The Grand Hyatt, inside the Jinmao Tower, Pudong © Rough Guides: Tim Draper (br)

Index

Maps are marked in **grey**

A ROUGH GUIDE TO
ROUGH GUIDES

Published in 1982, the first Rough Guide – to Greece – was a student scheme that became a publishing phenomenon. Mark Ellingham, a recent graduate in English from Bristol University, had been travelling in Greece the previous summer and couldn't find the right guidebook. With a small group of friends he wrote his own guide, combining a highly contemporary, journalistic style with a thoroughly practical approach to travellers' needs.

The immediate success of the book spawned a series that rapidly covered dozens of destinations. And, in addition to impecunious backpackers, Rough Guides soon acquired a much broader and older readership that relished the guides' wit and inquisitiveness as much as their enthusiastic, critical approach and value-for-money ethos.

These days, Rough Guides feature recommendations from shoestring to luxury and cover more than 200 destinations around the globe. Our ever-growing team of authors and photographers is spread all over the world, particularly in Europe, the US and Australia.

Rough Guides now number around 200 titles, including Pocket city guides, inspirational coffee-table books and comprehensive country and regional titles, plus technology guides from iPods to Android. As well as print books, we publish groundbreaking apps and eBooks for every major digital device.

Visit Ⓦ roughguides.com to see our latest publications.

Rough Guide travel images are available for commercial licensing at Ⓦ roughguidespictures.com.

Map index

Map symbols

- ✈ Airport
- ⓘ Tourist information
- ✉ Post office
- @ Internet access
- ✚ Hospital
-)(Bridge
- ⊠ Gate/park entrance
- ▲ Mountain peak
- ⊙ Metro station
- Ⓛ Bus station/depot
- ★ Minibus stand/bus stop
- ✡ Synagogue
- Chinese temple
- Pagoda
- Building
- Church/cathedral/chapel
- Market
- Park/national biodiversity
- Beach
- Cemetery

Listings key

- ■ Accommodation
- ● Restaurant/café
- ■ Bar/club
- ● Shop/market

City plan

The **city plan** on the pages that follow is divided as shown:

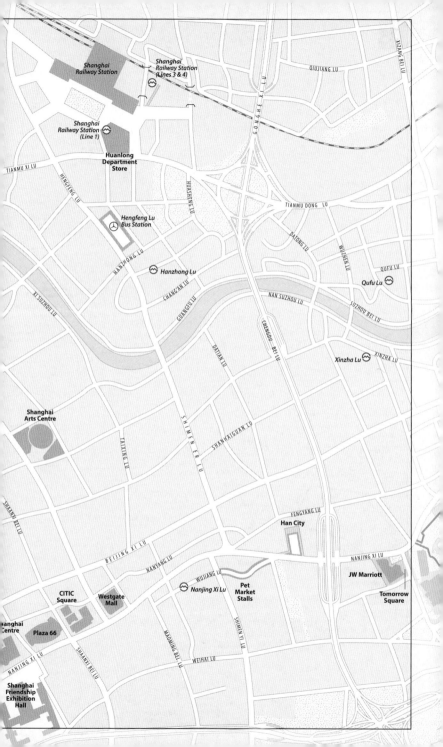

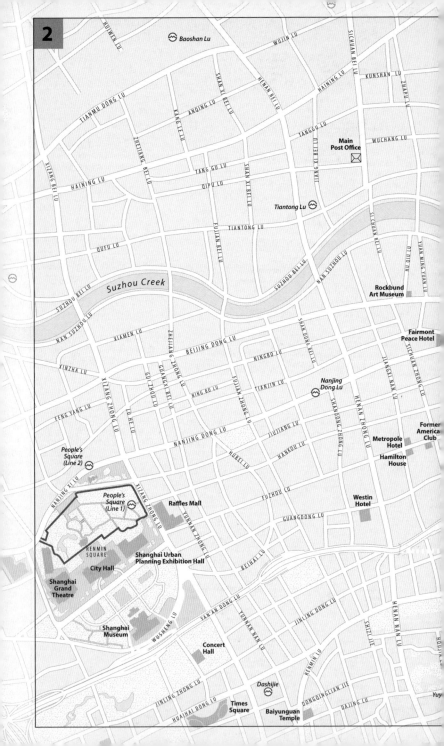

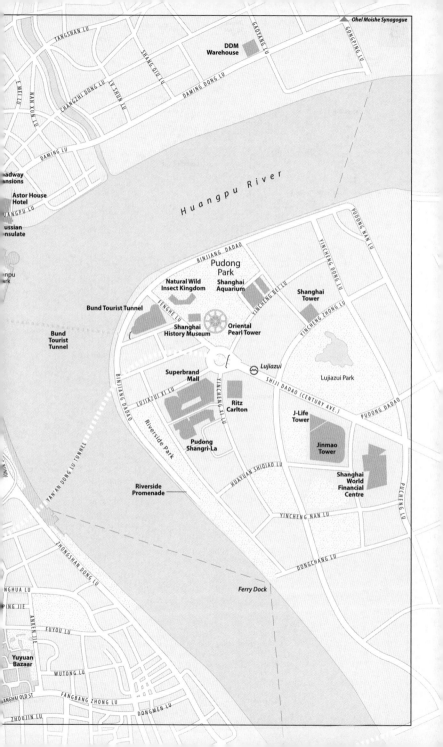

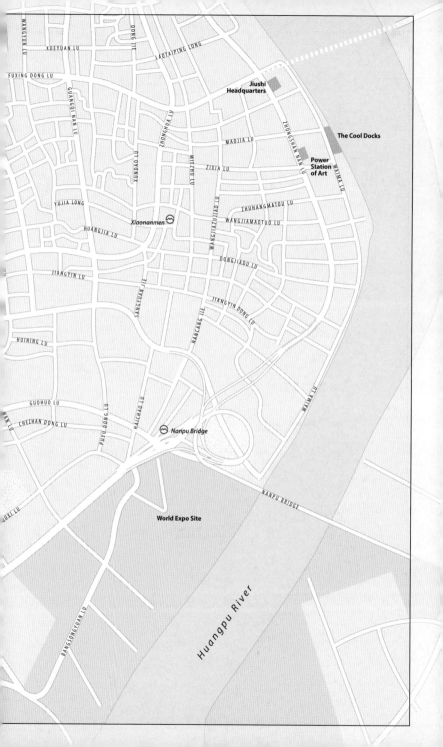

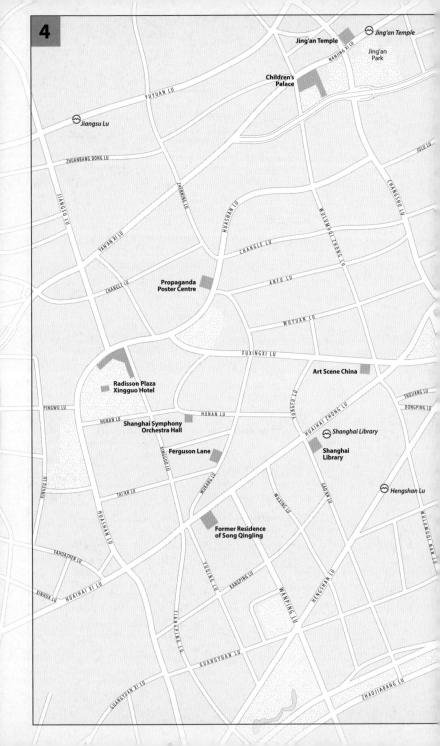

Jing'an Temple

Jing'an Temple

Jing'an Park

NANJING XI LU

VUYUAN LU

Children's Palace

Jiangsu Lu

JULU LU

ZHUANBANG DONG LU

ZHENNING LU

CHANGSHU LU

JIANGSU LU

HUASHAN LU

CHANGLE LU

WULUMUQI ZHONG LU

YANAN XI LU

CHANGLE LU

ANFU LU

CHANGLE LU

Propaganda Poster Centre

WUYUAN LU

FUXINGXI LU

Art Scene China

TAOJIANG LU

DONGPING LU

Radisson Plaza Xingguo Hotel

FUXINGXI LU

PINGWU LU

HUNAN LU

HUNAN LU

HUAIHAI ZHONG LU

Shanghai Library

Shanghai Symphony Orchestra Hall

Shanghai Library

XINGGUO LU

Ferguson Lane

GAOAN LU

Hengshan Lu

TAI'AN LU

WUKANG LU

WUKANG LU

XINGGUO LU

HUASHAN LU

Former Residence of Song Qingling

WULUMUQI NAN LU

FAHUAZHEN LU

YONGJIA LU

KANGPING LU

HENGSHAN LU

XINHUA LU

HUAIHAI XI LU

JIANGUO LU

WANPING LU

GUANGYUAN LU

ZHAOJIABANG LU

GUANGYUAN XI LU

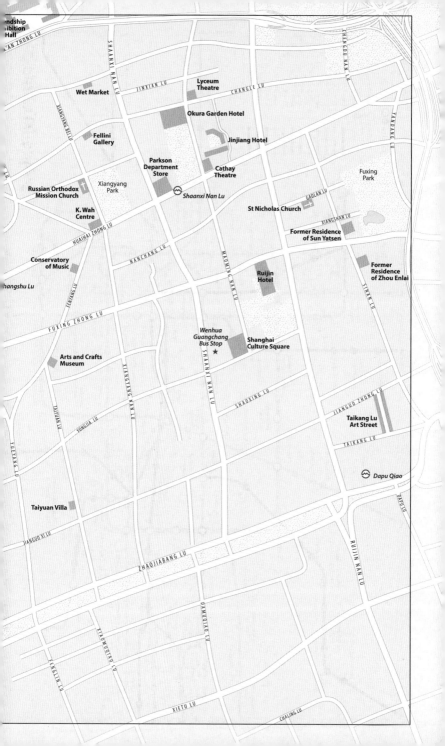

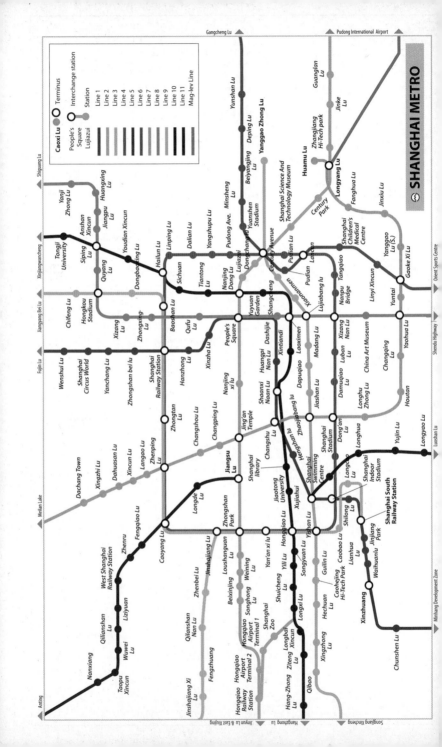